# Interest And Prices

## Knut Wicksell

INTEREST AND PRICES

MACMILLAN AND CO , Limited
LONDON · BOMBAY · CALCUTTA   MADRAS
MELBOURNE

THE MACMILLAN COMPANY
NEW YORK · BOSTON · CHICAGO
DALLAS   ATLANTA · SAN FRANCISCO

THE MACMILLAN COMPANY
OF CANADA, LIMITED
TORONTO

# INTEREST AND PRICES

## (*Geldzins und Güterpreise*)

### A STUDY OF THE CAUSES
### REGULATING THE VALUE OF MONEY

*By*

KNUT WICKSELL

*Translated from the German by*

R. F. KAHN

*With an Introduction by*

PROFESSOR BERTIL OHLIN

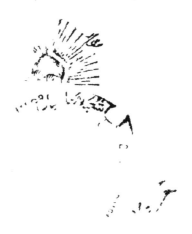

*Published on behalf of the Royal Economic Society by*

MACMILLAN AND CO., LIMITED
ST. MARTIN'S STREET, LONDON
1936

COPYRIGHT

PRINTED IN GREAT BRITAIN
BY R. & R CLARK, LIMITED, EDINBURGH

# TRANSLATOR'S NOTE

I HAVE to express my sincere thanks to Miss Anna Schwarz-schild, who read a portion of the manuscript with great care, and to Dr. Eduard Rosenbaum, who helped me out of many difficulties. The Appendix consists of Wicksell's last published article, translated from the original Swedish by Mrs H. Norberg.

Wicksell's *Geldzins und Guterpreise* was published at Jena by Gustav Fischer in 1898. Such footnotes as I have found it necessary to insert are enclosed in square brackets

R. F. K

# CONTENTS

|  | PAGE |
|---|---|
| INTRODUCTION BY PROFESSOR BERTIL OHLIN . . | VII |
| AUTHOR'S PREFACE . . . | XXIII |

CHAPTER 1
| INTRODUCTORY . . . . . | 1 |

CHAPTER 2
| PURCHASING POWER OF MONEY AND AVERAGE PRICES . | 7 |

CHAPTER 3
| RELATIVE PRICES AND MONEY PRICES . . . | 18 |

CHAPTER 4
| THE SO-CALLED COST OF PRODUCTION THEORY OF MONEY | 29 |

CHAPTER 5
| THE QUANTITY THEORY AND ITS OPPONENTS . . | 38 |

PAGE

## CHAPTER 6

THE VELOCITY OF CIRCULATION OF MONEY

A. *A Pure Cash Economy* . . . 51
B. *Simple Credit* . . . 59
C. *An Organised Credit Economy* . . . . 62

## CHAPTER 7

THE RATE OF INTEREST AS REGULATOR OF COMMODITY PRICES:

A *The Classical Theory and the School of Tooke* . . 81
B. *Simplest Hypothesis. Variations of the Rate of Interest when the Market Situation Remains otherwise Unaltered* 87

## CHAPTER 8

THE NATURAL RATE OF INTEREST ON CAPITAL AND THE RATE OF INTEREST ON LOANS . . . 102

## CHAPTER 9

SYSTEMATIC EXPOSITION OF THE THEORY

A. *The Causes which Determine the Natural Rate of Interest on Capital* . . . . . 122
B *The Use of Money* . . . . 134

## CHAPTER 10

INTERNATIONAL PRICE RELATIONSHIPS . 157

## CHAPTER 11

ACTUAL PRICE MOVEMENTS IN THE LIGHT OF THE PRECEDING THEORY . . . . . 165

## CHAPTER 12

PRACTICAL PROPOSALS FOR THE STABILISATION OF THE VALUE OF MONEY . . . . 178

## APPENDIX

THE MONETARY PROBLEM OF THE SCANDINAVIAN COUNTRIES . . . . . . . . 197

# INTRODUCTION

To judge the character and importance of Knut Wicksell's monetary doctrines, it is necessary to view them against the background of the monetary controversy of the late nineties. For some decades the organisation of an international gold standard had been the outstanding problem. Hardly had this organisation won its victory in the seventies, when its position was threatened by the continued fall in wholesale prices. A violent propaganda for bimetallism set in almost everywhere. The character, working, advantages, and disadvantages of this system naturally became the central topic of discussion in the monetary field. The old debate between the currency and the banking schools had died out and the latter undoubtedly held the field. The quantity theory of money was discredited, even in the Anglo-Saxon countries. Most writers agreed that if credits were granted on adequate security in accordance with sound banking principles, the supply of means of payment could not exceed "the requirements of the market". There was no discussion in that connection of the level of bank rate.

Two things seem to have caused Wicksell to adopt an entirely different attitude to monetary problems. First of all, he was a close student and admirer of the English classical school of economists, above all of Ricardo. To Wicksell's mathematical mind the quantity theory of money, as presented by Ricardo, made a much stronger appeal than the vague generalisations of the current banking discussions, which side-stepped the question "Why do prices rise or fall?" that Wicksell at an early stage came to regard as the main problem of monetary theory. The stress which the Ricardian school placed on the influence of discount policy on the quantity of money and on prices seemed to Wicksell entirely justified. On the other hand, he could not get round the fact that the rate of interest, as pointed out by Tooke, had on the whole been low during times of falling prices and high during times of rising prices, whereas the Ricardian doctrine seemed to suggest the opposite. The solution of this difficulty Wicksell found through his study and amplification of Böhm-Bawerk's theory of interest. Must not the "natural" rate of interest, governed by the marginal productivity of capital, *i e* of the roundabout methods of production which would exist if money were not used, have some connection with the rate of interest as it actually appears on the capital market? There was only one possible answer But what was this connection? These two rates of interest, the natural rate and the money rate which is quoted on the market, tend, of course, to coincide If the former differs from the latter, money can no longer be said to be neutral", and monetary consequences in the shape of changes in prices are bound to ensue. If the money rate were kept below the natural rate prices would rise, if above they would fall.

Wicksell always insisted that this reasoning did not mean more than an amplification of the old quantity theory [1] Moreover, he always regarded his own contribution as a doubtful hypothesis and never became as convinced of its tenability as did some of his pupils He explicitly rejected the idea that his theory provided an explanation of the business cycle. He was critical of Mises' idea that mistaken credit policy is the origin of the tendencies towards booms and depressions A brief quotation will indicate his position. "Our conclusion is, therefore, that although the changes in the purchasing power of money, caused by credit policy, are under present conditions intimately bound up with the business cycle and without any doubt also influence the latter, above all by giving rise to crises, yet it does not seem essential to assume that there is, by the nature of things, any necessary con-

---

[1] See, for instance, his preface to the German edition of his *Vorlesungen, II · Geld und Kredit,* 1922

nection between these two phenomena. The main cause of the business cycle, and a sufficient cause, seems to be the fact that technical and commercial progress cannot by its very nature give rise to a series which proceeds as evenly as the growth in our time of human needs—due above all to the organic increase in population—but is now accelerated now retarded. In the former case . a mass of circulating capital is transformed into fixed capital, a process which, as I have said, accompanies every rising business cycle it seems as a matter of fact to be the *one* really characteristic sign, or one in any case which it is impossible to conceive as being absent "[1] . . . "If the banks already at the beginning of a rising period *sufficiently raised their interest rates,* but on the other hand *reduced them energetically* when the depression was about to set in", then the price level would probably remain stable, although raw materials for fixed capital would rise in price during periods of good trade and fall during times of bad trade. "Under such circumstances the chief crises-causing factor would probably have disappeared, and what remained would be only a quiet wave movement between periods of accelerated formation of fixed capital and periods when the new capital assumed . other forms." . . "Increase in commodity stocks is probably the most important form of real investment during so-called bad trade."[2]

Wicksell's opinion of the character of the business cycle is perhaps most clearly presented in his paper "The Riddle of Crises"[3] Here he pointed out that there are two entirely different methods of explaining the comparatively regular ups and downs of business. One is to assume that some extraneous forces work intermittently and so cause oscillations. The other makes use of the hypothesis that the present economic system will, by its very nature, react in an oscillatory manner to any irregular forces which tend to make it move. It might be imagined to be like a

[1] *Lectures, II · On Money and Credit,* 3rd Swedish ed , p 197.
[2] *Ibid ,* p 198
[3] *Statsökonomisk Tidskrift,* Oslo, 1917.

rocking-horse. Wicksell undoubtedly inclined towards the latter view, while maintaining that intelligent credit policy—at least under most conditions—could prevent the rocking tendency from growing violent

As Wicksell worked on monetary problems for almost three decades after the publication of the *Geldzins*, it may be worth while to say something here about the changes which his views underwent. These were not, as a matter of fact, considerable. Although he was always ready to question his own reasoning, his lively discussions with other Swedish economists do not seem to have left many traces on his theory. Take, for instance, his discussion with Professor Davidson.[1] In 1906 Davidson, whom Wicksell held in the highest esteem, suggested that during periods of rapid technical progress and increasing productive efficiency a greater stability of business would be ensured if commodity prices fell in proportion to the increase in output than if they remained stable Davidson asserted that if the money rate of interest and business profits (Wicksell's natural rate) stood in a normal relation to one another before the increase in efficiency, then they would continue to do so if prices fell in proportion to the latter There would be no need for a change in the money rate of interest. If it were reduced[2] to prevent a fall in the price-level, it would be too low in relation to profits, and a process of an inflationary character would start. To this Wicksell replied "In the case which Davidson has chosen it may appear that the increase in profits due to increased productivity and the reduction in profits due to the fall in prices, caused on his assumption by the former, would offset

---

[1] See the following papers in the *Ekonomisk Tidskrift* (i) Davidson, "On the Concept of the Value of Money", 1906, (ii) Wicksell, "The Stabilisation of the Value of Money, a Means of Preventing Crises", 1908, (iii) Davidson, "On the Stabilisation of the Value of Money", 1909, (iv) Wicksell, "Money Rate of Interest and Commodity Prices", 1909. *Cf* also Brinley Thomas, "The Monetary Doctrines of Professor Davidson", *Economic Journal*, March 1935.

[2] In Wicksell's opinion the money rate should be *raised* to ensure equilibrium on the capital market and prevent a rise of the price level, see Wicksell's answer.

one another  But surely this would only happen if the price movement could be *anticipated beforehand and estimated*, or if it were so even and had lasted for so long that it had come to be generally regarded as something constant? In general, however, the individual business man will make his calculations for the future, and so fix his demand for labour, raw materials, and credit on the basis of *current* prices." [1] Hence, prices would rise if the money rate were not immediately raised, and when some time later the increase in productivity had led to a greater supply of finished goods, so that prices would fall, business men would make losses and the situation would be disturbed

Davidson retorted that this might happen, but he denied that it must happen  He was inclined rather to maintain that when the natural rate of interest, as a result of technical progress, tended to rise above the money rate, a fall in commodity prices would have a counteracting effect and, by keeping the natural rate down, would prevent any discrepancy from emerging.

In his rejoinder Wicksell admitted that this case required more attention than he had so far given to it. Davidson's reasoning depended, however, on "the tacit assumption that the supply of real capital has been increased in the same proportion as productivity Davidson is obviously of the opinion that money wages remain unaltered; thus if commodity prices have fallen, real wages would have been subject to an increase, but how can they be raised without an increased supply of real capital?" [2] Making reference to Bohm-Bawerk's theory of capital, Wicksell asserted that this is impossible, and continued: "If the quantity of real capital is increased the real [3] rate of interest will fall even if prices remain unaltered and thus money wages rise [4] .   . Naturally, however, my

---

[1] *Loc  cit* , 1908, p. 211.

[2] *Loc. cit* , 1909, p  64.

[3] This term is by Wicksell used as synonymous with "natural".

[4] The increased supply of real capital would raise real wages, thus, if the commodity price level were unchanged, money wages must rise.

assumption is that 'other things remain equal'; *i.e.* that real capital and real wages are *not* subject to any change. . . An increase in productivity when the supply of real capital is unaltered must necessarily mean a rise in the real rate of interest, and equilibrium on the market can never exist unless the money rate is made to coincide with the latter, *i.e.* unless it is in this case raised." [1] Although it was possible that prices might temporarily fall, a tendency for a cumulative rise in prices would set in unless the money rate was raised.

This discussion, although a little confused, is particularly interesting because it touched upon a line of reasoning which, had it been followed up, must have led to a reconsideration and revision of the fundamental concept of the "natural" or "real" rate of interest The outcome, as Wicksell pointed out, obviously depended on what business men believed about the future course of prices, it would influence their demand for credit as well as for wages and raw materials. The assertion that business calculations are as a rule made on the basis of current prices would not have withstood much criticism A discussion of what determines anticipations about the future would have been inevitable and the treatment of the factors which govern the volume of investment would, to some extent at least, have escaped from the domination of the curious concept of the natural rate of interest

The chief reason why Wicksell changed his views so little was undoubtedly that the criticism which his theory met did not go down to fundamentals. [2] During his last years Wicksell was again questioning the whole structure of monetary theory; this was not, however, due to the criticism which he had received but to his own doubts

---

[1] *Loc cit*, pp 65, 66.

[2] Only recently has a change in this respect come about as a result of Lindahl's *The Means of Monetary Policy* (in Swedish), 1930, and of Myrdal's "Der Gleichgewichtsbegriff als Instrument der geldtheoretischen Analyse", *Beiträge zur Geldtheorie*, edited by F A v Hayek, 1933, (published in Swedish in the *Ekonomisk Tidskrift*, volume of 1931 but printed in 1932)

about the reliability of the explanation of war-time inflation which he, like all other Swedish economists, had presented and defended.

Let me record very briefly the modifications and changes in Wicksell's theory, as indicated by himself In the preface to the first Swedish edition of his *Lectures, II: On Money and Credit*, 1906, we read· "Beside the somewhat too vague and abstract concept natural rate of interest I have defined the more concrete concept normal rate of interest, *i e* the rate at which the demand for new capital is exactly covered by simultaneous savings.    . Here I have on the whole tried more than formerly to deal with the problem of changes in the general commodity price level in terms of a simple and easily comprehensible formula of supply and demand for commodities and services "

The first of these two modifications brought Wicksell's theory on to lines of analysis and methods of thinking which later on proved to be acceptable to a wide range of economists, including some who regard as unfruitful his concept of the "natural rate of interest", *i e* the marginal productivity of capital as it would be in a moneyless society The relation between saving and investment, and the idea that there is some normal rate of interest, or rather credit policy, which brings about equilibrium between them, has played a dominating part in post-War monetary discussion. The second modification signified only a change in emphasis. Already in his *Geldzins*, Wicksell had stressed the idea that as a change in the price of *one* commodity is due to a change in the relation of supply to demand, the same must be true of a change in the general commodity price level This constituted a new approach to monetary theory Until then, and as a matter of fact for long afterwards, it was regarded as self-evident that, since commodities are exchanged for commodities, a change in the general price level must be due to entirely different circumstances from a change in individual prices Hence, the analysis of variations in the general price level, contained in economic text-books in the chapters on money,

started with a discussion of the monetary mechanism and
was not brought into any organic connection with the
theory of pricing and distribution.

Wicksell's most fruitful innovation in his analysis
is, I am inclined to think, the important step which
he took in bridging the gap between price theory and
monetary theory. Following up the idea that a rise in
the general price level is due to a rise in total demand in
relation to total supply, Wicksell intuitively realised that
it would be profitable to divide each of these two categories into two classes the supply of consumers' goods and
the supply of capital goods, on the one hand, the income
to be spent and the income to be saved, on the other hand.
A study of the relations between these four factors gave
him a deeper insight into the character of price movements than that obtained as a result of the analysis of
changes in price levels by means of the old quantity
theory, which ignored those changes in relative commodity prices which are so characteristic of price movements Furthermore, by Wicksell's line of approach the
analysis of the construction of the monetary mechanism —
the organisation of the monetary and banking system —is
given a secondary place This seems to me to carry with it
many advantages, *e.g* that the foundations of monetary
theory can be made more general than when they are expressed in terms of a monetary system of a special construction By means of his brilliant assumption of a pure
credit economy, Wicksell successfully escaped from the
tyranny which the concept "quantity of money" has until
recently exercised on monetary theory

I have come to regard this side of the Wicksellian
theory as more important than his other attempt to combine price theory and monetary theory—by his identifica-
tion of the rate of interest which would maintain the
price level constant with the rate as determined in the
theory of pricing and distribution, the latter being termed
alternatively natural rate, *i.e.* the marginal productivity
of capital, and normal rate, *i.e* the rate which equalises

supply and demand of savings. The general theory of
pricing and distribution is, after all, static in character
and its concepts are not likely to lend themselves to the
more dynamic analysis of, say, problems of inflation.
Rather than build monetary theory on this static analysis, it would seem more natural to pursue the monetary analysis of the actual determinants of the various
rates of interest in a dynamic world and then, in the light
of such analysis, to revise the theory of distribution  Work
along this line seems to me to be the natural consequence
of the first-mentioned innovation of Wicksell's  It would
bring monetary theory into harmony with price theory by
making the latter more dynamic and would probably give
up not only concepts like the natural rate of interest but
the whole idea of a monetary equilibrium and thus also
the concept of a normal rate of interest defined in equilibrium terms [1]

Let me return now to the third modification, introduced
by Wicksell in the first Swedish edition of his *Vorlesungen*
(1906). It concerns the influence of gold production on
prices. "I had formerly, in close accordance with the
opinion of the classical school, imagined that this influence
is mainly exercised chiefly through the intervention of the
rate of interest; gold production in excess of needs ought
in the first place to cause an increase in the gold stocks
of banks and thereby a reduction of their interest rates,
which in its turn should cause a rise in prices       After
further reflection I have, however, come to the conclusion
that the main emphasis ought rather to be placed on *the
demand for commodities* from the gold-producing countries,
if this demand is not offset by an equally large *supply of
goods* from other countries—in other words, by a need for
new gold—it must necessarily lead to a rise in prices, and
this *immediately*; thus the money rate of interest is perhaps
not at all affected or possibly affected even in the opposite

---

[1] An analysis of these questions is to be found in my Swedish book,
*Monetary Policy, Public Works, Subsidies and Tariffs as Remedies for
Unemployment*, 1934  A revised English version will appear in 1936
under the title *The Theory of Expansion*

direction."[1] "The increasing gold stocks would then serve as a sort of 'hook' *behind* the price movement, preventing it from receding again . . *i.e.* not as the first cause of the rise in prices but as a foundation which has been inserted *after* the beginning of the price movement . . I mention this only in passing as a conceivable hypothesis. . . . A similar treatment seems to be called for by the rapid reduction of the value of money which is as a rule the consequence of successive issues of *paper currency*"[2] "In this case, too, the rise in prices is, strictly speaking, the primary factor, the increase in the quantity of means of payment the secondary factor, and it is at least conceivable that under such conditions no real surplus of paper currency and consequent fall in the rate of interest emerges"[3] Two years later, however, in a discussion with Davidson, Wicksell seems to have returned to his old position; he made an attempt to deal with the case of gold production as a mere special instance of a discrepancy between the normal rate and the money rate of interest. "In so far as the new gold does not exercise a depressing influence on the interest rates of the banks, it will instead increase business profits, by enabling business men to sell in a market with higher prices after having bought in one with lower prices, in this way the discrepancy between the two factors, the money rate and the natural rate, will remain about the same."[4]

A few years after the War Wicksell changed his opinion once more. The lively monetary discussion which was then being conducted in Sweden, where several writers took an orthodox Wicksellian attitude, seems to have made Wicksell himself more and more sceptical.[5]

[1] Preface
[2] *Lectures, II* , 3rd Swedish ed , p 155.
[3] *Ibid* , p 157
[4] "The Stabilisation of the Value of Money, a Means of Preventing Crises", *Ekonomisk Tidskrift*, 1908, p 211
[5] See the following papers in the *Ekonomisk Tidskrift* (i) Davidson, "Some Theoretical Questions", 1919, (ii) Wicksell, "Professor Cassel's Economic Treatise", 1919, translated in the English edition of Wicksell's *Lectures*, vol 1, p 219 ff , (iii) Davidson, "The Theoretical Implica-

In the second Swedish edition of the *Lectures* (1915), Wicksell introduced a modification of more far-reaching character, although he did not himself regard it as important. In the Preface he writes: "I have not found myself called upon to modify my general standpoint, if one does not count as such a certain concession to my critics concerning the *mutual* effect on one another of the money rate and the natural rate of interest". This concession reads as follows. "It has been objected that a reduction of the money rate ought to have a depressing effect on the real (natural) rate; thus, the stimulus to a further rise in prices would disappear. This possibility cannot in general be denied. A reduction of the real rate requires, other things being equal, new real capital, *i e* increased savings " [1] Wicksell admits that the tendency towards an increase in savings may be much stronger than the opposite tendency, so that the rise in prices which has begun may stop. However, he regards this reaction between savings and the real rate of interest as a "secondary factor".

In my opinion, the bearing of this objection is much wider than Wicksell supposed. The analysis of Lindahl [2] and of Myrdal [3] has demonstrated that the existence of "credit and of money rates of interest are included as elements in the construction by which the natural rate is

---

tions of the Monetary Problem", 1920, (iv) Gustaf Åkerman, "Inflation, Quantity of Money, and Rate of Interest", 1921, (v) Wicksell, "Inflation, Quantity of Money, and Rate of Interest", 1921, (vi) Ohlin, "On Price Increases, Inflation, and Monetary Policy", 1921; (vii) Heckscher, "The Effect of a Too Low Rate of Interest", 1921, (viii) Brisman, "The Rate of Interest During Direct Inflation", 1922, (ix) Davidson, "On the Concept Normal Rate of Interest", 1922, (x) Åkerman, "Inflation, Quantity of Money, and Rate of Interest", 1922, (xi) Wicksell, "Answer to Mr Åkerman", 1922, (xii) Wicksell, 'Answer to Professor Heckscher", 1922, (xiii) Davidson, "On the Theory of the Value of Money", 1922, (xiv) Davidson, "On the Question of the Regulation of the Value of Money during the War and Thereafter", 1922–23

[1] *Lectures*, 2nd Swedish ed , p 202 See also Cassel, *Theory of Social Economy*, § 48

[2] *The Means of Monetary Policy* (in Swedish), 1930

[3] "Der Gleichgewichtsbegriff als Instrument der geldtheoretischen Analyse", *Beiträge zur Geldtheorie*, edited by F A v Hayek, 1933

determined" [1] "It is impossible to conceive of relative barter terms whose development is independent of the absolute monetary units in which credit contracts are concluded " [2] In other words, Wicksell's concept of a natural rate of interest proves to be of little use in dynamic analysis.

I now turn to another difference between Wicksell's presentation of his monetary theory in the *Geldzins* and in later works It did not mean any change in opinion and Wicksell does not himself seem to have discussed the relative merits of the two methods of analysis.

In the *Geldzins* Wicksell followed the line he had himself suggested a few years earlier [3] and dealt with long-lived capital goods—houses, canals, railways, etc —in the same manner as natural resources He termed them "rent goods" As capital in a narrow sense he regarded materials, tools, machines, etc., of shorter life Compared with the Bohm-Bawerkian analysis, this meant a relative return "to the classical distinction between fixed and mobile capital". [4] Only circulating capital was thus regarded as a fund of wages and rents, paid for the use both of natural resources and of fixed capital, on this basis the Bohm-Bawerkian theory of roundabout methods of production and the average period of investment was applied.

In the *Vorlesungen* (1906 and later editions), on the other hand, *total* capital was regarded as a wages fund. The average period of investment here refers to the time that passes between the investment of the original factors of production, *i.e.* labour and natural resources, and the consumption of the finished consumption goods. This latter method has the obvious advantage that, *e.g.* in a study of the effects of a reduction in the money rates of interest, the tendency for all new capital goods to become more durable is not overlooked. On the other hand, the concept of an average period of investment becomes

[1] *Ibid* , p 393
[2] *Ibid* , p 394.
[3] *Über Wert, Kapital und Rente*, 1893.
[4] P. 126, below

more concrete and is much easier to handle in a study of price movements, *e.g* during changing business cycles, if it is used as in the *Geldzins* If one tried to combine the advantages of both methods, the construction would seem to come closer to the latter. The futile attempt to divide non-human means of production into two classes, natural resources and capital goods, would have to be given up, thus, it would be impossible to speak of an average period of investment when looking backwards at investments that have already been undertaken, but the period of investment in respect to plans for the future would be of importance for the construction of capital goods of all sorts.

During his last years Wicksell came more and more to doubt the solidity of what had been regarded as the cornerstone of his monetary theory.—the idea that if the money rate coincided with a normal rate of interest, which brought about equality between savings and investment, the commodity price level would remain constant To what extent his earlier discussion with Davidson influenced him we cannot say. To judge from his last paper,[1] it was discussions with business men on the causes of war inflation, especially the influence of a reduction in the supply of commodities, which caused the alteration in his views.[2]

Briefly expressed, Wicksell's doctrine—which on this point coincided on the whole with Cassel's—amounted to this if more money is lent to investors, and used by them for real investment, than is saved, then total purchasing power is increased, and prices rise. But if equili-

---

[1] "The Monetary Problem of the Scandinavian Countries," *Ekonomisk Tidskrift*, 1925, translated below, p 199 ff

[2] Wicksell had frequently discussed this question in periodicals, newspapers, and in the "Economic Society" during the War, but along more conservative lines. See *e g* the following papers in the *Ekonomisk Tidskrift* (1) Wicksell, "Money Rate and Commodity Prices", with the ensuing discussion with Professor Cassel and the President of the Bank of Sweden, Moll, 1918, (11) Davidson, "Scattered Studies on the Rise in Prices, 1918; (111) Davidson, "Rationing of Capital", 1918, (1v) Heckscher, "The Question of the Regulation of the Value of Money", 1918

brium is maintained between savings and investment, purchasing power is kept constant and prices cannot rise, at least not more than in proportion to any reduction in the available volume of commodities Discussing the influence of war-time scarcity of commodities, Wicksell observed that in this kind of reasoning is reflected a "lack of a clear conception of the term *purchasing power*. It is only *money* purchasing power which here comes into question It therefore stands to reason that a general rise in the market prices of both goods and services *itself* creates the purchasing power required for meeting the higher prices" In addition is needed only "*an increase in volume of the medium of exchange* If all payments were made on a cheque basis this increase would, of course, take place quite automatically."[1] The velocity of means of payments of every kind would increase, for most people are more conservative in regard to their habits of consumption than in regard to their habits of making payments Besides, a new demand for credit would arise from people who wanted to increase their holdings of cash It cannot be regarded as certain that credit restrictions will keep down such a demand for credit. "A rise in the rate of interest is certainly an almost infallible means of restricting the demand for credit on the part of all *producers*, but it can hardly have a similar effect on those who merely desire to strengthen their cash position in view of the increase in the volume of exchange."[2]

These remarks are, in my opinion, worthy of the greatest attention The question of the reaction of the monetary mechanism is placed in the background and the movement of prices is discussed in terms of total incomes and the total supply of commodities It thus becomes evident that, as in the case discussed by Wicksell, a general rise in prices may well come about because consumers increase their demand, in terms of money, for consumption goods This need not imply any reduction of savings, for it increases

[1] Pp. 201, 202, below      [2] P 203, below

net incomes defined, *e g.*, as in book-keeping, hence, it may leave savings—the difference between income earned and income consumed—unchanged and need not have anything to do with too large credits to producers. The conclusion to be drawn, although it is not so formulated by Wicksell, is that, even if there is equilibrium between savings and investment, as commonly understood, incomes and prices may rise or fall *ad libitum*. Thus one of the very fundamentals of Wicksell's original theory would have to be given up.

Wicksell was, of course, quite right in pointing out that the fundamental concepts, not only of purchasing power or income, but also among others of savings and investment, had not been defined sufficiently clearly. When that has been done, it will, in my opinion, be possible to use the Wicksellian approach to the study of price movements with greater advantage. Although Wicksell's tools were deficient, his scientific genius led him to an insight into the character and morphology of the movements of the price system which will, I think, always be regarded as a great scientific achievement, even when such concepts as his natural or normal rate of interest have long since been discarded Nobody would have rejoiced more than Wicksell at the present questioning of the very fundamentals of monetary theory, his own contributions included, had he lived to witness it. His truly scientific and humble attitude towards monetary problems is well revealed in one of the concluding remarks, intended very seriously, in his last paper· "As to the period *after* the War, with its irrational and often puzzling price fluctuations, I am loth to confess that I would far sooner listen to somebody who could express an authoritative opinion on these matters than essay an explanation myself ".[1]

BERTIL OHLIN

[1] P 210, below

# AUTHOR'S PREFACE

THIS book is not very extensive, but it has occupied me for over two years of almost uninterrupted work  My original purpose was merely to provide a clear statement and a clear examination of the case for and against the Quantity Theory, and, in particular, for and against bimetallism (of which at that time I was inclined to be a supporter). My reflections soon forced me to give up this simple plan. I already had my suspicions—which were strengthened by a more thorough study, particularly of the writings of Tooke and his followers—that, as an alternative to the Quantity Theory, there is no complete and coherent theory of money  If the Quantity Theory is false —or to the extent that it is false—there is so far available only one false theory of money, and no true theory  In the criticisms advanced by the school of Tooke, there is on the *negative* side much that is correct and instructive, but in a positive sense they do not amount to more than a few aphorisms, of some ingenuity, which this school never succeeded, nor indeed so much as attempted, to organise into a connected whole  It is no exaggeration to say that even to-day many of the most distinguished economists lack any real, logically worked out theory of money, a circumstance which has not, of course, been particularly conducive to the success of modern discussions in this field.

The Quantity Theory, on the other hand, even in the form in which it is presented in Ricardo's truly classical writings about money, is open to too many objections, as pointed out by later writers, to be accepted without modification. The only possible course seemed to me to attempt to push on in the footsteps of the great master— to follow up the logical consequences of the fundamental conception which had given rise to the Quantity Theory, so as to arrive at a theory which should be both self-consistent and in full agreement with the facts.

The following line of thought seemed capable of leading to a useful conclusion An excess of money will, according to Ricardo, show itself in two ways—partly through a rise in all prices, partly through a fall in the rate of interest But the latter, Ricardo emphasises, can only be a *temporary* phenomenon, for as soon as prices have accommodated themselves to the increased quantity of money, the excess of money no longer exists and the rate of interest must return, other things being equal, to its former level. To bring about a fall in the rate of interest that is in any way *permanent*, the excess of money would have to be constantly renewed and the relative amount of money would have to be continually increasing Such a result would, therefore, be feasible only with commodity prices constantly rising This proposition should be capable of general application Indeed, in the developed credit economy of to-day it can claim an enhanced significance , for not only does an addition to the amount of material money act as a *cause* of easier credit but an increase (actual or virtual) in the velocity of circulation comes about as an *effect* . this will be shown below [1]

If the monetary institutions offer their money or their credit on abnormally favourable terms, this must logically lead to an intensified use of money or credit on the part of the public. A rise in prices is the result, and we have seen that prices will continue rising so long as credit remains easy. A tightening of credit has, of course, the opposite effect.

A very important qualification is, however, necessary. Though it is called for by the very nature of these phenomena, it is frequently overlooked, and hasty conclusions, which the facts fail to support, are the result. The rate of interest charged for loans can clearly never be either high

[1] The fact that, on the other hand, a *rise* in the rate of interest has a certain tendency to accelerate the circulation of money offers an apparent contradiction which is easily resolved, in the manner explained on p 119, below. See also what follows in the text.

or low in itself, but only in relation to the return which can, or is expected to, be obtained by the man who has possession of money. It is not a high or low rate of interest in the absolute sense which must be regarded as influencing the demand for raw materials, labour, and land or other productive resources, and so indirectly as determining the movement of prices. The causative factor is the current rate of interest on loans as compared with what I shall be calling the natural rate of interest on capital This natural rate is roughly the same thing as the real interest of actual business. A more accurate, though rather abstract, criterion is obtained by thinking of it as the rate which would be determined by supply and demand if real capital were lent in kind without the intervention of money

It is remarkable that this proposition—fundamentally very simple, indeed almost self-evident—though occasionally alluded to by economists, has never, to my knowledge, been used as the foundation for a complete theory of money and prices. The explanation, it seems to me, must lie in the defective condition of the theory of interest as it has so far been developed. Economists do not tire of impressing on their students that money and real capital are not the same thing, that interest on capital and interest on money are consequently different things. But as soon as it comes to applying these ideas, almost without exception "the two subjects are mixed up in the most inextricable confusion", as Mill puts it (at the opening of an argument[1] in the course of which, in spite of every effort, he merely succeeds in adding to the confusion).

It is only with the development of a real theory of capital, such as we owe to the genius of Jevons in his *Theory of Political Economy*[2] and of Bohm-Bawerk, who brought it to full completion in his famous *Positive Theorie des Kapitales*, that it has become possible to make a survey

---

[1] "Of the rate of interest", *Principles*, book iii , chap xxiii.

[2] His earlier works, as we shall see below, are based entirely on the older point of view.

of the phenomena of capital and interest, as they would be exhibited on the purely imaginary assumption that they could take place without the intervention of money or credit. At the same time the modifications which are called for by the appearance of money are brought to light These modifications are fundamental in nature. It is not true that "money is only one form of capital", that the lending of money constitutes "a lending of real capital goods in the form of money," etc. Liquid real capital (*i.e.* goods) are never lent (not even in a system of simple merchandise credit), it is *money* which is lent, and the commodity capital is then *sold* in exchange for this money.

There is nothing *so far* to bring the rate of interest on money into coincidence with the rate which would be determined by supply and demand if real capital goods were lent in kind. The supply of real capital is limited by purely physical conditions, while the supply of money is in theory unlimited and even in practice is held within fairly elastic boundaries· over a given period the same pieces of money can be lent almost any number of times to different individuals, or to one and the same individual [1]

It is, however, sufficiently certain that sooner or later the money rate will move into coincidence with the natural rate of interest on capital. In other words, the magnitude of the money rate is ultimately determined only by the relative excess or scarcity of real capital goods Precisely this, it seems to me, cannot be explained until it is possible to assume that the persistence of any deviation between the two rates of interest will lead to a change in commodity prices, and that this change will continue progressively, so that, with the monetary system of actual fact, the rate on loans is sooner or later drawn into line with the current level of the natural rate on capital

No better illustration of this proposition can, I think, be provided than in the famous letters exchanged between

---

[1] This is true even of merchandise credit, indeed to a marked degree. A lender cannot provide more *goods* than he actually possesses, but he can provide any amount of *money*—in fact he provides exactly the sum that the borrower promises to pay for the goods

Bastiat and Proudhon concerning the *Gratuité du crédit* (recently published in German by Muhlberger [1])

Not only Proudhon, but also his opponent Bastiat (as is made very clear in Bastiat's sixth letter [2]), were of the opinion that if the banks are permitted to issue paper without full metallic covering, they will be able to a corresponding degree to lower their rates of discount, and that under conditions of free competition this is what they will do On this line of approach not more than a hair's breadth separates us from the *gratuité du crédit* It is in any case easy to imagine a situation in which the credit system is so developed that the banks' necessary holdings of cash and their other expenses are reduced to a minimum. Then according to this view the money rate of interest could fall almost to zero *without any increase in the amount of real capital!* What becomes then of all the reasons put forward by economists, not least by Bastiat himself, for the economic justification and necessity for the lending rate of interest, and for its determination by the supply and demand for capital?!

The conflict is easily resolved It is only necessary to assume that a constant deviation of the rate of interest on loans below the natural rate on capital will bring about, not merely a rise in prices, as Bastiat himself maintains, but a *progressive* rise, proceeding without limit, so that sooner or later the banks will be led to raise their rates, *mutatis mutandis* in the opposite case where the money rate is above the natural rate It is at the same time clear, looking at the world as a whole, that if all banks behave in the same way, there is no reason for any *rapid* movement of the money rate into line with the natural rate, and a deviation between the two rates, with its due effect on prices, can persist for a considerable time. The question then arises whether this does not constitute an *adequate* explanation of all observed changes in prices, while I shall

---

[1] *Kapital und Zins, die Polemik zwischen Bastiat und Proudhon,* Jena, Gustav Fischer, 1896 [translation of *Intérêt et Principal,* Paris, 1850].

[2] *Ibid ,* pp 209-11 ff.

try below to show that all other explanations turn out to be logically untenable.

The Quantity Theory is correct in so far as it is true that an increase or relative diminution in the stock of money must always *tend* to raise or lower prices—by its opposite effect in the first place on rates of interest. But monetary conditions are only one factor in the situation, at any rate if the period under consideration is not too long. The other factor, which is often of more weight, takes the form of the independent movements of the natural capital rate itself, which must necessarily, but in general only gradually, be accompanied by corresponding movements of the money rate.

This completely disposes of the most important objection that has been advanced against this theory, which is clearly in complete accord with the observed fact that rising prices have seldom been associated with low or falling rates of interest, that far more often they are associated with high or rising rates of interest, and that falling prices accompany falling interest rates.

Though this line of approach turns out to be simple and clear, its detailed elaboration meets with great difficulties. Almost at every step opposite convictions are met with, in some of which not only laymen but experts too are deeply rooted ; or results are obtained which at first glance appear altogether paradoxical. I have made an honest attempt to meet these difficulties rather than to circumvent them by verbiage But I have the feeling that if I had at my disposal more time or more skill in exposition, it could all be a great deal simpler, more straightforward, and more convincing.

The worst of it is that the *more exact* test of the theory by means of the facts of experience still remains to be made. I am very far from regarding as adequate the little that I have been able to do in this direction in Chapter 11, where I give the reasons why a detailed investigation appears to me an extraordinarily difficult task, indeed as yet almost impossible. Until it has been fully endorsed by experience, every theory, no matter how plausible, remains no more than a *hypothesis* I would not pretend that mine is more than that. But I do not think that I have over-estimated the importance that would attach to it not only in theory but also in monetary practice if it should turn out eventually to be correct.

I start off with some introductory remarks about the concept of the average level of money prices and the possibility of measuring it They do not pretend to present any exhaustive treatment of this much debated matter, but it is to be hoped that they may contribute something towards clearing up the question.[1]

To facilitate the use of this book, certain passages are printed in smaller type They may be omitted, particularly at a first reading, without breaking the thread This applies also to the whole of Chapter 9. where I attempt, on the basis of certain hypothetical assumptions, a more systematic exposition of the theory. Towards the beginning of this chapter there is an exposition of Bohm-Bawerk's theory of production (his wages-fund theory), which may appear superfluous since I make no direct use of it This, however, is the case only because for the sake of simplicity I imagine a constant length (equal to one year) for the period of production At the same time I wanted at least to indicate how this restriction could be dispensed with. This is precisely where Bohm-Bawerk's teaching is useful —indeed it is the only economic theory which provides a rational explanation of the magnitude of the rate of interest on capital, wages, and rents, of the distribution of the final product between capitalists, workers, and landlords, etc

---

[1] Having failed to do so elsewhere I would here refer to Edgeworth's admirable treatment in his " Some new Methods of measuring Variation in General Prices " (*Journal of the Royal Statistical Society*, 1888) The idea of a rational definition of the purchasing power of money which, in the footnote to page 16, I ascribe to Pareto, is, it would appear, actually due to Edgeworth

I have on this occasion made next to no use of the mathematical method. This does not mean that I have changed my mind in regard to its validity and applicability, but simply that my subject does not appear to me to be ripe for methods of precision. In most other fields of political economy there is unanimity concerning at least the *direction* in which one cause or another reacts on economic processes ; the next step must then lie' in an attempt to introduce more precise quantitative relations. But in the subject to which this book is devoted the dispute still rages about *plus* as opposed to *minus*. As regards the influence on prices of easier credit, all three possible opinions are to be found among the most eminent writers that prices will tend to *rise*, that there is *no* effect, and finally (in the case of Tooke) that prices will tend to fall. I feel that for the moment I shall have accomplished sufficient if I convert the reader to *one* of these views.

I have, on the other hand, in an Appendix [1] ventured on a mathematical demonstration of Bernouilh's Law, the so-called Law of Large Numbers, which 1 make use of in dealing with the size of cash reserves and so with the velocity of circulation of money I am aware of no treatment of the theory of probability in which this beautiful and important law is deduced in a form accessible to non-mathematicians. I have attempted such a deduction, while confining myself to the simplest possible case, which is, however, adequate for most purposes.

---

I hold no teaching post, so that my scientific work is made possible only by special grants. I have in the first place to express my profound gratitude to the administrators of the Lorén Foundation, who for the third time have made me a generous grant.

It further gives me particular pleasure to express my respectful appreciation to the Government of Sweden for making me a grant towards this work.

[1] [Not included in the translation ]

Herr Otto Gutsche, of Breslau, with his usual care, has once again examined the manuscript on the linguistic side, and has also been so kind as to draw my attention to points of substance at which I had been careless or obscure

KNUT WICKSELL

Upsala, *January* 1898.

# CHAPTER I

CHANGES in the general level of prices have always excited great interest. Obscure in origin, they exert a profound and far-reaching influence on the whole economic and social life of a country.

*Relative* variations in the exchange values of individual groups of commodities are a necessary and obvious result of changes in the conditions of production and of technical improvements The damage which they cause to individual classes of producers and of consumers is, to a greater or lesser extent, adjusted as a result of changes in demand or of the movement of capital, labour, and land, from those spheres of production which are now less remunerative to those which have become more remunerative.

But it is a different matter when a rise or fall occurs in the money prices of all, or of most, commodities. Adjustment can no longer proceed through changes in demand or through a movement of factors of production from one branch of production to another. Its progress is much slower, being accomplished under continual difficulties, and it is never complete, so that a residue, either temporary or permanent, of social maladjustment is always left over.

A general *rise* in prices is, of course, to the disadvantage of all those who receive fixed money incomes, as is the case to-day with a constantly increasing number of social groups. It is also to the disadvantage of all those who derive the whole, or a large part, of their incomes by lending money capital of one kind or another (These constitute a class which is, of course, in no way confined to the class of real capitalists.) This is at any rate the case so long as a corresponding rise in the rate of interest does not happen to offset the fall in the purchasing power of money. Lastly, a general rise in prices is to the disadvantage of labour, so long as it has not the power to enforce a corresponding rise in wages But it must not be forgotten that a rise in wages may precede a rise in prices, acting as its direct cause. It will indeed appear later that this must be regarded as the most probable procedure whenever the rise in the price level is gradual and permanent, as opposed to those more fortuitous changes which are brought about by speculative buying and the like. That being so, it is not possible, without further qualification, to speak of a rise in prices as causing a general injury to labour. On the other hand, an upward movement of prices acts undoubtedly as a stimulus to the spirit of enterprise; though this advantage is possibly more apparent than real, for it is only too often associated with unhealthy speculation, based on what is a boom on paper rather than in actual economic fact, and culminates in over-expansion of credit, credit disturbances, and crisis.

A lasting *fall* in the prices of all commodities is generally recognised as no less significant an evil While it is true that with the same wages the workers would be able to obtain more of the necessaries of life, this advantage is frequently outweighed by the other consequences of a fall in prices. Business is paralysed, and growing unemployment and falling wages result Moreover, a low level of prices is often the *effect* of a previous reduction in wages, and it can then obviously do no more than offset this reduction. Lastly, and perhaps most important of all in this connection, direct and indirect taxation presses more heavily on the worker, and on the small man generally, when prices are low. Salaries of government and municipal officials seldom decrease in proportion to the cost of living. The state's creditors, like all other creditors, claim the same interest as before (apart from the possibility of conversion), which means a correspondingly greater burden on the nation as a whole if the majority of its creditors are abroad And if the amount of taxes and of other receipts collected by the state (or municipality) remains at its previous level in spite of the fall in prices, the temptation to some degree of government extravagance is generally inherent, and is seldom resisted with sufficient force.

In some cases, of course, there are considerable advantages to be gained by particular interests as a result of a rise or fall in the price level But if advantages and disadvantages are weighed against one another there can be no doubt that the latter always preponderate; both because every disturbance to the social mechanism is an evil in itself and because the gain due to a fortuitous and unexpected increase in a man's income is scarcely ever so significant as the injury caused by an unexpected decrease of equal magnitude

It is, however, widely believed that what is most desirable of all is a state of affairs in which prices are *rising* slowly but steadily. Many, indeed, look upon the reduction in the value of money that has taken place in the course of centuries as a contrivance of providence, successful in particular in curtailing the fatal consequences of irresponsible borrowing and of the thoughtless saddling of posterity with burdens incurred in the interests of the current generation, though opinions differ as to the wisdom of governments of former times in assisting providence by debasing the currency. That is as may be. As men become accustomed to rely more on their own strength and foresight and less on the beneficent influences of nature, so of course will it become less necessary to pay attention to such remedies for past blunders. Moreover, if a gradual rise in prices, in accordance with an approximately known schedule, could be reckoned on with certainty, it would be taken into account in all current business contracts; with the result that its supposed beneficial influence would necessarily be reduced to a minimum. Those people who prefer a continually upward moving to a stationary price level forcibly remind one of those who purposely keep their watches a little fast so as to be more certain of catching their trains But to achieve their purpose they must not be conscious or remain conscious of the fact that their watches are fast; otherwise they become accustomed to take the extra few minutes into account and so after all, in spite of their artfulness, arrive too late. . .

It follows that if it were in our power to regulate completely the price system of the future, the ideal position, affording common advantage to the overwhelming majority of the various groups of interests, would undoubtedly be one in which, without interfering with the inevitable variations in the relative prices of commodities, the general average level of money prices—in so far as this conception can be assigned a definite meaning, a point to which we shall return in a moment—would be perfectly invariable and stable.

And why should not such regulation lie within the scope of practical politics? So far as relative values are concerned, their variations, as has already been mentioned, are dependent on natural causes, which in part elude all human control. Attempts by means of tariffs, state subsidies, export bounties, and the like, to effect a partial modification of the natural order of these values almost inevitably involve some loss of utility to the community. Such attempts must so far be regarded as opposed to all reason. Absolute prices on the other hand– money prices—are a matter in the last analysis of pure convention, depending on the *choice of a standard of price* which it lies within our own power to make. Yet this choice too is to some extent conditioned by certain natural circumstances  It is only necessary to think of the external factors which have, as it were, forced us to adopt the precious metals, and in recent times gold in particular, as the material of coins. But fundamentally these circumstances are of only secondary importance; or, more correctly perhaps, a more than secondary importance should never be attributed to them. For it is the part of man to be master, not slave, of nature, and not least in a sphere of such extraordinary significance as that of monetary influences.

Little success has been achieved up till the present in satisfying such an ideal. The progress of monetary theory and practice has not done much to secure the desired stability of the standard of value and of prices Its failure is abundantly demonstrated by the history of prices of this last century, and particularly of its latter half It is true that opinions differ as to the actual magnitude of the *rise* in the general level of prices (in terms of gold) that took place between the middle of the century and about the year 1873 and of the succeeding *fall* which has continued up till to-day[1]—about the magnititude, that is to say, of the corresponding changes in the exchange value or purchasing power of money. But this is easily to be understood. In the first place, there is no reason why these changes should have proceeded equally in the different countries. It is, in fact, certain that, for various reasons to which we shall return later, the changes will be unequal. (This is probably the explanation of the minor deviations between the tables of prices constructed by Sauerbeck and Soetbeer, to which Sauerbeck has himself called attention.[2]) Then we have the not unimportant difficulty of ascribing an unambiguous meaning to the conception of an average level of prices Finally, there is the uncertainty as to which prices to take into account: whether to include only wholesale prices, as has usually been done up to the present, or also retail prices, whether to include only the prices of commodities or also the prices of services and, in particular, the wages of labour; and so on. In the next chapter we shall try to find a short answer to these questions.

In spite of these differences of opinion and in spite of the fact that the method which has hitherto been employed cannot be regarded as entirely unobjectionable, the substantial accuracy of its main results is not open to reasonable doubt. Examples of similar and even more violent oscillations of prices are provided in abundance by earlier periods of history, particularly for individual countries. But it has to be remembered that in those times a natural system of economy was in force to a very much more con-

---

[1] [1898.]

[2] See the discussion in the *Economic Journal,* 1895 and 1896

siderable extent than is the case to-day—over a wide range it was the rule in private as well as in public economy. Changes in the relative value of the precious metals or of money, even though very considerable, exerted a far smaller influence than does even the smallest movement of prices to-day, when a monetary system (in the widest sense of the term, including the credit system) has become almost universal.

It has already been pointed out that the prevention of these troubles by the provision of a constant measure of value cannot, in the present state of economic development, be regarded *a priori* as unthinkable. The difficulties of the problem are far more theoretical than practical. What is required is to be certain what is meant by the purchasing power of money and how it ought to be measured, and to obtain a clear view of the causes of changes in its value. There will then be no lack of practical means for converting theoretical judgments into appropriate measures. Of these two theoretical questions, it is the second, and by far the more difficult, that will mainly occupy our attention. But we will try in the first place to obtain as clear an answer as possible to the first

# CHAPTER 2

## PURCHASING POWER OF MONEY AND AVERAGE PRICES

IF between two different points of time the prices of all commodities had risen or fallen in exactly the same proportion, it would be perfectly justifiable to state that the purchasing power of money over commodities had decreased or increased in this same proportion. But such a case scarcely ever arises For even though there may be one general force operating on all prices in the same direction, calculated to bring about a perfectly uniform change, other forces usually come into play, arising out of the constantly changing conditions of production and consumption, and these must result in a different system of relative prices. The final result is shown in a somewhat greater rise in the prices of some commodities than of others, sometimes indeed in a fall in the prices of one or more groups of commodities when all other prices rise.

It is always possible to say that the real change in the purchasing power of money over commodities must lie somewhere between the two extreme values of all the various price changes. But to secure a more accurate measure, in a manner to which it would be impossible to object, constitutes a rather difficult problem.

It is clear *a priori* (as is now generally admitted) that a satisfactory solution is possible only if regard is paid to the quantities of goods actually exchanged; in other words, to the varying economic significance of different groups of commodities. If this is not done the whole question of average prices becomes vague and uncertain, and the method ordinarily employed may under certain circumstances lead to contradictory results. This can easily be demonstrated.—

In the interests of simplicity we consider only two

7

commodities, or groups of commodities. Let the prices (index numbers) of these commodities at a given point of time be denoted as usual by 100. At a later point of time it may be supposed that commodity A has doubled in price, so that its index number is now 200, while the price of commodity B has fallen by one-half, so that its index number is only 50. According to the ordinary method, involving the use of the arithmetic mean, the General Index Number, or average price, of the two commodities would now be $\frac{1}{2}(200+50)=125$; this would denote a *rise* in the average price level of 25 per cent.

But we might just as well have started off from the later point of time, denoting its prices by 100. Then at the earlier point of time the index numbers of the two groups of commodities would be expressed by 50 and 200 respectively, and the General Index Number would then be $\frac{1}{2}(50+200)=125$; this would indicate, in opposition to the conclusion of the last paragraph, that the average price had *decreased* by 20 per cent during the interval under consideration.

The mistake is not to be found in the adoption of the arithmetic mean but in the failure, already referred to, to take into consideration the quantities of the commodities. The ordinary method of determining index numbers has a true meaning only on the supposition that it is applied to such quantities of commodities as could each of them, at the moment adopted as a base, be purchased for the same sum of money, for instance for 100 million marks. If at a later point of time such a composite commodity, say $a$ kg. of coffee $+ b$ kg. of sugar, costs $200 + 50 = 250$ million marks instead of 200 million marks as at first, it can be said without a doubt that *its* price, and to that extent the average price of the two commodities, has risen by 25 per cent. If, on the other hand, the prices at the *later* point of time were each denoted by 100 we should be really presupposing quite a different composite commodity, made up of $\frac{1}{2} a$ kg of coffee $+ 2 b$ kg. of sugar—these being the quantities which can be purchased for 100 million marks—; and it can easily be seen that the price of *such* a composite does not rise but falls in the course of the period under consideration.

The method recommended by Jevons, of using the *geometric* mean, has the formal advantage that the same result is obtained whether one proceeds forwards or backwards. While that has to be admitted, in other respects the method is completely arbitrary It pays no regard whatever to the quantities of the various commodities and may thus lead under certain circumstances to impossible results. The employment of the so-called *harmonic* mean, which is sometimes recommended, offers no substantial advantages over the ordinary method. (As is well known, it involves taking the arithmetic mean of the reciprocals of the prices and then once again the reciprocal; in other words, instead of being applied to the money value of the unit of commodity it is applied, so to speak, to the commodity value of the unit of money.) And if no regard is paid to the quantities actually consumed this method, like the other one, would lead to impossible, or to contradictory, results.

Provided that it is possible to ascertain approximate values of the quantities actually consumed in an economic system, it is not difficult to obtain a measure of the rise or fall in the average level of prices; in other words, of the decrease or increase in the purchasing power of money But this is only feasible on the assumption that these quantities are the *same* at the two points of time which are under comparison, or that they all alter in the *same proportion* Taking the former case (from which the latter one can easily be deduced), let us call the quantities of the commodities, each measured in terms of some conventional unit, $m_1$, $m_2$, . ., and the prices per unit $p_1$, $p_2$, . . . . , at the earlier point of time, $p_{11}$, $p_{22}$, . . ., at the later point of time Then by solving for $x$ the equation

$$(m_1 p_1 + m_2 p_2 + \ldots) : (m_1 p_{11} + m_2 p_{22} + \ldots) = 100 \ (100 \pm x),$$

the percentage rise or fall in the average level of prices is obtained without any ambiguity.

In general the composition of the complex of commodities actually consumed will often be a quite different one, particularly when the two points of time are very widely separated.

When this happens, our problem is essentially *insoluble*, or rather the data are insufficient to provide a solution. This can be immediately demonstrated by assuming that consumption at the two points in question is made up of entirely different commodities, for instance a predominantly meat diet in the place of a vegetarian one, wheat in the place of rye, tea and coffee in the place of alcohol, coal and petroleum in the place of firewood and oil. To decide whether food, drink, heating, lighting, have become dearer or cheaper in the course of years, it would not be sufficient to know the various prices. It would at the very least be essential to be able to compare the different commodities in respect to their nutrition value, flavour, combustion value.

This point is rightly stressed by Lehr (in opposition to Drobisch). two different composite commodities involve quantities which are not directly comparable.[1] Nevertheless Lehr tries himself to solve the problem which he has already acknowledged to be insoluble This is of course made possible only by the introduction of new and arbitrary assumptions, which are sometimes in tolerably good agreement with the facts but sometimes in direct contradiction to them.

Lehr employs the conception "unit of satisfaction", by which he means that quantity of a given commodity which could on the average over the period in question be purchased for a unit of money (for instance, one mark). Retaining the symbolic representation employed above, let us call the quantities consumed at the later point of time $m_{11}$, $m_{22}$, . . . Then it can easily be seen that the magnitude of such a unit of satisfaction can be expressed as approximately $\dfrac{m_1 + m_{11}}{p_1 m_1 + p_{11} m_{11}}$ for commodity

---

[1] *Beitrage zur Statistik der Preise* (Frankfurt a/M , 1885) I quote from Lindsay, who in his *Die Preisbewegung der Edelmetalle seit 1850* (Jena, 1893) gives a fairly complete compilation of the various proposals for measuring the average level of prices; though I cannot agree with him at every point in his opinions of the methods which he mentions.

A, $\dfrac{m_2 + m_{22}}{p_2 m_2 + p_{22} m_{22}}$ for commodity B, and so on  The number of units of satisfaction of commodity A that are consumed at the earlier point of time is

$$\frac{m_1(p_1 m_1 + p_{11} m_{11})}{m_1 + m_{11}}$$

(i.e. the quantity $m_1$ divided by the magnitude of a unit of satisfaction), and at the later point of time the number is

$$\frac{m_{11}(p_1 m_1 + p_{11} m_{11})}{m_1 + m_{11}}.$$

Similarly for commodity B. And so on  Finally we obtain for the *average price of a unit of satisfaction* at the earlier point of time the quantity

$$P_1 = \frac{p_1 m_1 + p_2 m_2 + \ldots .}{\dfrac{m_1(p_1 m_1 + p_{11} m_{11})}{m_1 + m_{11}} + \dfrac{m_2(p_2 m_2 + p_{22} m_{22})}{m_2 + m_{22}} + \ldots .},$$

that is to say, the total amount of money paid out divided by the total number of units of satisfaction consumed. And, in the same way, at the later point of time

$$P_{11} = \frac{p_{11} m_{11} + p_{22} m_{22} + \ .  .}{\dfrac{m_{11}(p_1 m_1 + p_{11} m_{11})}{m_1 + m_{11}} + \dfrac{m_{22}(p_2 m_2 + p_{22} m_{22})}{m_2 + m_{22}} + \ldots .}.$$

The ratio of $P_{11}$ to $P_1$ is then supposed to express the average rise or fall in prices that takes place during the intervening interval.

Lindsay [1] regards this formula as "correct and sufficient for all reasonable demands", but objects that it "comprises too much", because it sets out "to measure at the same time the change in consumption, which does not form part of the problem". The objection does not seem to me to be either valid or indeed intelligible, for the various quantities of consumption are not *measured*, i e. deduced, but are *provided* as part of the necessary data for working out the change in prices  But I find it equally difficult to follow how Lindsay can accept the formula. In my opinion one is forced on *a priori* grounds to regard Lehr's method as theoretically inapplicable. It may under certain conditions lead to entirely anomalous results, as the following example will show

Suppose an economic system in which at a certain period, owing to the high price of wheat, bread is made almost entirely

[1] *Op. cit*

of *rye*. At a later period let the price of rye have fallen by 10 per cent. and the price of wheat by 25 per cent and suppose that in consequence of these changes bread is now made entirely of *wheat*, so that next to no rye is now consumed. If Lehr's formula were being used to determine the change in the purchasing power of money over bread, it would obviously be necessary to put $m_1 = 0$, $m_{22} = 0$ (wheat being commodity A and rye commodity B). Then

$$P_1 = \frac{p_2 m_2}{p_2 m_2} = 1, \ P_{11} = \frac{p_{11} m_{11}}{p_{11} m_{11}} = 1.$$

Therefore
$$\frac{P_{11}}{P_1} = 1.$$

In other words, the conclusion would be that the average price of the raw materials of bread has remained perfectly constant. But that cannot possibly be right, for both kinds have *ex hypothesi* fallen in price. (For a correct method of evaluation see below.)

It is of importance, in this as in all similar cases, to draw a sharp distinction between what is known and what so far is not, or cannot, be known  If the quantities actually consumed at the two points of time are known, it is possible for instance to start from the consumption of the first point and calculate what the cost of the composite commodity appropriate to it would be if each constituent were purchased at the price of the later point. Use of the above formula (p. 9) then clearly provides *one* measure of the change that has taken place in the average level of prices  Next it would be possible to take the quantities appropriate to the *later* point, $m_{11}$, $m_{22}$, etc , and work out how much this composite commodity would have cost at the prices that ruled at the earlier point  The corresponding relation

$$(m_{11} p_1 + m_{22} p_2 + \ \ldots) \ (m_{11} p_{11} + m_{22} p_{22} + \ldots)$$
$$= 100 : (100 \pm x)$$

provides a *different* measure of the change, but in itself it is just as natural and reliable.

If now these two ratios are almost *equal*—as will often be the case—it is justifiable to regard the concordant figure as the true measure of the change  If, on the other hand, there is a substantial divergence it is, I think, necessary to remain content with the results so far obtained  For practical purposes one might adopt some kind of average of the two figures—the arithmetic mean would be the simplest—; but it would have a purely arbitrary significance  The data are no longer sufficient to supply the required information. It would be necessary to undertake a more intimate study of the various kinds of commodities and of their relative importance to the individuals who comprise the community —in so far as such a comparison is at all feasible.

In the example given above, if we start from the consumption of corn in the earlier period, when it consisted entirely of rye, we come to the conclusion that the price of the raw material of bread has fallen by 10 per cent  This figure gives us a lower limit to the extent to which corn has in fact become cheaper, for it would have been applicable even if the members of the community had remained consumers of rye. But inasmuch as the transition to wheat would not have taken place if it had not offered some economic advantage, it may be concluded that the actual gain to consumers provided by the change in prices is somewhat greater. If, on the other hand, we were to calculate in terms of the consumption of the later period, when only wheat is purchased, we would conclude that prices have fallen by 25 per cent. But this is in excess of the actual cheapening of the raw materials of bread, because the consumption of corn in the earlier period was not made up of wheat, but of rye, which was then relatively cheaper  It follows that the real cheapening of the raw materials of bread lies somewhere between 10 and 25 per cent. To fix it more closely it would be necessary to compare the two nutriments. Suppose, for example, that it were known that, on account of its higher nutritive value, etc., wheat is 10 per cent. better than rye for most purposes of consumption. Let the price of rye in the earlier period be 200M , the price of wheat in the later period 187M  Then we have quite simply that

$$\frac{1 \cdot 1 \times 200}{187} = \frac{100}{100 - X}.$$

Hence $X = 15$, and the extent of the real cheapening is measured by 15 per cent., whereas the arithmetic mean of the two limiting values determined above would have suggested a cheapening of $\dfrac{10+25}{2}=17\frac{1}{2}$ per cent

It is obvious that this kind of reduction of one kind of commodity to terms of another kind is at best possible only in a rough and ready kind of way, and is often altogether impossible.

---

We come now to the no less difficult question as to which *objects* are to be included in considering the conception of average price level or average purchasing power of money. At first sight it would appear, at any rate from the theoretical point of view, as though it would be necessary to include everything in exchange for which money is taken or given It would in other words, as Wasserraab [1] expresses it, "make no difference whether it is articles of trade or real estate and houses which are involved, or whether it is services for which the money equivalent is paid in the form of daily or contract wage, salary, fee or honorarium, or of some other kind of price (for instance, freight or carriage in the case of transport undertakings, or tax or other due in the case of state services)".

Apart from these practical difficulties (which could possibly be overcome), it appears very doubtful whether such an extremely general statement of the problem does not involve too distant a goal and the introduction of extraneous elements.

Other authors, on the other hand, as for instance H. H Powers in his criticism of Irving Fisher's *Appreciation and Interest* (*Annals of the American Academy*, January 1897), regard it as obvious that the only thing which can be of importance is the determination of changes in the prices of actual commodities, indeed only wholesale commodities, for on these it entirely depends whether entrepreneurs and other large users of credit have been working at a profit or a loss. But this is going too far in the opposite direction, for the interests of the entrepreneur are by no means the only interests which are affected by an alteration in the purchasing power of money.

What one really wants to know is whether "living"—

[1] *Preise und Krisen* (Stuttgart, 1889), p. 75.

ordinary consumption—has become cheaper or dearer.    It
is true that this consumption comprises not only commodities in the strict sense of the term but also services and even
the use of capital—but only if they enter *directly* into
consumption, as in the case of domestic service, houses, etc
If, on the other hand, we include, *in addition to* the prices
of the products, the prices of the factors of production—
whether labour, the service of land, or the use of capital
—or of capital goods themselves (*e g.* houses, sites, etc ),
it can only result either in quite useless double counting
or even in more or less erroneous conclusions

If wages, for example, have gone up in proportion to the
prices of commodities, their rise can in general be regarded
as a simple corollary of the rise in prices—whether it is
considered to be cause or effect. If wages have gone up
more than prices, it must mean either that labour itself has
become more productive or that workers are now obtaining
a relatively greater share of the product as against land
owners or capitalists  But this has an influence on the
purchasing power of money over articles of consumption
only in so far as the general level of wages affects the
remuneration of those services that enter directly into
consumption.

In the same way the price or capital value of land will,
other things being equal, alter *pari passu* with the prices
of agricultural produce. Otherwise some cause or other
must have been at work to bring about a change in real
rents  This does not affect the general cost of living except
to the extent that a rise in urban ground rents usually
carries with it a rise in the rent of houses. But since the
former is already included in the latter, there is no need to
take special account of it.

It is quite true that increased activity in the sale of
houses and sites, or the payment of higher wages, dividends, rents, etc., increases the need for money and to this
extent may occasion a change in the value of money.
That, however, is an entirely different question. (It arises
equally when the same commodity changes hands several

times before entering into consumption, as is usually the case at times of crisis. But in calculating a General Index Number it would be undesirable to reckon one and the same commodity as many times over as it is sold and purchased.)

It seems to me, therefore, that the ideally correct procedure[1] for observing and measuring the general price level is to confine the calculation to objects of (direct) consumption, but over this range to make it as complete as possible, including not only commodities, but rents of houses, certain services, and the like. If the same money income serves at two different points of time to provide equally for the needs of nourishment, clothing, house-room, amusements, travel, education, etc , it is in accordance with ordinary usage to say that the purchasing power of money has remained constant. This is the case even though the prices of securities or sites have risen in the meantime, on account of a fall in the rate of interest or for some similar reason; or even though workers now receive higher wages than before.

If, on the contrary, house-rents or the cost of direct services have gone up it would certainly be said that things have become dearer and that the purchasing power of money has diminished, even though there has been no rise in the prices of actual commodities.

The problem being narrowed down in this way, it is scarcely necessary to point out that the usual methods of dealing with average prices are far removed from the condi-

---

[1] Perhaps something ought to be said about the view put forward by Pareto (*Cours d'économie politique*, vol 1 , p. 264 ff ) He holds that by the purchasing power of money ought really to be meant the *abstract marginal utility* that can be procured with one extra unit of money (*l'ophélimité élémentaire indirecte de l'or*). It follows that this quantity would never be the same for two individuals or classes of the community, but would vary according to their wealth. In the same way, for example, at a time of increasing national welfare it would be necessary to speak of a falling purchasing power of money, even though the prices of all commodities remain perfectly constant This is scarcely in accordance with ordinary usage Yet such a definition of the value of money ought fundamentally to be the least open to theoretical objection I confess that I do not venture to come to a decision as to its practical usefulness.

tions here stipulated for a satisfactory computation. These
methods are, for the most part, applied only to wholesale
prices. That is to say, raw materials and half-finished goods
have in part to take the place of finished consumption
goods. Services and the use of capital are entirely omitted,
and the relative importance of different commodities is
taken into account only in a very superficial kind of way
But it must be remembered that the main purpose of these
estimates was merely to establish the much disputed *fact* of
fluctuations of prices. We owe them to the diligence of a
few scholars who had to work with limited means and on
material which, collected originally for quite other purposes,
was in many respects incomplete  In this connection the
labour of men like Soetbeer and Sauerbeck must not be
supposed to be wasted  Indeed, the control calculations of
Palgrave and others have shown that the introduction of
the quantities of the commodities involves no such substantial modification to the final results as might *a priori*
have been expected

But a much more precise calculation of the average
price level will become essential once it is generally
accepted that appropriate choice and management of the
measure of value would result in a stable level of prices and
a constant purchasing power of money. When the goal is
set as high as this the means of reaching it will be provided
by an appropriate development of official statistics

It all therefore depends on obtaining a clear view of
the *causes* that influence the value of money and of the
means that are available for *regulating* it  This is the
question which forms the subject-matter of the following
chapters and to which we now turn

# CHAPTER 3

## RELATIVE PRICES AND MONEY PRICES

MODERN investigations in the field of the theory of value have thrown much light on the origin and determination of the exchange values, or relative prices, of commodities. But they have, unfortunately, done nothing to promote directly the theory of money—of the value of money and money prices

It is true that many of the well-known workers on the theory of value, such as Jevons, Walras, and Menger, have entered fairly deeply into questions concerning money. But their treatment of such questions runs, for the most part, in the old ruts  For instance, Walras' exposition consists fundamentally of nothing more than a mathematical version of the quantity theory which will be discussed below  there is no substantial development or extension of the theory itself  In most writings on the theory of value the question of the nature and origin of money prices is almost entirely neglected.

There is, however, nothing remarkable in this  For the whole study of relative prices is based on the conception of marginal utility, and in the determination of the *average* price level, and consequently of the actual level of money prices, this principle plays practically no part, or only a very indirect part

To make this clear, let us try to recapitulate quite shortly the main conclusions of the modern theory of value.

Free exchange in an open market is governed by the general law of proportionality between the exchange values of commodities and their *marginal utilities*  The marginal utility is the utility of the last unit of a commodity that is acquired or disposed of (*i.e* exchanged), or, what comes to the same thing, it is the strength of the *least* pressing need which is met by any unit of the com-

18

modity; or (still on the assumption of very small units, that is to say, of commodities that are perfectly divisible) the strength of the *most* pressing need which could be met by the acquisition (or retention) of an additional unit of the commodity but which in fact has to remain unsatisfied.

The existence of such a proportionality between relative exchange value and the utility of the *last* unit given or received in exchange, for each person engaged in the exchange, is immediately obvious It follows from the economic principle by which there is a tendency for everyone to continue the process of exchange for so long as, but no longer than, he continues to acquire commodities which represent more than the equivalent of the commodities that he gives in exchange.

But it does not follow from this principle that the relation between marginal utilities must apply to the *whole* quantity of a commodity given in exchange This is rather a consequence of what Stanley Jevons called The Law of Indifference, according to which only one price — only one ratio of interchange with other commodities—can rule for any commodity in an open market (competition between buyers and sellers being general and sufficiently keen).

This rule does not apply to an *isolated* exchange between two, or a small number of, individuals. Successive portions of the commodities may then be exchanged at varying prices The problem of relative price in an isolated exchange is for this reason indeterminate, or insufficiently determined, according to the varying degree of calculating ability, cold-bloodedness, and so on, of the individuals engaged in the exchange, the average ratio of interchange of the commodities can fall anywhere within wide limits.

It is true that if on an open market the owners of a particular commodity hold back temporarily with the object of raising the price it can easily happen that some of them are able to get rid of their complete stocks (or so much of them as they desire to sell) at the higher price which they exact at the start. But the more pressing requirements of the buyers are now satisfied, and consequently the remaining owners of the commodity must eventually resign themselves to much lower prices for the greater part of their stocks. Similarly, if the buyers hold back temporarily with the purpose of lowering the price it can easily happen that some buyers are able to cover their full needs at a relatively low price. But the stocks of the sellers are now for the most part cleared out, and so the remaining buyers must eventually pay a correspondingly higher price.

As a result of the prevalence of competition on both sides, among the sellers and among the buyers, an approximately uniform price for each commodity soon pervades the market This price is the one at which supply and demand just balance. Such a balance is only possible when the marginal utility is proportional to the price (ratio of interchange) for each commodity and for each individual who takes part in the market.

If longer periods of time are being considered, this equilibrium between supply and demand gives way to an equilibrium between production and consumption. As a corollary we find that the price and the cost of production of a commodity are proportional or equal—in so far as the phrase "cost of production" is capable of correct application, or of any application whatever

It is evident that all this is only an approximation. This can be seen by examining the record of any market or exchange. The existence of a single market price, in the strictest sense, is merely a theoretical ideal, from which reality diverges to a more or less significant degree—particularly if the producers or owners of a commodity are united in a combination or cartel or if the consumers, in their turn, protect their interests by means of a consumers' organisation or some similar body

It can now be seen that money has a *double* rôle to play in relation to the exchange of commodities.

l  If there are only *two* kinds of commodities they could,

at any rate when appropriate quantities of each are at hand, be *directly* exchanged for one another in the market, without the intervention of money or any other medium of exchange; and the above law of exchange would operate But as soon as *more than two* kinds of commodities appear on the market the situation is different (the general proof is due to Walras[1]). If the commodities are directly exchanged for one another in pairs, buyers only receiving what they require for their own consumption, it is no longer possible for the participants to attain complete satisfaction of their wants and there is no definite point of market equilibrium. In addition to, or instead of, the process of direct exchange, a process of *indirect* exchange must intervene.

Let us suppose, to take the simplest case, that commodity (A) is desired only by the owners of commodity (B), that commodity (B) is desired by the owners, not of commodity (A), but of a third commodity (C), which, in its turn, is demanded by the possessors of commodity (A) and by no others. It is then obvious that no direct exchange can take place. Only an indirect exchange is possible For instance, the possessors of (A) might exchange their commodity for commodity (B) with the intention, not of consuming it, but of offering it to the owners of commodity (C), and so of acquiring this commodity (C), which is the one that they desire.

But this kind of intermediate trade would soon prove too clumsy and troublesome for any developed economic system unless it were conducted on organised lines. It has therefore become an immemorial custom among all nations to hold stocks of some commodity for which there is a universal demand and to employ it as a *medium of exchange* (in the narrower sense of the term). A commodity is particularly suitable for this purpose if it can be easily

[1] Walras, *Éléments d'économie politique pure*, Leç 19-21   *Cf* also Launhardt, *Mathematische Begründung der Volkswirtschaftslehre*, § 12, and my own work *Über Wert, Kapital und Rente*, p. 50 The problem is very inadequately treated by Jevons (*Theory of Political Economy*, p 124)

transported and if it is not susceptible to rapid decay, so that everyone willingly accepts quantities that are in excess of his immediate requirements. Let us call such a commodity, (M). Then in our example the possessors of commodity (A), assuming that they were provided with a sufficient supply of (M), would obtain the commodity (C), which they desire, in direct exchange for a certain quantity of (M). Then the owners of (C) can use the quantity of (M) which they acquire in this way to buy the commodity (B), and the owners of (B) can then use it to buy the commodity (A) If the quantities that are exchanged of the commodities (A), (B), and (C) are exactly equivalent, commodity (M)—*the money*—has in this way merely executed a cyclical movement in the direction A—C—B, and so back to A. But the other commodities, which are the real objects of exchange, have each advanced one step of the reverse cycle.

2 In actual practice, however, perfect equivalence of the quantities exchanged will not be *immediately* attained It may be that some of the people engaged in the market do not for the moment possess any goods that are suitable for sale, or possess but a small quantity, and can temporarily cover their purchases only by means of money. Others may be in possession of a surplus of goods and may desire to provide themselves with money for the immediate, or more remote, future. In short, money as such serves the purpose not only of a medium of exchange in the narrow sense but also of a store of value, it is used to remunerate services, and it is only later, when the money once again changes hands, that, in exchange for these services, other services are rendered and received.

Nowadays the word "market" is commonly used in a purely metaphorical sense—it no longer denotes a concrete reality Purchases and sales tend to be spread more or less uniformly over the whole year, and a considerable time often elapses after a man makes a sale before he makes the ensuing purchase This function of money would thus be of considerable importance in the real world if it were not ıendered unnecessary, for the most part, by the development of credit facilities, as will be explained later

For the sake of simplicity, we shall now leave on one side the function that money fulfils as a store of value We shall suppose that we are dealing with an actual, though indirect, exchange of goods which are already in existence and which are destined for immediate consumption. It is then obvious that the fundamental conditions of exchange are not affected by the intervention of money. For every buyer and seller there holds good, ıust as before, a direct proportionality between the price of each commodity and the marginal utility of the quantity that ıs acquired or retained Moreover, the total value of the goods that are acquired ıs everywhere equal to the total value of the goods that are sold, so that ın the end everyone pays out just as much money as he receives. Either each single coin returns to its original owner or ıt ıs replaced by one of equal value So the function of money is here purely that of an intermediary, it comes to an *end* as soon as the exchange has been effected.

Hence we arrive at an important, if self-evident, fact the neglect of which has constantly resulted ın false conclusions. The exchange of commodities in itself, and the conditions of pıoduction and consumption on which it depends, affect only exchange values or *relative* prices. they can exert *no direct influence whatever on the absolute level of money prices.*

For a single commodity or group of commodities, the establishment on the market of an incorrect relative price results ın an inequality between supply and demand, between production and consumption, and this sooner or later effects the necessary correction But ıf, on the other hand, the prices of all commodities, or the average price level, ıs for any reason forced up or depressed there is nothing in the conditions of the *commodity* market that is calculated to bring about a reaction. After the exchange has taken place, each coin returns, on our assumption,

either actually or virtually to its original owner, to whom
it is a matter of complete indifference whether he pays
more or less for the goods that are offered to him provided
that at the same time he obtains a correspondingly higher
price for his own goods.

If there is any reaction whatever away from a *general*
level of prices that is too high or too low, it must originate
somehow or other from *outside* the commodity market
proper. Either the commodity which serves as money,
being traded on its particular market, where it appears as
an article of use or of consumption, derives a marginal
utility, and an exchange value against other commodities. depending on its properties in use and on the
conditions of its production; or this exchange value is
influenced by the circumstance, which we have hitherto
neglected, that the exchange of commodities is never in
actual practice an instantaneous process, but always ex-
tends over some period of time, during which money
fulfils the function of a store of value We shall later
undertake a closer examination of both these views, one
of which is connected with the so-called Cost of Production
Theory of Money and the other with the so-called Quantity
Theory. Whichever of these views may be regarded as
the more correct (they are in no sense opposed to one
another) one thing is certain: money prices, as opposed to
relative prices, can never be governed by the conditions
of the commodity market itself (or of the production of
goods); it is rather in the relations of this market to the
*money market,* in the widest sense of the term, that it is
necessary to search for the causes that regulate money
prices

These considerations are sufficient to enable us to examine a view which is so widespread that to question it at
all would seem almost paradoxical. In discussions of the
causes that have led to the fall of commodity prices during
recent decades, it is constantly asserted that in part,
perhaps for the most part, the cause resides "on the side
of goods". By this is meant that technical progress in

production and transport must have led *pro tanto* to a cheapening of all, or of most, commodities, and so to a fall in the general price level.

Such a statement can be formally derived from one or other of the independent theories of the origin and causes of the value of money, for instance, from the Cost of Production Theory or from the Quantity Theory, which have just been mentioned  On the basis of the Cost of Production Theory, it could be said that the cost of production of commodities has fallen more than the cost of production of gold, or that the former has fallen while the latter has remained unchanged. From the point of view of the Quantity Theory, one would refer to the fact that the total volume of production, and still more the volume of commodities exchanged, has expanded enormously—on account of an increase in population, greater efficiency of production, a more general use of money, and so on—while no corresponding expansion has taken place in the total stock of money. Such explanations obviously stand or fall with the particular theory on which they are based

But the decrease in the cost of production of commodities, the improvements in transport, etc., are often put forward without further explanation as independent causes of the fall of commodity prices by writers who actually reject the theories that have just been referred to as well as every other independent theory of money  It is as though this kind of explanation replaces every other theory of the value of money. The reasoning is somewhat as follows. Technical progress results in a fall in the cost of production, *and so in the price*, first of one group of commodities, then of another. The extension of this fall in price to all, or to most, groups of commodities means a fall in the general level of prices and a corresponding rise in the purchasing power of money over commodities. When, on the other hand, the question is one of a *rise* in the prices of commodities an explanation is looked for (as in the case of Thomas Tooke and his followers) in bad harvests, in an increase in the demand for particular commodities of which the supply remains unaltered, and in the effect of tariffs and indirect taxes in raising the prices of such commodities. In short, the same causes which can, as a matter of experience, be cited to account for a rise or fall in the price of *any single commodity* are put forward without further explanation, as soon as they extend to several of the most important groups of commodities, as the source of changes in the general level of prices.

This conclusion comes to grief over a logical fallacy, the nature of which is easily made clear in the light of the above discussion. When a single commodity can be produced more "cheaply" than was formerly the case - that is to say, when its production involves the use of less labour, land, or capital—its price, on the assumption of perfect competition, must certainly fall *in relation to the prices of the other commodities*, of which the costs of production are supposed to remain appreciably unaltered. But this by itself does not necessarily imply that the *money price* of the commodity is lowered by the whole of the difference between the former and the present exchange values. It may easily happen that the actual fall in price accounts for only a part of this difference, though most probably for a very large part; the remainder being made up by a small *rise* in the prices of the other groups of commodities. If this is so the changes that occur in prices may result in a rise of the average price level just as easily as in a fall; or it might remain unaltered. The same is true if the production of each of the other commodities in turn becomes successively facilitated.

Whether the price level will actually rise or fall cannot be decided *a priori*. The decisive factors are obscure and complicated, but so far as they lend themselves to a general survey, it appears that the outcome must chiefly depend on the *temporal* sequence of the changes in the supply of the particular commodity and in the demand of the producers of this commodity for all other commodities, and in the supply and demand of commodities in general. This sequence must in its turn depend on what happens to be the condition of the *money market* If the money market is in a fluid condition producers are provided with ample funds or can easily procure them by borrowing; supply then follows a more restrained course, and producers can satisfy their need for raw materials, labour, etc., without having first to await the sale of their own goods. In other words, the demand for commodities increases, directly and indirectly, while the supply is restricted or expands only by degrees; demand moves ahead of supply and prices tend to rise. Although a relative fall in the price of the commodity that is now produced more cheaply is in the long run inevitable, the absolute fall is relatively insignificant whilst the prices of all other commodities have gone up.

If, on the other hand, conditions in the money market are tight, producers hasten to dispose of their stocks of goods in order to obtain money, supply moves ahead of demand and prices give way The fall in price is, of course, greatest and most noticeable for those commodities of which the production has been cheapened as a result of technical improvements, and it may therefore easily look as though it was these improvements that constituted the true cause of the general fall in prices.

We may examine the matter from a different aspect The well-known law that the prices of commodities tend towards their costs of production is comprehensible only if it refers to *relative* costs and prices. In its essence it is only a corollary—in fact, merely an alternative expression—of the approximately correct observation that under free competition the returns to the factors of production—wages, rent of land, and earnings of capital—are equal in all occupations, or at any rate are continually tending towards equality Provided that the improvements in production are introduced only over a small area, so that there is no appreciable influence on the general level of remuneration of the factors of production, it is certainly justifiable to state that wages or profits over this area, which begin by being raised, must sooner or later be forced down by competition to the level of wages and profits elsewhere. We may now employ the usual argument in regard to the effect on commodity prices. But here too it would be more correct to state that there is in reality a *rise*, even though it may be a very small rise, in (real) wages or profits over the whole field of production.

If, however, the technical improvements apply over a considerable range of total production, it would be quite absurd to continue to suppose that the general level of wages, rents, and earnings of capital remains unchanged It *must*, on the contrary, rise (in *this* connection it is a matter of indifference whether one category rises more than the others or even at the expense of the others): for increased productivity of labour and natural resources is in general synonymous with greater remuneration of the factors of production. This *may* be secured through commodity prices falling while wages, rents, etc., as measured in money, remain temporarily unchanged; but it may just as well happen that these are *increased* while commodity prices remain unchanged or even rise a little. The law of equality between prices and costs of production is not capable of being utilised to determine what will happen in actual fact It depends rather on whether entrepreneurs' demand for labour, land, etc., and so finally the demand, direct or indirect, for commodities, is more vigorous and pronounced than the supply of commodities And this, as we have seen, must depend on the conditions that prevail in the *money market*.

These considerations, which to some extent forestall the discussion that follows, cannot here be pursued any further. We now proceed to a short treatment of the most important of the actual *theories* which have hitherto been advanced concerning the causes affecting the value of money.

# CHAPTER 4

## THE SO-CALLED COST OF PRODUCTION THEORY OF MONEY

No theorist can to-day lend his support to the traditional conception that money possesses in itself an independent, and more or less invariable, intrinsic value, against which the exchange values of real commodities are, as it were, compared or measured, though echoes of this doctrine are sometimes observed even in modern monetary literature. The $\pi\acute{a}\nu\tau a$ $\acute{\rho}\epsilon\hat{\iota}$ of the modern theory of value must have put a definite end to this manner of approach. The value of an object is merely the importance that we ascribe to its possession for the purpose of gratifying our wants. This importance *varies* according to the extent of the range of those wants which, beginning with the most urgent, have already secured their gratification.

It is generally admitted that money provides no exception to this universal rule. But whether or not in this connection it can be regarded "exactly like any other commodity" is quite a different question.

The answer has already been provided Money as such, *i e* so long as it fulfils the functions of money, is of significance in the economic world only as an intermediary. It is its purchasing power over commodities that determines its utility and marginal utility, and it is not determined by them.

But even though there is nothing to determine or set limits to the exchange value of our commodity (M), as we have called it, in the market in which it plays the part purely and simply of a medium of exchange, there is no reason why its exchange value should not be determined, more or less completely, through the influence of other markets in which it appears as a commodity proper (These markets may be materially distinct from the first or may

29

in fact be more or less closely bound up with it, the distinction then being a purely conceptual one. But that
does not concern us here.)

This would in fact be the case where the commodity
that is used as money is one of the ordinary articles of
consumption of the country or perhaps one of its principal
staple commodities—for instance, in early times hunting
tribes used skins, tobacco was used in Virginia.

An example of the same kind is provided by copper, which
in fairly recent times still provided the main part of the
coinage in certain countries, *e g.* during large portions of the
seventeenth and eighteenth centuries in Sweden (and also in
Russia). But it proved quite unsuitable for this purpose because
of the violent fluctuations in its value.

Even though it may be quite common for people to
accept this "money commodity" in payment for goods and
services, having no other object in view than again to pass
it on in exchange for other goods and services at the prices
that are then current, yet there always remains the possibility of employing it as an article of actual consumption
or of trade and speculation. This possibility will be realised
as soon as a shift, no matter how small, of the general level
of prices causes the exchange value of the money commodity to move above or below the position that is
called for by the conditions of production and sale; or, on
the other hand, as soon as a change occurs in these factors,
so that they no longer remain in equilibrium with the ruling
prices, *i.e.* with the purchasing power of the money commodity over other commodities.

But the case is a different one where the employment of
the money commodity as an article of use, and particularly its *actual* consumption (in gilding, silver-plating, etc.),
have come to occupy a position altogether secondary
to its employment as a medium of exchange, and
where, in addition, the yearly production results only in a
relatively slow increase in monetary stocks. Such is the
case with the precious-metal standard of to-day, and with
the instruments of exchange that are based upon it. Not

one man in a thousand would ever ask himself, on completing a piece of business, whether it would pay him better to convert into jewellery the gold coins that he receives rather than to continue to employ them as money, scarcely one in several hundred would actually carry out such a course even though commodity prices were rising very considerably and the exchange value of the money commodity were suffering a corresponding reduction.

A cheapening, however, of the precious metal in terms of commodities will at least set up a tendency for its production to decrease and for its consumption to increase, or rather for its consumption by *actual use* to increase (for it must not be forgotten that a portion of the consumption of the precious metal goes into what may be regarded as a kind of *treasure-store*, and a portion also, closely related to it, into what is principally a *display of wealth*, and that these portions are subject to their own peculiar laws and may sometimes follow an opposite course to consumption by actual use) But it is a matter of experience that any direct reaction on prices of the conditions of production and consumption is scarcely noticeable. This may be because movements of prices are not appreciably affected, up to a certain point, by the conditions of production and consumption, or it may be because their effects are temporarily obscured or neutralised by *other* factors At the present stage of development of the monetary system, the output of the precious metal—or let us simply say the newly extracted *gold*—passes, for the most part, not into circulation but into the stocks of cash of monetary institutions, and gold for industrial uses is mainly taken either out of these stocks or directly out of imported stocks of uncoined metal. In neither case can it be supposed that there is any *direct* effect on prices

It was W. N Senior, an Englishman, who played a preeminent part in developing the theory that the exchange value of gold must be determined by its cost of production (or, more generally, by its cost of *extraction*). Though several of Senior's assertions suffered at the hands of later critics, his treatment, which shows great powers of penetration, has not entirely failed to be of permanent value to learning. Even Senior has to admit that this line of causation is in practice exceedingly slow in operation. He mentions himself [1] that, at the time when he wrote (1828), the Mexican mines, which then supplied by far the greatest part of the metal (silver) needed for the world's coinage, had as a result of political unrest "been almost totally unproductive for the past fifteen years, so much so indeed, that silver has been sent to Mexico from Europe, and yet neither the general value of silver, nor its specific value in gold, has suffered any perceptible alteration".

But the train of thought may have been carried too far At any rate Jevons assumes that the decrease in the production of silver between 1810 and 1830 helped to bring about the fall in prices which, as he computed for England from Tooke's tables of prices, began in 1818 [2]

This view is supported by the experience of more recent times. That the conditions of production of the precious metals have an effect on the purchasing power of money cannot logically be denied Indeed it is *a priori* evident that if this influence continues to operate in the same direction over a very long period of time, it must eventually transcend all other factors in importance· one has only to think of the probable consequences of the discovery of inexhaustibly rich mines of precious ores, or on the other hand of the complete exhaustion of all deposits of gold or silver But it is never possible to detect any precise parallelism from year to year, or even from decade to decade, between the level of commodity prices and the ease or difficulty with which gold is being produced. All attempts to discover such a relation have hitherto proved a failure.

[1] *Three Lectures on the Value of Money* (London, 1840), p. 73 (printed for private circulation; the lectures were delivered in Oxford in 1829) [a reprint was published in 1931].

[2] *Investigations in Currency and Finance*, p. 132 [second edition, p 124]

Some authors, for instance W. Roscher, attempt to uphold the Cost of Production Theory of Money on the basis that "the value in exchange of the precious metals is determined by the cost of producing them from the poorest mines which must be worked in order to supply the aggregate want of them".[1]

It is rather the Quantity Theory of Money which is involved in such an argument. For the marginal cost of production is primarily an effect, rather than a cause, in relation to the exchange value of money. The exchange values of the precious metals might conceivably be subject to considerable fluctuations in either direction, on account, for instance, of changes in the demand for money, while the natural conditions that govern their production remained completely unaltered.

Now it is precisely changes in prices and fluctuations in the value of money over relatively *short* periods—ten, fifteen, or twenty years—which have the most serious consequences for trade. The more gradual changes —secular they may be called —in the value of money are of far less importance in this connection, even though they mount up considerably in the course of centuries. To some extent their interest is purely historical. The Cost of Production Theory may appear sufficiently logical, and it may indeed appear self-evident, but it is just when enlightenment is most urgently needed that this theory leaves us sadly in the lurch  The treatment of money (or rather of the substance of which money consists) as a *commodity*, and the theory of the value of money that is based on this treatment, lead to almost entirely negative conclusions as soon as we have to deal with these questions of real practical importance which arise in modern monetary systems. We must therefore look for other means of elucidation.

Here is to be found our answer to the question, which though frequently discussed is essentially rather an idle one, whether money is a "commodity". In Roscher's opinion, "the wrong definitions of money may be divided into two classes. those

[1] Roscher, *Principles of Political Economy*, book ii , chap iii , section cxxii [Lalor's translation, vol i , p. 365].

D

which convey the idea that it is more than the most current of all commodities, and those which imply that it is less"[1]

In sharp antithesis to this conception we have R. Hildebrand's assertion that, so far from being a commodity like any other commodity, money is "the very opposite of a commodity".[2]

In spite of these contradictions it may safely be stated that there is really no essential difference of opinion. In origin and substance, money—I mean concrete money, specie, which is the only kind of money that we are at present discussing—is undoubtedly a commodity  But so long as it circulates from hand to hand, it obviously cannot play the part of a commodity. On the other hand, as soon as it assumes the rôle of a commodity its rôle as money is at an end, or has not yet begun  How far its use as money, or how far its use as a commodity, is the predominant determinant of the exchange value of the money commodity, and consequently of the level of commodity prices, really depends, as we have already seen, upon purely quantitative relations  It is just because the metal used in coinage is employed so little for industrial purposes, and because, above all, its real consumption proceeds at so small a rate, that the value of money, at any rate over short periods of time, is not dependent on these factors, but is governed by quite different laws, which we still have to discuss.

In passing, there is a point to be noticed. The growth in the use of money, and the increase in monetary stocks, tends more and more to reduce the significance of the commodity characteristics of money  On the other hand, the development of the monetary system results in a displacement of specie by credit instruments and so-called money substitutes, and there exists, therefore, an important tendency towards a *strengthening* of the commodity aspect of money and of its influence on prices

It is sometimes said to be feasible to *base* a monetary system upon gold and yet to dispense entirely, or almost entirely, with the employment of gold both in circulation and in the banks' reserves. This would be done by extending the use of cheques, by the issue of notes of which the cover is of a purely banking

---

[1] *Ibid*, section cxvi, note [p  342; Lalor's translation has had to be slightly modified].

[2] *Theorie des Geldes*, p  10. This rather obscure statement depends on a point of view which is not, in my opinion, consistently adhered to in the later portions of Hildebrand's work.

nature, and so on. This view, which is held by some of the most prominent writers on monetary questions, must be regarded as utopian. In such a system the value of money would be *directly* exposed to the effects of every fortuitous incident on the side of the production of the precious metal and every caprice on the side of its consumption. It would undergo the same violent fluctuations as do the values of most other commodities

But it would be quite possible to maintain a stable value of money without the use of reserves of a precious metal Only it would be necessary for the *metal to cease to serve as a standard of value.* To these questions also we shall be returning later.

Among the attempts that have been made to attribute to the cost of production of money the dominating influence on its value in exchange, that of Karl Marx deserves special notice. Marx fits the value of money in with his general conception of the origin of all value, and regards it as determined by the amount of labour which is necessary for its production. But this process is not instantaneous. If the measure of value itself falls in value, "this fact is first evidenced by a change in the prices of those commodities that are directly bartered for the precious metals at the sources of their production", it is only gradually that "one commodity infects another through their common value-relation, . . . , until finally the values of all commodities are estimated in terms of the new value of the metal that constitutes money. This process", he continues, "is *accompanied*[1] by the continued increase in the quantity of the precious metals, an increase caused by their streaming in to replace the articles directly bartered for them at their sources of production".[2] Marx refuses to admit that the quantity of money may possibly exert an influence on prices. Such an opinion would, he says, be based on the "hypothesis that commodities are without a price, and money without a value, when they first enter into circulation, and that, once in the circulation, an aliquot part of the medley of

[1] The italics are mine.
[2] *Capital* (English translation by S. Moore and E Aveling), 1887, vol i., p 93

commodities is exchanged for an aliquot part of the heap
of precious metals".[1]

If the medium of exchange becomes greater in quantity
than "the circulation can absorb", its velocity of circulation is retarded or a portion "falls out of circulation" altogether. "All that is necessary in order to abstract a given
number of sovereigns from the circulation is to throw the
same number of one-pound notes into it, a trick well known
to all bankers." [2]

This gives rise, of course, to the same objections as does
Marx's general theory of value. It is only on the margin of
production that the value of a commodity is equal to its cost
of production in the narrowest sense, that is to say, to the
cost of labour (true interest being left out of account). It is
on this margin, if it exists at all, that the value of a commodity is just sufficient to cover the cost of labour, and
nothing is left over for the rent of land. But this margin is
not fixed in position. If an improvement is effected in the
general conditions under which the commodity—in this
case gold—is produced, or if its exchange value rises,
capital and labour flow in and the margin is pushed back,
in the reverse case the margin moves forward. There is,
therefore, as was emphasised above, no logical reason why
a change in the conditions of production of gold (a rise or
fall in the *average* cost of production) should not at first,
and perhaps for a fairly long period of time, be consistent
with a temporarily constant exchange value of gold

But in the actual locality where the gold is produced it is
very probable that increased output will result at first in
a certain lowering of the value of money, this is fully
confirmed by the fabulous rise in prices which took place in
California and Australia upon the discovery of gold. But
such a tempestuous wave of upward-moving prices is very
soon dissipated in the neighbourhood of its origin.[3] There

---

[1] *Ibid.*, p. 99          [2] *Ibid*, pp 95, 96
[3] *Cf* Tooke and Newmarch, *History of Prices*, vol. vi, Appendix
xxxii., p. 854 "In the palmy days of 1848 and '49 ' (in California) "all
were purchasers at any price; . . . a Dollar was paid for a pill, and the

is usually only a very small direct effect on the general level of world prices, and it is so often obscured by other factors that it is impossible to regard it as the most important, much less the sole, source of the price changes which occur in practice.

It is no easier, in my opinion, to justify Marx's second conception, which is not peculiar to him but is to be found in the works of very many other writers on monetary questions. The money which has "fallen out of circulation" must have fallen into some other use. But so long as conditions remain unaltered it is not possible that there should arise some new need which the money could serve to satisfy. It is, therefore, hard to see how the money which is released in this way can fail to bring about an upward movement of prices. But this matter is best discussed in connection with a more detailed analysis of the theory to which the next chapter is devoted.

same sum for an egg, a hundred dollars for a pair of Boots", etc "But in '51, bales of valuable Goods were sometimes not worth their storage", etc.

# CHAPTER 5

## THE QUANTITY THEORY AND ITS OPPONENTS

IT is clear that the higher is the price of a commodity the greater is the amount of money required for the purpose of its sale and purchase. But the whole function of the available supply of money—so long at any rate as it retains the form of money—is to be exchanged, sooner or later, for commodities. It is now but a small step to recognising that the total volume of money instruments in existence in an economic system, or rather their volume taken in relation to the quantity of commodities exchanged, is the regulator of commodity prices. This doctrine is usually ascribed to the English philosopher Hume, but in origin it goes back very much earlier; it may even date back to ancient times.[1] It marks a decided theoretical advance, by bringing into prominence the purely formal or conventional character of the value of money—or rather, of the function of money—in antithesis to the "mercantilist" conception, referred to above, of money as possessing a more or less unchangeable value of an intrinsic kind, which in the course of exchange is merely compared with the value of other commodities. (The Cost of Production Theory of Money belongs, of course, to a much more recent date.)

It cannot, I think, be denied that *under given conditions* the Quantity Theory is capable of being correct, and that in any case a significant degree of truth attaches to it But it must not be imagined that the quantity of the available

---

[1] *Cf* the often quoted fragment from the Roman lawyer Paulus (L.1, Dig xviii 1), *Origo emendi vendendique* etc , contained in it are the words "eaque materia" (money) "forma publica percussa usum dominiumque *non tam ex substantia praebet quam ex quantitate*".

For an account of Hume's immediate forerunners, see Marx, *op cit* , p 99, note, also p. 82, notes

stock of money or of individual balances serves as a *direct* measure of commodity prices and determines their level. Rather is the phenomenon to be pictured somewhat as follows

We saw above[1] that the laws which govern the exchange of commodities have no significance in themselves in regard to the absolute level of money prices· it is of no consequence whatever to a purchaser that he has to pay more for one commodity provided that he can be certain of himself obtaining a correspondingly higher price for some other commodity. But this is on the supposition that the purchase and the sale which succeeds it both take place within the same indefinitely short interval of time In practice this does not happen. Even if I have in stock the full equivalent of the goods that I purchase I am not always certain of being able to dispose of my goods at any moment to the best advantage Still less so if my own products, by means of which I intend to regain the money that I spend, cannot be available until later—indeed they may involve the use of the very goods that I am purchasing Buying, or spending money, on the one hand, and selling on the other hand, are usually concentrated over different parts of the month, quarter, or year. It follows that everyone, and particularly every business man, has to keep by him a certain sum of money—his till money—of which the average amount depends on the nature of his business, so as to defray such expenditure as is not covered by simultaneous receipts. (We are at present abstracting from the special arrangements by means of which, in a developed credit economy, this necessity can be curtailed and partly dispensed with.)

Now let us suppose that for some reason or other commodity prices rise while the stock of money remains unchanged, or that the stock of money is diminished while prices remain temporarily unchanged. The cash balances will gradually appear to be *too small in relation to the new level of prices* (though in the first case they have not on

[1] P. 23.

the average altered in absolute amount. It is true that in
this case I can rely on a higher level of receipts in the
future. But meanwhile I run the risk of being unable to
meet my obligations punctually, and at best I may easily
be forced by shortage of ready money to forgo some purchase that would otherwise have been profitable.) I therefore seek to enlarge my balance. This can only be done—
neglecting for the present the possibility of borrowing, etc.
—through a *reduction* in my *demand* for goods and services,
or through an *increase* in the *supply* of my own commodity
(forthcoming either earlier or at a lower price than would
otherwise have been the case), or through both together.
The same is true of all other owners and consumers of commodities  But in fact nobody will succeed in realising the
object at which each is aiming—to increase his cash
balance, for the sum of individual cash balances is limited
by the amount of the available stock of money, or rather is
identical with it. On the other hand, the universal reduction in demand and increase in supply of commodities will
necessarily bring about a continuous fall in all prices. This
can only cease when prices have fallen to the level at which
the cash balances are regarded as *adequate*  (In the first
case prices will now have fallen to their original level )

The reverse process will take place as the result of a
fortuitous fall in prices, the stock of money remaining unchanged, or of a permanent increase in the available quantity of money. But in the latter case (as in the case of a
diminution in the stock of money), the nature of the effects
depends to some extent upon the *route* by which the additional supply of money reaches the economic system
Eventually, however, it must become distributed in the
"channels of circulation"—at any rate this can be adopted
as an assumption—and a rise in prices, if it has not already
occurred, must now come about. It is not as though a man
who accidentally possesses twice as many ten-mark pieces
as usual would now proceed to bid double the price for
every commodity. But he will probably desire to complete
some purchase that he would otherwise have postponed, or

he will be more hesitant in disposing of some commodity that necessity would otherwise have compelled him to sell In short, the result of the increase in the quantity of money is a rise in the demand for commodities, and a fall in their supply, with the consequence that all prices rise continuously—until cash balances stand once again in their normal relation to the level of prices.

Both the strength and the weakness of the Quantity Theory are now adequately revealed. It consists of more than a mere *"truism"*, *i.e.* a truth which is self-evident but barren, it consists of more than the rule that the sum of the quantities purchased, each multiplied by its respective price, must be equal to the amount of money paid for them. The Theory provides a real explanation of its subject matter, and in a manner that is logically incontestable; but only on assumptions that unfortunately have little relation to practice, and in some respects none whatever.

For it assumes an almost completely individualistic system of holding cash balances In fact, over a wide field of economic activity, the individual balance has become scarcely anything more than an accounting magnitude, a legal conception, and is replaced in practice by a kind of collective holding of balances, arising out of the acceptance by banks of deposits

It assumes that everybody maintains, or at least strives to maintain, his balance at an average level that is constant (relatively to the extent of his business or of his payments) Or, what really comes to the same thing, that the *velocity of circulation* of money is, as it were, a fixed, inflexible magnitude, fluctuating about a constant average level, whereas in practice it expands and contracts quite automatically and at the same time is capable, particularly as a result of economic progress, of almost any desired increase, while in theory its elasticity is unlimited.

It assumes, in the third place, that an almost constant *proportion* of all the business of exchange, even if not the whole of it, is transacted by means of money in the sense of coin or notes. In actual fact the border line between money in this sense and true instruments of credit (ordinary book credit, bills, cheques, etc.) is extremely vague; and over a wide range one can be substituted for the other —and on occasion is so substituted, as is demonstrated at every period of crisis.

Finally, the Quantity Theory assumes that the portion of the total stock of metal which is employed in actual circulation can be sharply differentiated from the portion which is kept in the form of hoards against future needs or which, in the form of ornaments and jewellery, is withdrawn from use as money This too is, of course, an untrue assumption Money is treasured up only with the object of being sooner or later returned into circulation, a process that may under certain conditions be hastened or delayed; and the same is to some extent true of jewellery made of precious metals. It is true that hoarding in the real sense cannot be significant except in undeveloped communities—in progressive countries it has usually assumed other forms—and that the cost of manufacture of metallic jewellery usually forms so large a proportion of the total value that melting down would not be an economic proposition (the possibility of melting down arises in practice only in the case of old-fashioned or worn-out objects)

To sum up: The Quantity Theory is *theoretically* valid so long as the assumption of *ceteris paribus* is firmly adhered to. But among the "things" that have to be supposed to remain "equal" are some of the flimsiest and most intangible factors in the whole of economics—in particular the velocity of circulation of money, to which in fact all the others can be more or less directly referred back It is consequently impossible to decide *a priori* whether the Quantity Theory is *in actual fact* true—in other words, whether prices and the quantity of money move together in practice.

These difficulties have, of course, never been completely overlooked by supporters of the Quantity Theory. But they are open to the reproach that they have passed over the

difficulties rather too lightly and have not subjected the
details of the question to any comprehensive examination
They sometimes in fact express themselves as though the
quantity of money, or of that part that at any moment finds
itself in the hands of the public, must act as a *direct*
and *proximate* price-determining force. That, of course, is
putting the matter the wrong way round, and is open to a
simple line of criticism

This is also true to some extent of J. S Mill, whose views,
moreover, on this point seem to fail to be altogether clear or
self-consistent (see *Principles*, Book III , cap. viii , § 2 ff ).
Marx was, in my opinion, not entirely without justification
when he wrote[1] that Mill, "with his usual eclectic logic, under-
stands how to hold at the same time the view of his father,
James Mill, and the opposite view" (but the acidity is uncalled
for, and furthermore unreasonable, inasmuch as Marx himself
had in no way succeeded in overcoming the difficulties involved).

There are also many modern writers (for instance Charles
Gide in his *Principes d'économie politique*) who adopt a very
peculiar attitude towards the Quantity Theory. In some passages they write as though the theory is absolutely correct in
principle and at the most is in need of simple modification,
while elsewhere they would appear to hold that at the present
stage of economic development it has lost almost all foundation and validity.

———————

Meanwhile it is far easier to criticise the Quantity Theory
than to replace it by a better and more correct one. Up to
the present every attempt in this direction has come to
grief; or rather, scarcely a single serious attempt has been
made, apart from the Cost of Production Theory, which
to-day, except in orthodox Marxist circles, can no longer
reckon on any direct supporters

It is usual to speak of a *Credit Theory* of Money, which
is supposed to originate from Thomas Tooke and provide a
scientific antithesis to the Quantity Theory But I find
myself unable to say where such a theory is developed in
Tooke's writings. His monetary contributions—no matter

[1] *Op cit.*, p. 100, note; *cf ibid* , p  82

how highly one may regard them in other respects—are on
the theoretical side purely critical in general outlook and
negative in concept It is quite impossible, I think, to con-
struct out of them a positive theory of money He frequently mentions factors—and usually quite correctly—
as being *without* influence on the value of money, but he
never mentions the factors on which the value of money
must ultimately depend.

Let us, for instance take the twelfth of the celebrated
seventeen conclusions, in which Tooke formulated his objections to the Quantity Theory.[1] It reads as follows:

"That the prices of commodities do not depend upon the
quantity of money indicated by the amount of bank notes,
nor upon the amount of the whole of the circulating
medium, but that, on the contrary, the amount of the circulating medium is the consequence of prices."

There can be no doubt that there is much truth in this,
but clearly it provides no clue to the causes that determine the value of money; it simply leaves the question an
open one

And in fact almost all these conclusions of Tooke's are of
the same negative character We shall later be considering
the validity of some of them in more detail (particularly his
criticism of the Quantity Theory). Only one of them, the
thirteenth, attempts to provide a positive answer to the
question at issue. It reads as follows:

"That it is the quantity of money, constituting the
revenues of the different orders of the State, under the head
of rents, profits, salaries, and wages, destined for current
expenditure, that alone forms the limiting principle of
the aggregate of money prices, . . As the cost of production is the limiting principle of supply, so the aggregate
of money incomes devoted to expenditure for consumption
is the determining and limiting principle of demand "

Now this would indeed be a piece of positive elucidation
if the method of elucidation itself were not unfortunately

---

[1] *An Inquiry into the Currency Principle*, 1844, pp 121-4 *Cf History
of Prices*, vol vi , Appendix xv., pp. 635-7

almost as obscure and in need of elucidation as the phenomenon under discussion  Incomes determine prices; but we might just as well say—so at least it would appear —that the former are determined by the latter  With the possible exception of interest on loans (debentures, government securities, etc.), there is no category of income that is not, to a greater or less degree, dependent on, or regulated by, the prices of goods and services. Indeed we can go further  since almost every adult is a *producer* in the wide sense of the word, in consequence either of his labour or of his ownership of land or capital, costs of production and money incomes are really only two different aspects of the very same thing, and the sum of *each* must be equal to the sum of the prices of all the goods (and services) produced and consumed. It might therefore appear that this method of elucidation is taking us quite hopelessly round a circle; or that, to quote Launhardt,[1] it is no easier to decide "where in this endless, ring-shaped maze the beginning and the end are to be found than it is to decide which came first, the hen or the egg"

For my part, I do not share this view. It is my belief that this observation of Tooke's, or more precisely its *first* half, does really provide a starting-point from which a theory of the value of money and of prices can be developed  This I shall try to show later on. But Tooke himself never elaborated his suggestion, which makes an appearance in other sections of his works. As soon as he deals with changes that take place in the value of money in actual practice he ascribes them mainly—like many writers before and since—to changes in the conditions of production of the commodities themselves, to a greater or smaller yield of the harvests, etc (apart from the more temporary influences of business speculation and the like). The unscientific and illogical character of such a method of exposition, as soon as it ceases to be regarded as a corollary of the (Cost of Production or of the) Quantity Theory of Money, has already been indicated.

[1] *Das Wesen des Geldes,* p  42

In his report to the Royal Commission on the Depression of Trade and Industry,[1] Professor A Marshall remarks that it is not possible, in the manner of Tooke and also of many recent writers, to put forward a diminution of the cost of production of commodities as an additional cause of a fall of prices, when its effects in increasing the supply of commodities relatively to gold have already been allowed for.

But it is to be noticed that according to Tooke's view —which was expressed with ever-increasing precision as the years went by--an increase or decrease in the supply of commodities in relation to the available supply of money is *not* to be regarded as a cause of variations in prices; rather, the quantity of money in circulation depends, in accordance with the principle quoted above, on the level of prices (and the amount of business activity).

The inadequacy of Tooke's method of explanation was further exposed by Jevons,[2] as we shall see later, in so far as it relates to the great rise in prices in England at the beginning of the nineteenth century.

This gap in Tooke's line of approach has not been bridged by his followers, among whom the chief German representatives are the distinguished scholars Adolf Wagner (in his earlier writings on banking) and E Nasse Wagner's famous work, *Die Geld- und Kredittheorie der Peelschen Bankakte*, contains next to nothing that is *positive* about the causes that determine the value of money. He makes the assertion[3] that a money system which changes into a pure credit system as a result of the general adoption of "giro" and cheque methods of transaction "can be regarded as perfect" and "offers the advantage of an unchangeable standard". This assertion is made without any explanation and is not supported by the slightest investigation of the circumstances that are responsible for variations, or for the constancy, of the standard of value. Later in his life Wagner began to come round to the Quantity

---

[1] Third Report, 1886, Appendix C, p 421, Marshall, *Official Papers*, p. 5

[2] *Investigations in Currency and Finance*, p 131 [second edition, p. 123].

[3] *Die Geld- und Kredittheorie der Peelschen Bankakte*, p. 127.

Theory, as seems to be indicated by his intercession for bimetallism. Nasse's work will be referred to at a later stage.

Nor have the more recent opponents of the Quantity Theory succeeded in providing a real substitute. On the contrary, they fall only too easily into the still older way of thinking of the money substance as possessing an *intrinsic* value, or at any rate they incline towards this point of view. Thus R. Hildebrand, although, as we have seen, he had explained that money is "the very [1] opposite of a commodity", was eventually led to ascribe the origin of the value of money purely to the substance of which this "*Nichtware*" is composed  Bank notes, and irredeemable government paper money, constitute for him "only money tokens, not money, only means of payment, not means of exchange"  "Let us even suppose", he goes on, [2] "that, as a result of the issue of inconvertible paper money, coins disappear almost entirely out of circulation, *i e.* that in the country under discussion they become an ordinary commodity or that an agio comes into existence. . . . Even then the real seat of the purchasing power of money, the origin of its value, is still only to be found in the coins, although they no longer serve as a means of payment in this country and it is only in the imagination of the purchaser or seller that they continue to play the rôle of money  Even then the paper money is merely a money token, that is to say a representative means of payment playing the part of a deputy,—it is not money."

It does not appear to me that such a conception has any foundation. It is not some vague ritual, but the palpable facts of exchange and of credit, of commodity markets and of the money market, which day by day determine individual commodity prices and consequently (in a country that has a paper standard) the average purchasing power

---

[1] [In the original "*wahre*" is presumably a misprint for "*gerade*"; *cf.* p. 34 ]

[2] *Theorie des Geldes,* p 64.

of the nation's paper money.[1] On the other hand, it is the facts of the metal market and of foreign trade which determine the purchasing power of metallic money, or rather of the monetary metal Let us now suppose that first of all paper is made irredeemable and that then free coinage is suspended. Every link between notes and the monetary metal is consequently broken (as is the case with silver in Austria and Russia), and the determination of the value of each takes place relatively independently—never *quite* independently, however, because the one can always be substituted to *some* extent for the other,—and the value of the one can lie either below or above the value of the other, as is borne out by experience. It may at first seem paradoxical that "worthless scraps of paper" can possess a value in themselves The explanation is simple. these particular scraps of paper, furnished with a certain form of inscription, may not be manufactured or drawn up by anybody; it is essential to have some means of exchange (in spite of Hildebrand, it is impossible to deny such a title to paper money without flying too much in the face of common usage), and no other is available. Consequently the "scraps of paper" are accepted at the price at which they are obtainable.

It is not difficult to discover the origin of Hildebrand's view. The essential similarity between paper money and redeemable notes is often denied, but it is recognised, quite rightly I think, by Hildebrand, who consequently refuses to ascribe the value of the one to a different factor from the value of the other. But even redeemable notes do not derive their value from that of coins. Their redeemability guarantees their value in terms of the metal of coinage, but the value in terms of commodities equally of the notes and of the metal is determined by the general situation in the

---

[1] It cannot be denied that the adoption of a legally enforced rate, the acceptance of notes in payment of taxes, etc., assist in maintaining the value of a paper currency, for the supply and demand of paper means of payment is not then determined entirely by the condition of the market. But there is no reason, I think, for regarding them as the sole, or indeed as the predominant, influence

money market; and this in its turn is influenced just as much by the presence of notes—and indeed of any other instruments of exchange and credit—as by the presence of coins.

Strictly speaking, we can assert that *all* money—including metallic money—is *credit money.* For the force which is directly responsible for the generation of value always lies in the *belief* of the receiver of an instrument of exchange that he will be able to obtain for it a certain quantity of commodities  However, notes and paper usually enjoy a purely local credit, while the precious metals—or at any rate gold—are accepted on a more or less international scale. But it is all a question of degree. This is shown by the behaviour of silver in recent times, since the suspension of free coinage, the value of silver has fallen far below the value of notes based on silver.

Among the most zealous opponents of the Quantity Theory at the present time is Professor G. Luzzatti,[1] an Italian. His views on the causes responsible for the value of money are so fantastic and confused that they almost lie outside the scope of serious criticism. According to this writer, it is *the amount of the community's wealth,* and particularly the relation between the whole and its individual parts, which determine the level of prices  The quantity of money exerts an influence only in so far as the money itself forms a part of the wealth [2]

As a result of an increase of the community's wealth, and particularly of a more equal distribution (which increases the purchasing power of the working classes), all prices would tend to rise; in the opposite case they would fall; and

---

[1] *Prezzi ideali e prezzi effettivi,* Milan, Ulrico Hoepli, 1892.

[2] *Ibid*, p. 3. "Non è la moneta che fa i prezzi alle cose, ma è la *valuta,* ma è il *complessivo valor d'uso sociale,* ma è specialmente il rapporto fra il tutto e le singole parti che li prefinisce a una certa misura"  And p 5· "il corpo di questi beni (the commodities employed as money) per la sua abbondanza o per la sua scarsezza, non ha alcun effetto sul valore del denaro raffigurato da essi, se non in quanto l'abbondanza determini un accrescimento del valor d'uso sociale e la scarsezza una qualche diminuzione".

so on [1] Luzzatti supplies no logical deduction of these propositions, which are not, it seems to me, very well confirmed by the experience of recent decades—except perhaps by that of Italy. Luzzatti's reasoning becomes eventually so loose that it is impossible to tell whether by the value of money he means its value in *exchange* with commodities, or its *subjective* value, varying from individual to individual.[2]

---

So it is no good; the Quantity Theory cannot just be thrown overboard  The above instances illustrate the danger of running into even less perfect, and quite untenable, conceptions or semi-mystical speculations. Relatively, at any rate, the Quantity Theory is the most competent of all the methods of interpretation that have so far been advanced of the oscillations of the general price level; indeed, it is the only one which attempts in some degree to provide a rational explanation. It must be put up with, in the hope that a more intimate analysis of the underlying facts might remove the blemishes from which it undoubtedly suffers.

Above all, it is important to have a clear picture of the phenomenon of *velocity of circulation* of money and of the causes which are responsible for variations in this factor.

[1] *Ibid.*, p. 7 ff.          [2] *Cf Ibid.*, p. 36 ff.

# CHAPTER 6

### THE VELOCITY OF CIRCULATION OF MONEY

## A. *A Pure Cash Economy*

THE subject of velocity of circulation, so important for a proper appreciation of monetary questions, is treated very scantily in most economic text-books. Even the best writers sometimes display a certain lack of conviction with regard to the true meaning and bearing of the conception. Thus we find J S. Mill making the singular assertion[1] that "rapidity of circulation . . must *not*[2] be understood to mean the number of purchases made by each piece of money in a given time Time is not", states Mill, "the thing to be considered. . The essential point is, not how often the same money changes hands in a given time, but how often it changes hands in order to perform a given amount of traffic", and so on.[3]

If Mill were taken literally the whole definition would end up as a mere tautology. For in order to discover how often a certain sum of money changes hands in effecting the sale and purchase of a given quantity of goods, it is necessary to know the average *price* of the goods in question, which is precisely the quantity for the determination of which the (amount and) velocity of circulation of money are to be utilised. In other words, velocity of circulation as defined by Mill could not be regarded as an independent factor in the determination of average price. The real purport of Mill's somewhat obscure explanations is as follows· The commodity price level depends not only on the quan-

---

[1] *Principles*, book III , chap VIII , § 3.

[2] [The italics are the author's ]

[3] Similarly James Mill "By rapidity circulation is meant, of course, the number of times the money must change hands to effect one sale of all the commodities" (*Elements of Political Economy*, third edition, p. 134)

tity of available money and its velocity of circulation (in
the sense in which everywhere else Mill himself uses the
term), but also on the quantity of goods which are exchanged in the appropriate interval of time with the aid of
this quantity of money. This, however, is obvious and
applies generally to the Quantity Theory· excess or deficiency of money can be thought of only in a relative sense,
that is to say, in relation to the quantity of goods exchanged
for cash.

So our definition of velocity of circulation is simply this.
the average number of times the available pieces of money
change hands during the unit of time, say a year, in connection with buying and selling (excluding lending).

Just as important a conception is the reciprocal of velocity of circulation, the average *interval of rest* of money
It is the mean interval which elapses between two purchases effected by means of the same sum of money.
During this interval the money lies idle in safe or coffer.

To arrive at these quantities, several routes are theoretically
available. Though they all lead to the same goal, it is of some
interest to compare them

(1) If we know the total value, P, of goods exchanged against
cash in the course of the year and also the quantity, M, of
money in circulation, then clearly the mean velocity of circulation of money is given by the ratio of P to M.

(2) If it were possible to trace the movements of the individual pieces of money (units of money) through the economic
system and to discover how often each one changes hands in the
course of the year, the arithmetic mean of the individual fre-
quencies of circulation would give the value of the mean velocity of circulation of money  The result would be precisely the
same as before. For the total number of circulations of all the
money units is the same as the total value of goods exchanged,
and the number of money units is equal to the quantity of
money.

(3) Thirdly, an attempt could be made to ascertain the
*intervals of rest* of all the pieces of money during the given
period, the actual processes of exchange being regarded as confined to single points of time  The arithmetic mean of these
intervals of rest could then be obtained (intervals at the begin-

ning and end of the given period would not be counted separately but would be combined) This would give *the mean
interval of rest* of money, and, expressed as a fraction of the
unit of time (the year), its value would be equal to the reciprocal of the velocity of circulation of money, as worked out
above This is as it should be For the arithmetic mean of the
intervals of rest of all the units of money is equal to their sum
divided by their number, and consequently the reciprocal is
equal to the number of intervals of rest divided by their sum
But the *number* of intervals of rest (as defined above) is clearly
equal to the number of circulations of all the units of money, or,
what is the same thing, the total value, P, of the goods exchanged. And the *sum* of the intervals of rest clearly comprises
all the intervals of rest of each individual piece of money,
which, expressed as fractions of the unit of time, add up in
each case to exactly a year (to the unit of time itself) The total
sum is therefore equal to the number of units of money, *i e* to
the quantity, M, of money in circulation The ratio of P to M
is thus once more obtained.

(4) This calculation takes no account of the *sequence* in
which the intervals succeed one another. It can therefore be
carried out in a different manner. The practical feasibility of
this method is not to be altogether excluded from consideration,
and we shall see in any case that it has a certain theoretical
significance. Suppose that it were possible, for each individual
till, to calculate the amount of money which (in the processes of
exchange) flows through it in the course of the year (most
simply, if not quite accurately, regarded as half the sum of
receipts and payments), and also the mean interval of rest of
this money in the till Let the former quantities be represented
for the various tills by $a$, $b$, $c$, etc., the latter by $r$, $s$, $t$, etc.
Then the mean interval of rest is given by the formula

$$\frac{ar + bs + ct + \ \ldots}{a + b + c + \ \ldots},$$

and its reciprocal

$$\frac{a + b + c + \ \ldots}{ar + bs + ct + \ \ldots}$$

is the mean velocity of circulation of the money in circulation
in the given economic system. The numerator of the latter
fraction, $a + b + c + \ \ldots$ , is clearly equal to the sum of
receipts, or of payments, in the system, that is to say, to
the total value of the goods exchanged. It follows that the

denominator, $ar + bs + ct + \ldots$, must measure the quantity of money in circulation, as can be proved directly in the manner indicated above.

The question now arises whether the magnitude of this velocity of circulation can be regarded as determined by *independent factors*, or whether rather, as is sometimes maintained, it is not merely the *resultant*, given the quantity of goods exchanged and of available money, of the particular level of commodity prices, themselves determined by *quite different* causes.

That there is *some* degree of truth in this is not only probable, but quite understandable. For instance, if the general level of prices or of business activity rises or falls while the quantity of money remains initially unchanged, the velocity of circulation suffers a purely automatic increase or decrease

At a higher price level, other things being equal, everybody pays out more from his till; more, however, flows in. This necessarily results in a shorter interval of rest of money in the tills and so to a higher velocity of circulation. Or if money is lacking for certain purchases, they are *postponed* until sufficient money has been accumulated; if we think in terms of a circular flow of money between people in economic relations with one another, A buys from B, B from C, C from D, and so on, in more rapid succession than was the case before—the circulation of money is accelerated. The situation is reversed when prices fall.

It is a big jump to the assertion that velocity of circulation has no independent existence at all—that rather the whole theory which is based on the influence of this factor on the demand for money "proves to be nothing more than empty and barren formalism".[1] It is at once clear that the purely physical conditions under which money can be paid and transported set a definite limit to the magnitude of the velocity of circulation. Money cannot circulate faster—at any rate in a pure cash economy—than a messenger boy can run, its speed cannot exceed that of the

---

[1] R. Hildebrand, *Theorie des Geldes*, p. 41.

mail van, train, or steamer to which is consigned the cash used for making a payment. For it is clearly impossible for a sum of money, in the course of its journey to the recipient, to effect a second payment. But the importance of this consideration is very greatly diminished by the modern developments of transport, by the concentration of population in large towns, etc. Moreover, payments over greater distances have, of course, for a long time been made by means of the transfer, or rather the exchange, of claims (bills of exchange), with the result that at the most it is merely a residual balance that has actually to be paid over in money. It is only at times of severe crisis that at one and the same moment money is being sent in opposite directions between distant places, for instance between London and New York. Ordinarily, the well-known procedure, often explained, is in operation. Suppose A in London desires to make a payment to B in New York. He purchases the money claim which C in London holds against D in New York. And so on  The result is that the two sums of money which are owed, instead of having to be taken across the ocean in opposite directions, need only travel over the shorter distances between different business houses inside London and New York

There is, however, in actual practice an important factor which sets both upper and lower limits to the magnitude of the velocity of circulation. It is the time during which each piece of money has to lie unused in the till between two successive payments. This interval, which depends on the conditions of the market and on the purchasers' arrangements, is subject to exceedingly great variation from one period to another and from one piece of money to another. It might therefore appear that its mean value, averaged over considerable sums of money and over long periods of time, is again a purely arbitrary factor, having no independent importance. But this is not so  It is easy to see that the average interval of rest of the money in my till is the same thing as the ratio of the amount of money in the till to my average daily (weekly, or monthly) payments.

That the size of a cash holding is in no sense arbitrary (when credit is unobtainable) but within fairly narrow limits bears a definite relation to the turnover of the business, is a fact of which every business man is aware.

Retaining our supposition of a pure cash economy, in which credit is neither given nor received, let us now try to specify the most important factors which influence the size of the cash holding.

First of all, there are certain technical and natural features which sometimes cause a concentration of receipts at one time and of payments at another time, for instance at different seasons. If, as a result of the nature of his business, a man obtains most of his receipts in the spring and, on the other hand, has to make most of his payments in the autumn, then on the above supposition he must necessarily keep by him a fairly considerable sum of money throughout the summer. In the opposite case, where the receipts accrue mainly in the autumn and the payments become due in the spring, an appropriate holding of cash is necessary through the winter. Imagine a case where the whole of the annual business of a country is concentrated in two markets, at each of which one half of the population appear as buyers and the other half as sellers, nobody being both buyer and seller at one and the same market. Then the mean period of circulation (or rather interval of rest) of money would be just a half-year, and twice the total quantity of money would be equal to the total value of the goods annually exchanged.

It is unnecessary to point out that this case is purely imaginary. Though formerly it was very usual for the business of exchange to be concentrated into a few big markets or fairs, an overwhelming proportion of the goods were not disposed of in final exchange for money, but by means of the intervention of money (or of temporary credits) for other goods; this is in contradiction to the above assumption, with the result that in actual fact the circulation of money could proceed very much faster.

There is a point which may be noted in passing. In a

pure cash economy the most essential cash holdings are those which are destined for definite payments at given points of times in the future. It is precisely these which in an advanced credit economy can most easily be dispensed with, for loans or commodity credits, falling due on definite dates, provide a perfect substitute.

So much for payments which can be foreseen  In the second place, we have to consider those more or less *unforeseen* disbursements which occur in every business. To meet them, a larger or smaller amount of money must be kept in *reserve*. It is true that the size of this reserve depends, not only on the nature of the particular business, but in part also on the personal predilection of the owner. Yet the extreme upper and lower limits are much closer than might at first sight be supposed "Chance" is never, of course, completely irregular, and the truth of the so-called "Law of Large Numbers" can be verified under the most diverse conditions. According to this law, chance deviations in one direction or the other are most of them densely concentrated about a certain mean value, much bigger deviations are rare, the probability of the occurrence of a particular deviation, or its relative frequency, falling off much faster proportionally than the magnitude of the deviation.

Suppose that experience has shown that in a particular business the sum of the payments (or rather the excess of payments over simultaneous receipts) at a certain season tends to oscillate from year to year about a certain mean value, $a$  Let the "probable deviation" be $b$. this means that the odds are even— on the basis, once again, of the experience of this particular business—in favour of the payments over the period in question lying between $a+b$ and $a-b$. If the business man is satisfied with this so-called simple margin of safety, he must have by him a cash holding of $a+b$. But if he demands a greater degree of security against the possible exhaustion of his till, his cash holding must of course be somewhat larger. With a cash holding of as little as $a+2b$, the betting on the total exhaustion of his till over the period in question would, according to the laws of probability, be more than 9 to 1; with a cash holding of

$a + 3b$ it would be more than 44 to 1, and with one of $a + 5b$ it would actually be more than 2600 to 1, *i.e.* the till would be exhausted only about *once in three thousand five hundred years.*

The business man has never heard of the Calculus of Probability, but his empirical line of reasoning is on the whole valid: deviations from the normal course of business which have not occurred either in his own experience or in the experience of his predecessors are not very likely to occur in the future; and although the business man's experience seems to be the result of pure chance, the measures that he adopts in regard to his holding of cash will be scarcely altered from year to year so long as the circumstances remain the same. This stability becomes even more marked when it is the average of all businesses in a particular field that is under consideration.

In the third place, considerable sums of money accumulate from time to time, particularly in the hands of people who possess large fortunes, as a result of the sale of individual blocks of capital or the like, whose owners cannot for the moment find suitable employment for the proceeds. These money balances are, strictly speaking, merely a particular kind of cash holding, for here too the money is destined to return sooner or later into circulation. But their magnitude is clearly subject far more than that of real business holdings to individual caprice and to the influence of trade conditions. In an undeveloped economic system, where security is lacking, the most prominent function of gold is, of course, to act as a store of value; the large and small hoards, which are withheld from circulation for years on end, may constitute the major portion of the available stock of money. At times of stress in India, for instance, in the regularly recurring years of famine, an enormous quantity of little hoards emerge from under the bedsteads, where they have been buried in the ground, and serve to push up prices, particularly those of corn, to an abnormal level. But in the civilised countries of Western Europe this kind of thing no longer happens.

Moreover, the development of banking ensures that all large sums of money are temporarily entrusted to the banks, so that they are never *completely* withdrawn from circulation at all.

It would thus appear, on the assumptions that have been made, that, with the possible exception of the last-mentioned category, the average interval of rest, and consequently the average velocity of circulation of money, is of almost constant magnitude. It would react immediately against accidental expansion or contraction.

### B. *Simple Credit*

So far we have imagined a pure cash economy without credit or the lending of money. This is a purely hypothetical case, for at no stage of economic progress can the phenomenon of credit have been entirely absent. If we proceed now to take it into account the whole situation would appear to be altered, the ground would at once seem to have been cut away from under the Quantity Theory. But no substitute for money is provided by simple merchandise credit or simple lending of money from one person to another. What they do is to provide a powerful pulley for accelerating the circulation of money. Indeed there would be *absolutely no theoretical limit* to the extent of this influence if it were possible to leave out of account those practical obstacles of which we shall be speaking shortly.

In the example discussed above, one half of the population appeared as sellers in the spring and to an equal extent as buyers in the autumn, while the other half appeared as buyers in the spring and as sellers in the autumn It followed that in a pure cash economy the necessary stock of money would be equal to half the value of the total annual output But with the aid of some form of credit, the need for money and the amount of cash holdings could be diminished to an *unlimited* extent According to our assumption, the sellers are able to find a use for their money only after half a year has passed. It follows that they might just as well deliver their goods on half-yearly credit (and, in the absence of risk, without charging any interest). At the next annual market, which takes place after six months have elapsed, buyers and sellers will not group themselves in the same pairs as before, and it would not be possible simply to annul the old claims against the new ones which now come into existence as a result of the new transactions. But as soon as a sum of money, no matter how small, were brought into circulation in the market, it would zigzag rapidly backwards and forwards between buyers and sellers; the money received at any moment in exchange for goods would immediately be employed for the repayment of debt, and the money thus received in the repayment of debt would find a use in the purchase of goods.

And equally in the case where credit takes the form of loans rather than of merchandise credit. Any sum of money, no matter how small, would be sufficient. It might, for example, be lent by a seller A to a buyer B, who in his turn might employ the money for the purchase of goods from a seller C, C might then in his turn lend the sum of money to a buyer D; and so on.

It is easy to see that the procedure here outlined is *perfectly general*. No matter how great the economic complications, money must always be somewhere, and provided that it is not at the actual moment being employed in effecting a payment, it can be lent by its present owner to some other person, who can complete a payment with its aid. So there is no "theoretical" limit to the velocity of circulation of money other than that provided by its physical mobility or speed of transport. Were it possible to increase these to an unlimited extent a very large proportion of all the world's business of exchange and lending could actually be paid for *in cash* by sending backwards and forwards (*very* rapidly, it is true) one single ten-mark piece (or, for all I care, one single ten-pfennig piece). This may sound odd, but it is essentially less remarkable than the well-known fact that nowadays an enormous amount of such business is settled *entirely without the use of money*— through the transfer and exchange of claims.

Reality is, of course, far removed from this ideal representation, so far as it is simple credit between private individuals, not *organised* credit (as provided by a banking system), that is being taken into consideration. The reason is obvious. In the first place, many people, in fact the overwhelming majority of people, are so poor that they have little or no facilities for obtaining credit—an evil which can be alleviated by no system of credit; only a general improvement in economic welfare can make a difference. But quite apart from that, it is of course only in a very limited circle of people that it is possible to enter into individual transactions of credit or lending, whether in the capacity of creditor or of debtor. Moreover, if abuse of confidence is to be prevented such transactions involve precautionary measures which are burdensome and tedious both to the creditor and the debtor. Consequently, it will never occur to anybody, so long as he is actuated merely by his own interests, to consent to a loan or to a delay in payment when he is confronted with the prospect of himself running short of funds and having to borrow, perhaps in a few days' time. Or at least he would have to be certain of being able to satisfy his own needs for money on more advantageous conditions than he himself demands. Otherwise he would be undertaking, all to no purpose, the trouble of a double transaction, and be running in addition the risk involved by lending.

The matter can be put in other words as follows: A system of simple, unorganised credit certainly does to some extent reduce the necessity for holding cash balances; but the necessity still exists, particularly in regard to those balances which serve as *reserves* against unforeseen payments. The velocity of circulation of money is now seen to be a somewhat elastic quantity, but it still

possesses sufficient powers of resistance against expansion
or contraction for the conclusions of the Quantity Theory
to retain the appearance of substantial validity.

Under special conditions simple credit may itself be
capable of a significant degree of expansion, for instance
at times of speculation as a result of the attractiveness of
higher profits, or of the offer of ever higher prices or of
a higher rate of interest. But as soon as this incentive
disappears, the contraction is correspondingly catastrophic,
as is revealed in the period of crisis that ensues. Everybody now hastens to fortify his balances, which appear
much too small in relation to the new level of prices.
The demand for goods contracts, their supply increases,
and prices fall, for a time possibly far below their normal
level—particularly if confidence has been strained and
general mistrust prevails. We shall return to this subject
in another connection.

### C  *An Organised Credit Economy*

We have seen how simple merchandise credit and the
lending of money from one individual to another, while not
capable of providing a definite substitute for money, do give
rise to an increase in the velocity of circulation. And theoretically there is no limit at all to the extent of this influence. But in practice it is held in narrow bounds; for, in the
first place, the opportunities which are open to any single
individual for receiving and providing credit are usually
very limited, while at the same time an acceleration in
the circulation of money is necessarily bound up with a
(relative) fall in the size of balances below the level which
is dictated in an undeveloped credit economy by foresight,
and to some extent by custom.

In a developed credit economy both these obstacles are
removed, and either actually or *virtually* a higher velocity
of circulation is provided— or, more correctly, the velocity
of circulation is *capable* of being increased more or less at

will. The available means can be placed in two main categories· the *transfer of claims* (the use of bills of exchange) and the *centralisation of lending* in monetary institutions; and in addition there is the combination of the two classes which characterises the modern system of banking and bourses (discounting, the use of cheques, clearings, notes, etc.).

Let us suppose that several individuals, A, B, C, D, etc., have been given credit (*e.g.* merchandise credit) by one another, so that A owes money to B, B to C, C to D, etc. The repayment of these debts requires that a certain sum of money shall pass from A to B, from B to C, etc. If all the promissory notes fall due on the same date and involve equal sums, then repayment can be accomplished in a very short space of time and with the aid of the same pieces of money. Now if at least one of these individuals, for example A, is a man whose credit is generally accepted, his promissory note can be utilised by B, C, D, etc. for making their payments, so that one single payment in money is all that is in fact necessary, namely, from A to the last person in the line  It is of course usual for the acceptability of such a promissory note to be further strengthened through each endorser undertaking by means of his endorsement a subsidiary liability. A payment made by means of a bill of exchange is therefore not final, for if the bill fails to be met the money can be demanded from the endorser  It is precisely for this reason that bills provide a great source of strength to the credit system (this was particularly the case in earlier times)  While every expansion of simple credit is necessarily bound up with increasing risk, the security of a bill as a commercial instrument increases with the number of endorsements that it carries, and consequently with the number of money payments that it has provided the means of obviating.

Let us suppose that the standing of each individual endorser (including the acceptor and the drawer) is so small that the odds are no more than even in favour of his remaining solvent during the currency of the bill. Then if the bill carries, let us say, ten names, the probability of all these individuals becoming insolvent simultaneously is only one in $2^{10}$, $i.e$ $\frac{1}{1024}$, assuming that they are commercially independent of one another, an assumption which is not of course always valid.

It is only on account of their relative inconvenience, and for similar reasons (taxation of bills, etc.), that this *original* use of bills has gradually become less prevalent since banking was perfected. Bills no longer pass from hand to hand so much as formerly; they are discounted at some bank, and usually then remain in the bank's portfolio until they become due (at any rate so far as domestic bills are concerned). In other words, the employment of a bill of exchange has become purely a form of lending money.

But let us leave this out of account and consider the original system of bills, as for instance it took shape at the beginning of the century[1] in Lancashire and elsewhere. We have seen that the subsidiary liabilities which are incurred as a result of endorsement are completely discharged only when the bill is finally paid. It might thus be imagined that the sum of money in question had actually been passed along the whole line of intermediaries, B, C, D, etc. It turns out therefore that bills merely provide once again a method of causing a virtual acceleration in the circulation of money. Their superiority over simple merchandise credit here lies in the greater security and negotiability of the promissory documents, which can be included in cash holdings and in reserves almost in the same way as money (sometimes, indeed, when the coinage is in bad condition, they are better than money), and they can thus actually dispense with money.

As the monetary system becomes more developed, particularly if bills are mainly accepted by great business or banking houses which are furnished with numerous connections, it will more and more frequently happen that, in the process of effecting payments, a bill returns into the hands of the acceptor before the date on which it falls due, or that the acceptor exchanges it when it falls due

[1] [Of the nineteenth century ]

for some other bill that he has in his possession. The circle of payments is then completed without the employment of any money whatever  This need be no matter for wonder when it is remembered that in its essence money plays a purely formal part as an instrument of exchange, being really destined to return to its original owner after passing round a greater or smaller circuit

This procedure too might be regarded as an *acceleration* of the circulation of money  For the necessary quantity of money can be supposed to be infinitely small, and its (virtual) velocity of circulation to be infinitely great. Then its power of making payments would be represented mathematically by the expression $0 \times \infty$. The bills might be finally discharged by an indefinitely small sum of money being passed round among the interested parties, paying off at each step the outstanding debt.

There can scarcely be any doubt that the use of bills might, under favourable conditions, have developed so far as to have dispensed almost completely with the use of money.

A more powerful influence in this direction has been exerted under the head of our second category, the development of the *banking system*  When a man does not require his money until a certain date in the future he has no longer to rely upon the former method—insecure and tedious, and therefore often not used at all—which involved searching out a private borrower of sufficient solidity  He simply entrusts his money to a bank,[1] which is usually in the position to lend it immediately to some second person. The money now serves as an instrument of exchange or payment, and when it has accumulated in the hands of individuals in sufficiently great sums it is deposited for the same reasons as before in the same or another bank, which lends it out once again  And so on. So that during the time when it would otherwise have lain idle with its original owner it changes hands, and effects purchases, perhaps ten or twenty times.

[1] Or what is essentially the same thing, he buys securities or bills on the bourse.

F

This centralisation of lending in the banks (or on the bourse) has an important effect in gradually obviating the necessity for any precise insistence on fixed dates of repayment when loans are granted or received The increase in the velocity of circulation or the diminution in cash holdings may thus extend even to money which is intended to serve as a stock of cash for immediate payments or as a reserve against unforeseen payments.

Let us suppose that a number of business men keep their holdings, no matter for what reason, in one and the same place, for instance that they entrust them to the management of a bank. Then experience shows that the aggregate holding is subject to relatively much smaller variations than the individual holdings This is partly due to the regularity of chance, the "Law of Large Numbers",[1] but still more to the real interdependence of firms, a payment by one firm resulting, directly and indirectly, in a corresponding receipt by another. The consequence is that the bank, with the permission of the owners, can always lend a part of the sums that are entrusted to it, either to some different party or to the depositors themselves by granting them the right to withdraw up to a certain limit in excess of their balances. If the bank is intelligently managed it can do this without running any danger of being unable to meet its liabilities, even though the money may be repayable on demand.

It may happen in a particular business that in the course of each month the regularly recurring receipts and payments balance one another. Or it may be that at certain seasons there is an excess of payments but that this can be largely foreseen, so that the necessary funds can be secured by the normal use of credit—on the basis of claims falling due and the like But at the same time the business man needs a certain reserve against irregular receipts or unforeseen payments. We have already discussed the amount of this reserve, from both the theoretical and the practical points of view Let us suppose that experience has

[1] *Cf* Knies, *Der Credit*, vol. 2, 1879, p 247 A fuller account is given by Edgeworth in his "Mathematical Theory of Banking", *Journal of the Royal Statistical Society*, 1888.

shown that over a course of years the excess of payments has never varied in one direction or the other by more than a certain amount. If the business man is provided on the average (for instance at the beginning of each month) with, say, two or three times this amount he is secured to a high degree of probability against the exhaustion of his holding. Let us call the amount of this reserve $r$. Imagine now a collection of one hundred such firms, which have to be supposed to be completely independent of one another  Then according to the laws of probability the variations of the aggregate holding would only be $\sqrt{100} = 10$ times as great as that of the individual holdings (and so *relatively* only one-tenth as great)  It follows that to the same very high degree of probability an aggregate holding of $10r$ would be sufficient to cover the unforeseen payments of all the firms.

If a bank were acting as cashier to all the firms it could content itself with laying by the sum of $\frac{1}{10}r$ in respect to each individual firm without running any risk of impinging on its other funds  It could then concede to these firms the right to withdraw, if necessary, in excess of their balances *without limit*. Such a right would be available only in a *bona-fide* case of real need. This would be shown in practice by each firm's balance standing as often above as below the sum originally deposited  The necessary reserve of each firm would then be diminished to one-tenth of what would be necessary in the absence of a banking system, and the velocity of circulation of the money would be increased ten times. With a greater number of depositors the necessary amount of the aggregate holding would be relatively still less, the absolute amount increasing only with the *square root* of the number of customers.

(It should be mentioned that this does not purport to be a mathematical system for the running of a bank. We are merely utilising a simple numerical example in an attempt to throw some light on what appears to be the essential nature of these very complicated phenomena )

But in all applications of the theory of probability there is always the possibility of so-called *constant errors*  If the bank's customers belong to one and the same branch of industry—if, for example, they are all agriculturists or all cattle dealers—not only will their regular payments all be greatest at the same time of year but the random variations will probably be closely correlated.   The result is that the aggregate holding of reserves has to be substantially greater.

On the other hand, the variations will be even *smaller* than is indicated by the above calculation if the bank's customers have business relations *with one another*; so that a payment by one *necessarily* implies a receipt by another Finally, if the bank rules over a completely closed system it is clearly no longer a question merely of "chance", but the algebraical sum of deposits and withdrawals will always remain equal to zero.

The greater the number of the bank's customers, and the more diverse their occupations and their positions in life, the smaller is the stock of cash which the bank has to maintain in relation to the total extent of its business , and the greater *pro tanto* is the velocity of circulation of money When the bank's customers do business with *one another* cash may be withdrawn for the purpose of making a payment and be returned to the bank before the day is over

It is possible to go even further There is no real need for any money at all if a payment between two customers can be accomplished by simply transferring the appropriate sum of money *in the books of the bank* It can be written off the account of the debtor (the buyer) and credited to the account of the creditor (the seller). Suppose now that this system, which is known by the name of the *Virement, Giro,* or cheque system, is developed up to the point where everybody possesses a banking account Then all payments could be effected by such bookkeeping transfers, except possibly those for which small change suffices It is true that a substantial amount of *capital* would be required to instil confidence and to meet unavoidable risks But whether the banks are branches of one single monetary institution serving the whole country (like the Austrian Post Office Savings Bank [1]) or independent establishments connected by a common clearing house (on the English or American pattern), they would require *no stock of cash* —not at any rate for purely domestic business

A pure credit system has not yet, even in England, been

---

[1] For an account of the much discussed development of this quite unique institution, see an article by Ed. Tobisch, "Der Check- und Clearingverkehr des k. k osterreichischen Postsparkassenamts" *Conrad's Jahrbuch,* 1892.

completely developed in *this* form  But here and there it
is to be found in the somewhat different guise of the *bank-note system*  A bank note is essentially to be regarded as a
kind of deposit-receipt or cheque, which passes through
a number of hands before it is presented to the bank either
for redemption or as a deposit  In those countries where
notes can be issued for small denominations, they are
always preferred to coins on account of their greater convenience  In Holland, Sweden, and the United States, for
instance, a gold coin may not be seen for years on end
This is the case in Sweden in spite of the fact that all the
banks of issue are obliged to redeem their notes in gold
Such an obligation is, of course, of the greatest significance
For it causes the discount policy of the banks to be regulated, more or less automatically, by the state of the exchanges , so that the general level of commodity prices
is governed by that in foreign countries. This will be a
matter for later discussion. But so far as purely domestic
business is concerned, the cash reserves of such countries
are now nothing more than a matter of tradition

In Sweden it rarely happens that gold is consigned even to
foreign countries, for the big banks prefer to maintain balances
with foreign banks, and to draw on these balances or, in case
of necessity, on foreign credits

The bank-note system presents a rather complicated
phenomenon, partly for inherent reasons and partly as a
result of legal restrictions of a somewhat arbitrary nature
Notes can be obtained only on payment of interest (or in
exchange for commodities), but they earn no interest for
their owners  Private individuals are therefore unwilling
to stock them in large quantities, and they flow back to
the banks in the shape of deposits or are lent to others in
return for interest. At the same time, temporary use is made
of other instruments of credit, such as bills or merchandise
credit, "in order to economise notes"  The matter can be
put in other words as follows . Notes provide in themselves
the basis for a more or less elastic system of credit, and

they circulate with a velocity which is more or less variable. It is for this reason that it was never possible for even the older supporters of the Quantity Theory to provide a satisfactory demonstration of the exact relationship which they held to exist between the price level and the quantity of notes (and coin).

The essential characteristic of notes, regarded as a substitute for metallic money, does not consist in their being used for making *payments* in the place of coin. For even where notes are in common use, payments could in fact be effected by means of metallic money. It would merely be necessary for each buyer and seller to arrange to meet at the bank, and instantaneously to convert notes into coin and then the coin back again into notes. (This is to some extent what actually took place at earlier stages of the history of banking and note issue ) The essential characteristic of notes consists in their taking the place of coin in the *cash reserves* of private individuals and of those banks which do not themselves issue notes

Current accounts (under the *Giro* system) provide a similar service, and they have the further advantage that they usually earn interest, so that they tend more easily than notes to dispense with other forms of credit. Cheques scarcely ever circulate: they effect but a single payment. Theoretically they have the advantage of greater simplicity, but in practice notes are far more convenient, at any rate for small payments (provided that notes of small denominations are available)

We intend therefore, as a basis for the following discussion, to imagine a state of affairs in which money does not actually circulate at all, neither in the form of coin (except perhaps as small change) nor in the form of notes, but where all domestic payments are effected by means of the *Giro* system and bookkeeping transfers. A thorough analysis of this purely imaginary case seems to me to be worth while, for it provides a precise antithesis to the equally imaginary case of a pure cash system, in which credit plays no part whatever. The monetary systems actually employed in various countries can then be regarded as *combinations* of these two extreme types If we can obtain a clear picture of the causes responsible for the value of money in *both* of these imaginary cases, we shall, I think, have found the right key to a solution of the complications which monetary phenomena exhibit in practice. (A close examination of such a simplified system should also be of service, as we shall see, in settling certain other economic questions )

For the sake of simplicity, let us then assume that the whole monetary system of a country is in the hands of a single credit institution, provided with an adequate number of branches, at which each independent economic individual keeps an account on which he can draw cheques. In order to meet foreign, and perhaps also industrial, demands, the Bank must maintain a certain stock of gold. It may be imagined that this stock of gold, or rather its average value, $R$, comprises the property of the Bank itself. On this assumption, the Bank's claims on the public must be exactly equal to its debts to the public. If the sum of the credit balances is $K$, the sum of the debit balances must be $K$, or rather $-K$; so that the algebraical sum of all balances always remains equal to zero.

But this is true only in respect to pure domestic transactions. When the foreign balance of trade or balance of payments is such that the Bank has to give up part of its cash to foreign countries, it finds itself with an equal excess of domestic claims. And, on the other hand, when gold flows into the country and is delivered to the Bank, the sum of the credit balances rises correspondingly above the sum of the debit balances; and the Bank owes more to the public than the public owes to the Bank. A similar situation is created according as more or less gold is being devoted to industrial uses at home than is being imported (or mined).

On these assumptions, the more important kinds of credit and monetary transactions would be conducted in the following kind of way.

The actual exchange of commodities proceeds very simply The buyer draws a cheque on his balance (or on his credit) for the appropriate sum, and the seller cashes the cheque, the sum being thus credited to him by the Bank. But within a short space of time goods must be paid for by goods It follows that the sum of the amounts debited must be equal to the sum of the amounts credited, not only for all the Bank's customers taken together (for that must *always* be the case), but also for *each individual* customer ; so that by the end of the day or of the week each account will always show the same balance as at the beginning.

A certain interval will, however, elapse between the sale of one lot of goods and the purchase of another equivalent lot During this time, the sellers are in reality extending credit to the buyers to the amount of the sum in question (or a part of it), although on the surface the payment has the appearance of being immediate. This is brought about as a result of the facilities and the guarantees provided by the Bank Let us return to our former illustration, where one half of the inhabitants of a country offer their produce for sale in the spring and the other half in the autumn In the extreme case, the first half would appear as creditors in the books of the Bank during, say, the summer and the second half as debtors, to a total sum equal to half the value of the annual produce But in the winter claims and debts would be completely cancelled, and all the accounts would show zero balances. Or, to take a more probable case, the aggregate amount of claims and of debts might remain almost constant during the whole year, and equal to a *quarter* of the value of the annual produce, each half of the population appearing in the books of the Bank *alternately* as creditors and debtors Finally, every possible combination of these two extreme cases is possible , but, in accordance with our assumption, the average amount over the year of claims and of debts must always be equal to a quarter of the value of the annual produce. The period of circulation of money in such a pure cash economy would be half a year ; but if it is assumed that cash is turned over $n$ times a year, then it is easy to see that the average amount of claims and of debts in the

Bank's books would be $\dfrac{W}{2n}$, where $W$ stands for the value of the annual produce, or rather of the annual turnover of commodities.

Even if the Bank held a stock of gold equal in value to the amount of deposits paid in (though on our assumptions this is in no way necessary), the velocity of circulation of money would be doubled.

According to Essar's [1] figures, the aggregate turnover on current account (half the sum of the amounts credited and debited) in 1890 was in the case of the French Bank equal to 135 times the average amount outstanding on current account, 146 times for the Belgian Bank, and as much as 190 times for the German Reichsbank The turnover of the French Bank was 54 thousand million francs and this was effected by an amount of money of about 400 million francs

But these figures do not fully indicate the velocity of actual circulation Essar is concerned purely with *credit* balances, where the account cannot be overdrawn The Bank would be all the less anxious to keep in reserve the full amount of such balances, and would lend most of them away or employ them as cover for the note issue The same money would thus in fact be fulfilling its function even more frequently

We have so far dealt with the interval of time, dependent on nature and technique, which separates a purchase from the corresponding sale But actual long-term credit itself has a part to play. Many people require in their businesses, either regularly or at certain periods, more capital than they themselves possess, while others possess more capital than they are able or willing to find a use for The resultant lending and borrowing can be supposed to be effected through the intervention of our Bank. Capital is accumulated (or saved) when a customer allows part of his balance to remain at the Bank, and increases it from time to time by depositing fresh sums (in the shape of cheques received in exchange for goods and the like). The Bank must of course pay interest, at any rate on long-term deposits (the

---

[1] "La Vitesse de la circulation de la monnaie", *Journal de la société de statistique de Paris*, 1895, p 113 ff.

rate bearing little relation to the rate which it itself demands). For otherwise its depositors would withdraw their money, and lend it out on their own account But all that they would have to do would be to draw cheques on the Bank, and there need be no drain on its cash reserves, though an approximately equal amount of its outstanding loans would probably be repaid by borrowers anxious to avail themselves of the more favourable terms now offered by private lenders, and the extent of its business would be contracted

Against these long-term deposits there stand loans, which are renewed when they fall due and run on in actual fact for a lengthy term. But we have seen that there is no need to postulate any precise equivalence. It might well be that the greater part of the deposits are kept at the Bank for several years, while the corresponding loans are granted for only three months and are never directly renewed On the other hand, it might happen that the deposits are frequently withdrawn, while the loans are granted for a long term. The total sum deposited is nevertheless equal to the total sum withdrawn. This is a purely mechanical relationship, necessitated by our assumptions, which indicate that, at any rate in the case of domestic transactions, for every cheque drawn an equal sum of money must be deposited in the Bank

It would be quite possible for all the country's lending to be concentrated in the Bank, but there is no need to make such a supposition In practice, every bank avoids locking up money in risky and protracted enterprises. This is far more the business of individual capitalists, who risk a portion of their property, or stake their rights to it over a long period of time, in order to take a share in such profits as the enterprise will secure if it meets with success. This does not upset our system. Such individuals form no part of the circle entailed in the Bank's credit activities; they deal directly with one another by way of debentures, shares, mortgages, limited companies, and the like. A simple illustration is afforded by the case of an entrepreneur who is enabled to build, let us say, a house through the temporary provision of bank credit. When his under-taking is completed, he either sells the house or raises a mortgage upon it The money raised in this way is with-drawn from the purchaser's or lender's banking accounts by means of cheques, and the entrepreneur uses these cheques to repay the loan extended to him by the Bank

It is important to notice that the long-term rate of in-terest (the *bond rate of interest*[1]) must correspond some-what closely to the short-term rate of interest (the *bank rate of interest*), or at any rate that a certain connection must be maintained between them. It is not possible for the long-term rate to stand much higher than the short-term rate, for otherwise entrepreneurs would run their businesses on bank credit—this is usually feasible, at any rate by indirect means. Similarly it cannot stand lower than the short-term rate, for otherwise most capitalists would prefer to leave their money at the Bank (or to use it in discounting bills of exchange).

It is to be remarked in passing that we have not yet come across anything which corresponds to the customary method of explaining how the rate of interest is determined by the supply and demand of "capital" It would appear rather that the rate of interest—the short-term rate in the first place, and so indirectly the long-term rate— is com-pletely subject to the discretion of the Bank. The rights of this matter will be examined later

An extremely interesting question now arises . What is it in our system, and so by inference in the real world, in so far as its conditions correspond to those which we are postulating, that determines the exchange value of money and the general level of commodity prices? No money circulates, and for the purposes of domestic trade no money need be kept in reserve Means of payment, or purchasing power, can be provided in accordance with the

[1] ["*Börsenzinsfuss*" in original ]

dictates of choice and necessity. The Quantity Theory of Money would appear to be deprived of its very foundations.

This question calls for an answer: that is to-day almost universally recognised It ran like a red thread through the familiar, and in many ways so instructive, discussions of the English Commission of 1887–88, which had to examine the causes of relative variations in the value of silver and gold. In the course of the evidence, the question arose again and again how it was possible at the present stage of economic development for the quantity of gold in the banks, or anywhere else, to exert an influence on prices , and how, in particular, the surplus of gold possessed at that time by the banks and the prevailing low rates of discount could be compatible in the light of the Quantity Theory with the falling level of prices. England's most distinguished monetary theorists and practitioners were summoned before the Commission, but I have not been able to discover that this fundamental question received any solution worthy of the name. Some of the witnesses, for instance H. H Gibbs,[1] a Bank director who appeared several times, became involved in a veritable net of self-contradictory argument. At one time they would ascribe the low rates of interest and the ease with which the banks could maintain their stocks of gold to the decline in business and to the low level of prices, and then they would explain these latter phenomena as being due to a relative scarcity of gold By far the most valuable contribution towards a solution of this question was, in my opinion, supplied by Professor Alfred Marshall in the course of an examination which lasted for three days [2] But Marshall seems to me to lay too much emphasis on the *direct* influence that he alleges is exerted by the magnitude of banking reserves on the rate of interest and consequently on prices. This view cannot easily be reconciled with the instances which the members of the Commission themselves brought against him, and still less with the increase

---

[1] Gold and Silver Commission, *First Report*, Q 5328 ff
[2] [Marshall, *Official Papers*, pp 32-169 ]

which took place later in the reserves of the Bank of England and in the cash holdings of the other central banks of the world  Nevertheless, the second volume of Marshall's *Principles*, in which he intends to publish a full discussion of monetary questions, will be awaited with the greatest interest.

This question is also touched upon in the well-known, and often quoted, discussion of Erwin Nasse, "Uber das Sinken der Warenpreise wahrend der letzten funfzehn Jahre".[1] In order to demonstrate the difficulty of ascribing the fall in prices which had actually taken place to a scarcity of gold, Nasse mentions the astonishing development in almost all countries during recent decades in the use of instruments of credit as a means of payment  This development had gone "hand in hand with the growth in trade and the increase in the need for means of payment" and had brought about an "ever-growing independence" of "the available stock of gold"  "It will be contended", continues Nasse, "that the foregoing considerations leave the value of gold entirely in the air, since they free it from the influence of the scarcity of the precious metals. If the means of payment could be increased at will according to the needs of trade, no limit would be set by monetary conditions to the most arbitrary rise in prices, such as takes place when speculation is rife and enterprise feverishly active. It is impossible to see how the available quantity of means of payment, if it could be increased at will, could determine and limit the purchasing capacity of buyers and consequently the general level of prices "[2]

Nasse then answers this objection himself  "International trade provides a rôle for cash payments which is entirely different from the rôle which they fulfil in connection with domestic payments in highly developed countries." . . . "An unhealthy movement which is proceeding faster in some country or area than in the rest of the world causes the balance of payments to become

[1] *Jahrbucher fur Nationalökonomie und Statistik*, vol. 51 , 1888
[2] *Ibid* , p  156.

unfavourable, the country's cash reserves, that is to say, its Bank's stock of cash, is consequently contracted; and an arbitrary rise in prices is prevented. For it then lies with those in control of the Bank to restrict credit, and so, by exerting a downward pressure on prices and putting an end to unhealthy speculation, to restore the international equilibrium of prices."[1]

There is no need to emphasise the inadequacy of this account of the determination of "the general level of prices" It does not really amount to more than saying that the level of prices in one country cannot move entirely independently of that of other countries, and so of the level of world prices That is of course perfectly true, but it fails to provide any information on the question which awaits an answer It merely gives rise to the further question of what it is that determines the prices of the "other" countries—the world prices themselves. The situation may be such, as we shall see later, as to cause prices to move in the same direction in several, or all, countries. Clearly then there will be no occasion for international movements of gold, and it is difficult to see what it is that can govern such a general movement of prices It might be that prices would ultimately rise until the banks' stocks of gold appear inadequate to the needs of international payments, or, on the other hand, prices might fall so low that the superabundance of these stocks becomes intolerable. But having regard to the actual size of the central banks' stocks of gold and to the relative insignificance of such shipments of gold as do in fact take place between them, it is clear that the limits provided by these factors are too wide to be regarded as directly governing the level of prices.

But Nasse does not adhere to this opinion He is inclined rather to adopt the view, popularised by Tooke, that the real cause of movements in prices is to be found "on the side of goods", that is to say, in changes in the conditions of production and transportation of the commodities themselves.

[1] *Ibid*, p 157.

This view was carefully examined above,[1] and it was argued that only a supporter of the strict Quantity Theory or of the Cost of Production Theory of Money could find such a position tenable Nasse has declared himself an opponent of both these theories, and it seems clear that his argument about the probable influence of increases of efficiency on prices [2] is without any logical foundation.

But even if it were justifiable to regard the magnitude of bank reserves as definitely governing commodity prices, it would still be necessary to examine the mechanism by which this result is brought about Nasse has done no more than to point out, quite correctly, that when an "unhealthy" (disproportionately great) rise in prices takes place in a single country, and money consequently leaves that country, the banks, particularly the Central Bank, have the power to "exert a downward pressure on (domestic) prices" "by means of restriction of credit" (raising the discount rate, selling securities, and so forth).

This must not be held to support the somewhat one-sided view of the school of Ricardo, according to which every shipment of gold must be caused or accompanied by a change in prices in the countries concerned Moreover, credit restriction is by no means the *only* method by which the international equilibrium of prices can be re-established after a disturbance. A more important factor is the rise in the supply of imports, and the fall in the demand for exports, which is brought about by a rise in domestic prices, for this in itself exerts a downward pressure on prices The main purpose of a temporary rise in the banks' rate of discount is merely to bring about a postponement of the payments that are immediately falling due to foreigners until such time as a change in the conditions of export and import has produced a more favourable balance of payments. On these and similar points the objections of the school of Tooke against the classical theory may in many ways be justified [3] But they seem to touch purely upon side issues, and they are without fundamental importance in deciding the main question

But, it might well be asked, does the power of monetary

---

[1] P 26 ff    [2] *Loc cit*, p 55 ff
[3] See p 82 ff, below

institutions over prices operate only in this direction?
Is it not logically necessary to suppose that under suitable conditions they can exert an influence in the opposite direction—that is to say, that they can raise prices?
And is it reasonable to maintain that this influence in
either direction can only appear in exceptional circumstances, such as the extreme conditions presented by a
crisis? Should it not rather be supposed that the banks'
discount policy, or more generally their credit policy—no
matter how it may be determined—is *always* exerting a
certain influence on the level of prices, either maintaining
or disturbing it? If so, is this influence to be regarded as
confined within *narrow limits*, such changes in the general
level of prices as actually occur being brought about by
other forces? If so, what is the nature of these forces? Or
is it a characteristic of the banks that their power is *unlimited*, so that in a pure credit economy they could bring
about any desired rise or fall in prices by pursuing a uniform policy with regard to the rate of interest? Is it possible
that we have here found the general cause of the price
fluctuations which occur under present conditions, when
it is becoming more and more usual for instruments of
trade and credit to pass through the hands of the banks?
Does it follow that the most powerful instrument for
stabilising prices lies in appropriate regulation of banking
policy?

In the following chapters we will try to find answers
to these questions, which are clearly of the greatest importance for a final solution of the monetary problem,
though they are seldom referred to in current monetary
discussions.

# CHAPTER 7

## THE RATE OF INTEREST AS REGULATOR OF COMMODITY PRICES

### A. *The Classical Theory and the School of Tooke*

THE above question, as to whether it is in the power of the banks to regulate at will the exchange value of money and commodity prices, was answered by Ricardo with a decisive affirmative. His answer was not, as Wagner asserts,[1] confined to the supposition of irredeemable paper money (as was current in England at the time at which Ricardo was writing) It applied equally well where the notes were redeemable in metal, though it must, it is true, be assumed that the banks of issue of the various countries pursue a uniform policy. There is a passage in Ricardo's reply to Bosanquet which leaves no room for doubt on this point. "Let us suppose", he says, "a case in which money could not be profitably exported—Let us suppose all the countries of Europe to carry on their circulation by means of the precious metals, and that each were at the same moment to establish a Bank on the same principles as the Bank of England—Could they, or could they not, each add to the metallic circulation a certain portion of money? and could or could they not permanently maintain that paper in circulation? If they could, the question is at an end, an addition might then be made to a circulation already sufficient, without occasioning the notes to return to the Bank in payment of bills due If it is said they could not, then I appeal to experience, and ask for some explanation of the manner in which bank notes were originally called into existence, and how they are permanently kept in circulation."[2]

[1] *Geld- und Kredittheorie der Peelschen Bankakte*, p 47.
[2] Ricardo, *Reply to Mr Bosanquet's Observations*, chap. v (*Works*, M'Culloch's edition, p. 343) At the time of Ricardo the rate of interest

According to Ricardo, such a new issue of notes must necessarily bring about a *rise in prices* In principle this seems correct, though it is not to be expected that prices will rise in exact proportion to the increase in the note issue, for the notes may release or displace other instruments of credit and the velocity of circulation may decline.

It is to be observed in passing that Ricardo is here inconsistent with the view which he expresses elsewhere [1] on the question of the relatively stable value of the precious metals. If it is possible for the banks (to be accurate, for the banks of the world as a whole) to regulate the value of money through the issue of notes even though the notes are perfectly redeemable, then it is clear that a constant value of money is not ensured simply by the provision that the notes shall be redeemable. Yet this was Ricardo's belief. A certain touch of logic must therefore be allowed to the later Currency School, no matter what view is taken of Peel's Bank Act, for which they were responsible.

Quite a different line of approach is to be found in the writings of the school of Tooke (Tooke, Fullarton, Wilson, and also Mill, Nasse, and to some extent Wagner, etc.) It is here maintained that on the assumption that the banks issue notes *purely by way of lending* on adequate security—and not through advancing large sums to the government and the like—the banks are entirely dependent on the requirements of the business world for means of payment and have no means of affecting these requirements or of influencing prices.

For example, the eighth and ninth of Tooke's propositions, already referred to, run as follows·

on loans was still limited by English law to a maximum of 5 per cent (The restriction was not definitely removed until 1837 ) This explains why Ricardo and other economists were in the habit of referring to a restriction or expansion of the banks' note issue rather than to a rise or fall in their rates of interest The difference is not very significant, other means are available for restricting credit which are just as effective, and indeed even more sensitive, than actually raising the rate of interest

[1] *Proposals for an Economical and Secure Currency (ibid.,* p 391 ff ) Ricardo's suggestion (Section II , pp 400-402) that an ideal standard of value is an impossibility would to-day be regarded as old-fashioned and is no longer tenable in view of the possibility of employing index numbers

"That it is not in the power of Banks of Issue, including the Bank of England" (or any other Central Bank), "to make any direct addition to the amount of notes circulating in their respective districts, however disposed they may be to do so. In the competition of Banks of Issue to get out their notes, there may be an extension of the circulation of some one or more of them in a large district, but it can only be by displacing the notes of rival banks

"That neither is it in the power of Banks of Issue *directly* to diminish the total amount of the circulation, particular banks may withhold loans and discounts, and may refuse any longer to issue their own notes, but their notes so withdrawn will be replaced by the notes of other banks, or by other expedients calculated to answer the same purpose." [1]

It is particularly the second of these propositions that sounds rather paradoxical. It is quite certain that it must be possible for all the banks of a country, provided that they are solvent, to *diminish* the quantity of notes in circulation, or indeed to withdraw them altogether What "other expedients" could then take their place? Would it be some makeshift, such as direct exchange credit or private bills, circulating from hand to hand without being discounted and taking the place of means of payment? But how small would be the extent to which these makeshifts of a more primitive system could take the place of our instruments of organised credit! Or would it be precious metals flowing in from abroad? It is a fact that such a flow would finally set in—though only gradually at first—but it would occur only as a result of the fall in prices and the rise in the value of gold, which would take place in precise contradiction to the view expressed by Tooke. And even this makeshift ceases to be available as soon as we adopt an international point of view and assume that all banks pursue a uniform policy

It is necessary then to admit that it lies within the power of the banks to *diminish* the quantity of means of

---

[1] *An Inquiry into the Currency Principle*, p. 122, *History of Prices*, vol vi., Appendix xv., p 636

exchange, for instance by raising the discount rate. It is scarcely logical to deny that, by means of the reverse operation, the banks can bring about an *increase*.

An apparent confirmation of Tooke's theory is provided by the famous unanimous assurance of the country bankers summoned before a Parliamentary Committee. Fullarton has set out their statements in the following words: "The amount of their issues is exclusively regulated by the extent of local dealings and expenditure in their respective districts, fluctuating with the fluctuations of production and price, and that they neither can increase their issues beyond the limits which the range of such dealings and expenditure prescribe, without the certainty of having their notes immediately returned to them, nor diminish them, but at an almost equal certainty of the vacancy being filled up from some other source."[1]

But it must not be forgotten that it was here a question purely of provincial banks, of which the notes (as Ricardo had already pointed out) could circulate only in their own districts, but not in London, while the notes of the Bank of England were of course freely accepted everywhere If provincial banks unduly enlarged their issue, then according to Ricardo a local rise in prices would result, and this would lead to increased imports of goods into the district and to diminished exports to London, so that the district's balance of payments would rapidly become unfavourable. But on *this* matter Tooke's treatment is certainly more accurate. Tooke would say that the cheaper terms of credit provided by the provincial banks would lead to a transfer of capital from the provinces to London. In either case the result is the same. A portion of the provincial banks' notes would be returned to them for exchange into Bank of England notes, which would be employed in making payments in London; or, what comes to the same thing, the banks would be asked to supply bills or cheques on London.

[1] Fullarton, *Regulation of Currencies*, p. 85, quoted by J S Mill, *Principles*, book iii., chap. xxiv., § 1.

Only if the provincial banks were acting in co-operation with the Central Bank, never if they were acting alone, would it be possible for them, having once displaced all Bank of England notes from their district, to expand their own circulation. This would be true even where paper money was irredeemable. In the same way a contraction of the Bank of England's circulation would force the provincial banks to bring about a corresponding *diminution* in their own circulation. The provincial bankers' statement was evidently based on the facts. But these facts have no relevance whatever to the question which lies before us. It is only within very narrow limits that a single bank can increase the extent of its lending, whether by means of notes or by means of cheques. If a bank provides credit on too liberal a scale it is in direct danger of its notes or cheques becoming concentrated in the hands of the other banks and being presented by them for *redemption* ; or, at best, it might have to pay a higher rate of interest on its current account with the other banks than the rate that it receives In connection with the influence of "the banks" on the circulation of money and on prices, it is therefore essential to think of the aggregate of all the banks of a country, or, in the extreme case, of the world. In economics false conclusions are all too easily drawn by applying to a national, or to an international, economy knowledge which, before further examination is undertaken, is appropriate only to the private economy from which it is derived

It is on the basis of these and similar facts that people like Fullarton and Tooke absolutely deny the possibility of banking policy being in any way responsible for such fluctuations in prices as occur in practice. J. S Mill took up a middle position on monetary questions. His views were rather inconsistent [1] and of no great significance for the further development of theory, either in his own country or abroad; but he comes to the same negative conclusion, making an exception of periods of speculation and crisis. In a "quiescent state of the market", Mill regards Tooke's

[1] This has already been emphasised; see p. 51.

theory as perfectly correct. Then "each person transacts his ordinary amount of business . . . or increases it only in correspondence with the increase of his capital or connexion, or with the gradual growth of the demand for his commodity, occasioned by the public prosperity" At such times, "producers and dealers do not need more than the usual accommodation", and "as it is only by extending their loans that bankers increase their issues, none but a momentary augmentation of issues is in these circumstances possible" "Even if we suppose, as we may do, that bankers create an artificial increase of the demand for loans, by offering them *below* [1] the market rate of interest, the notes they issue will not", Mill assures us, "remain in circulation; for when the borrower, having completed the transaction for which he availed himself of them, has paid them away, the creditor or dealer who receives them, having no demand for the immediate use of an extra quantity of notes, sends them into deposit In this case, therefore," concludes Mill, "there can be no addition, at the discretion of bankers, to the general circulating medium· any increase of their issues either comes back to them, or remains idle in the hands of the public, and no rise takes place in prices " [2]

It is a great pity that on a question of such far reaching importance Mill relies for his exposition on one single example—worked out, moreover, very inadequately. It is quite impossible to state whether a given quantity of notes will remain in circulation for a longer or for a shorter period of time. It is equally easy to imagine the opposite of Mill's example. It might be supposed that instead of being passed into the hands of a single trader and from him back into the Bank, notes are paid out in small quantities to a large number of separate individuals, and so disappear into circulation. But this, too, would prove nothing, for it is impossible to say whether a corresponding quantity of other notes might not be pushed out

---

[1] [The italics are Wicksell's ]
[2] *Principles*, book iii., chap. xxiv , § 2

of circulation. Whether or not the result of such behaviour on the part of the Bank is to increase the circulation must ultimately depend on whether this procedure *in itself* is calculated to bring about *a rise in prices* In other words, the real cause of the rise in prices is to be looked for, not in the expansion of the note issue as such, but in the provision by the Bank of easier credit, which is itself the cause of the expansion.

This becomes very clear if, instead of this rather complicated system, we imagine a system in which all payments are made by means of cheques [1] There is then no "circulation of money" at all The cheques regularly return after a day or two to the Bank (or rather to one of the banks, and so to the bankers' clearing house). To an expansion of the note issue in the case which we have been discussing there now corresponds an increase in banking turnover. It is clear that whether this occurs or not depends mainly on whether the lowering of the Bank's discount rate is calculated *in itself* to bring about a rise in prices.

B *Simplest Hypothesis Variations of the Rate of Interest when the Market Situation Remains otherwise Unaltered*

That such is the case is obvious in regard to *current* prices —given the assumption, which we are retaining throughout this chapter, that a fall in the rate of interest, or more generally an easing of credit, takes place *without any other change in the market situation*, so that it really increases the profitability of enterprise. In subsequent chapters we shall abandon this purely hypothetical assumption and consider the far more general case, in which an alteration in the rate of interest is accompanied by, or more frequently is caused by, economic changes in other quarters. Quite half the controversy which has arisen in this field can be ascribed to lack of attention to this important distinction.

[1] *Cf* p 70.

In the example taken from Mill, it was a question, as is expressly stated, of "an artificial increase of the demand for loans", such as would not occur under ordinary conditions. The borrower is intending to make some payment which otherwise he would have dispensed with or would have postponed. Either he desires to buy some commodity which otherwise he would not have bought at all, or would only have bought later; or he intends to make a payment in cash where otherwise he would have had to buy on credit, or finally he wishes temporarily to keep some or all of his own goods off the market, and he asks the Bank for money with which to meet his immediate or pending liabilities without having to sell his goods. In the first case (other things being equal), the demand for goods in general is raised; in the second case, the rise is concentrated into the field of cash purchases, in the third case, the supply of goods is lowered. Thus all three cases provide the basis for a rise of prices—of current prices.

This is precisely the proposition which is passionately contested by Tooke and his followers, with a display of instances which, on the face of them, are not unconvincing A low rate of interest is by no means always accompanied by high, or by rising, prices. In fact the opposite is the general rule. "At the great trading centres", remarks E. Nasse,[1] "the rate of discount and the prices of the more important groups of commodities often fall almost simultaneously, and persist for a long time in deep depression, until" some outside cause "at last arouses entrepreneur activity" .. "It is impossible for a country's credit institutions, acting by themselves, to bring about an upward movement of prices, no matter how willing they may be to supply capital at the lowest possible rate of interest. Some other stimulus must first be provided before real use can be made of the available purchasing capacity."

We shall be giving a full account of the nature of this case and of its probable explanation. For the moment,

---

[1] Nasse, "Ueber den Einfluss des Kredits auf den Tauschwert der edlen Metalle", *Zeitschrift fur die ges. Staatswissensch.*, vol xxi , 1865, p 146

we must say a word about the reasoning itself. The "other stimulus" of which Nasse speaks cannot possibly reside in anything else but the *hope of higher profits* This may result from the expectation of an increased demand for particular groups of commodities, or from technical discoveries, lower wages, and the like, which hold out the promise of a higher return to producers. Now it must be a matter of indifference to the individual business man whether he derives his profit from higher gross receipts, from lower costs, in the narrow sense of the word, or from cheaper credit. It follows obviously that unless the fall in the rate of discount *is neutralised by simultaneous changes elsewhere*,[1] it must, when it has persisted long enough to exert a depressing influence on long-term rates of interest, provide a stimulus to trade and production, and alter the relation between supply and demand of goods and productive services in such a way as necessarily to bring about a rise in all prices

It is quite true that there are businesses to which a rise or fall in the rate of interest is of very little consequence, since an expansion or contraction of their activities is prevented by technical considerations. It is equally true that there are many other businesses in regard to which such an occurrence is the decisive factor Some enterprises are in a state of complete preparation, for others the plans for expansion have long been ready, and their execution only awaits a favourable opportunity, in yet others business is bad, and it is being debated whether they shall be carried on or closed down In all such cases an easing or tightening of credit may be the last drop which causes the vessel to overflow, so that the plans which have been worked out are brought into execution. It is impossible to conceive that to-day, when almost every enterprise works on borrowed capital of one shape or another, it should be a matter of *complete* indifference whether the need for credit is met at 3 per cent or 4 per cent., or only at 6 or 8 per cent.

[1] *Cf.* p. 100, below.

Easier credit sets up a *tendency* for production (and trade in general) to expand, but this does not in any way imply that production will *in fact* increase. There will in general be no such increase, or only a relatively small one, if the available means of production, labour and so on, are already almost fully occupied [1] (An individual business may indeed expand, but only at the expense of another, which must suffer a corresponding contraction ) But this is far from saying that there is any obstacle to a rise in prices, the excess of demand (brought about by easier credit) *over supply* of raw materials, labour, land, and the like, and directly and indirectly of consumption goods, is the decisive factor in forcing up prices.

Neglect of this important difference between tendency and fact is, if I am not mistaken, one of the chief reasons why the nature of the influence of credit on prices has up till now been so completely veiled in darkness. We shall soon be meeting with an even more important reason for this confusion.

It is usually unnecessary to concentrate attention on *speculation*, in the narrow sense of the word ; and that is the case here. Tooke points out [2] that real speculative purchases (excluding trading in futures, etc ) will scarcely take place unless the speculator can reckon on a rise in price of ten per cent , and that it is then of little importance whether he has to pay one per cent  more or less for his credit. This may be substantially correct, but such transactions belong to the class of exceptions. They are of importance in connection with times of speculation and crisis, but in dealing with an organic movement of prices, persisting over several years, it is not the exceptions which have to be taken into consideration but the ordinary regular and recurrent transactions, and the question that has to be asked is at what prices, taking into account the situation in the money and commodity markets, they can and will be effected.

In practice, the rate of interest is altered only in steps of one-half to one per cent., and only after lengthy intervals of time, during which the rate of interest (or at any rate the Bank rate of interest) remains completely unaltered. It would therefore appear that these changes are *too small* to exert more than a very diminutive influence on the structure of prices. Suppose that I am a business man and that, having sold my goods against bills drawn for three

---

[1] *Cf* p  143, below          [2] *History of Prices*, vol. iii , p  153

months, I can now discount these bills at 3 per cent per annum instead of the 4 per cent. which formerly I had to pay The result is that *ipso facto* I have received a higher cash price for my goods, and the transaction has put "into circulation" a greater sum of money But it is easy to see that the rise amounts only to $\frac{1}{4}$ per cent. of the normal price Moreover the contract may be as yet incomplete, so that it may be impossible for the seller to retain the whole of the extra profit for himself He may be forced by competition to share part of it with the purchaser. Let us suppose that they participate equally in the advantage provided by the easier credit. Then the seller will have to reckon with a credit price which has *fallen* by $\frac{1}{8}$ per cent , but as the result of the fall in the rate of discount, he receives a cash price which has *risen* by $\frac{1}{8}$ per cent Now suppose that the purchaser prefers to pay cash and raises the necessary sum himself by means of borrowing Then if he intends to dispose of the commodity in three months' time, the fall of 1 per cent in the annual rate of interest means that at the most he can afford to raise the price which he offers by $\frac{1}{4}$ per cent.—always on the assumption that he cannot reckon on a rise in the price which he will himself obtain in the future. But here, too, the price will not actually rise to the maximum extent; it may only rise by, say, $\frac{1}{8}$ per cent

It is, however. frequently the case that quite a small fall in the rate of interest would *immediately* bring about a much greater rise in prices. The price which can be paid for goods obtained by means of credit is higher the longer is the period during which the credit is utilised Take, for instance, the case where raw materials or labour will be employed for *one, two, three* or more years before the finished product emerges Then a fall of 1 per cent in the rate of interest will clearly be responsible in the extreme case for a rise in the current prices of these raw materials and services of 1, 2, 3, or more per cent Where the investment is to all intents and purposes being undertaken "for eternity", as in the case of such things as buildings, railways, and durable machinery, the possible rise in price is considerably greater. If railway companies could issue debentures at 3 per cent instead of 4 per cent., they would be able, *ceteris paribus*, to pay almost 33⅓ per cent. more for all their requirements: 4 per cent. on 100 million marks comes to the same thing as 3 per cent on 133⅓ million marks.

It is, of course, possible for the rise in the prices of particular goods and services to be even greater It is probable that the prices of some of the factors of production will rise only slowly. This is likely to be the case with labour, because the market in ordinary day-labour is so large The other factors—such as the land and property which have to be expropriated, and the iron and wood which are used as materials—can then be paid at a correspondingly higher rate.

It is commonly observed that at times of so-called expansion the commodities which are the first to show a substantial rise in price are precisely those raw materials which are employed for the purpose of further production. There is now no room for doubt as to the correctness of this observation nor as to its probable explanation. But it is a necessary condition that the easier terms of short-term lending shall have persisted sufficiently long to influence the long-term rate, the so-called bond rate of interest, so long as the upward movement is brought about by easier credit and not merely by other causes, such as technical progress. We have seen that a casual and temporary change in the discount rate would not in itself exert any marked influence on prices To this extent it can be granted that Tooke was quite right in maintaining, in contradiction to Ricardo, that the banks' discount policy is in itself of direct significance in respect only to such matters as international or interregional movements of capital and the postponement of payment of fluctuating liabilities, but that it is of smaller importance in respect to the structure of prices.

This, it may be noted, is in itself a reason for not expecting any precise correlation between movements in the discount rate and in commodity prices. The direct influence of the one on the other is at first trivial and may easily be masked by other factors or altogether annulled.[1] But as soon as the long-term rate of interest moves in sympathy, *and provided that conditions remain otherwise unaltered,* prices suddenly rise and the whole world knows that "the upward phase" has started. We shall be referring later to some statistical data supplied by R. Giffen which seem to confirm this principle.

If we leave on one side these violent changes in the prices of such raw materials and services as are required for the purpose of long-term investment, and their reaction on the prices of other commodities, it would appear that a large change in the rate of interest could exert only an extremely trivial influence on prices.

It might even be supposed that prices would soon return of their own accord to their original level, or perhaps sink below it. In our first illustration the credit price which would have to be paid in three months' time would be entirely unaffected by the fall in the discount rate, and in the second illustration it would actually be depressed. But it would be fallacious to draw any such deduction about the future level of prices. Prices accepted to-day for an immediate delivery of goods which will not be paid for until some point in the future, are not the *prices of the future.* They are current prices with an addition for interest, and have nothing in common with prices which will have to be paid in the future for goods or services supplied *in the future,* of which the level will be determined by the relation existing in the future between the conditions of supply and of demand. The one exception that I can think of is the case where the *sellers' services* are also to be supplied in the future—in other words, where work is undertaken to order or where sales are made on a forward basis. This will be discussed more fully at a later stage in connection with a pertinent observation of Tooke's on the alleged influence of the rate of interest on *costs of production.*

Such would certainly be the case if it could be assumed that the effect of a single but permanent change in the rate of interest was *confined to the immediate impact,* so that any further rise in prices would require a further fall in the

[1] *Cf* below.

rate of interest. But this assumption immediately leads to absurd conclusions.

On every consideration of probability things happen quite differently. It is to be supposed that the maintenance of a lower rate of interest has effects, *ceteris paribus*, which are not only permanent, but also *cumulative*. To understand the connection, attention must be devoted to the rather formal nature of money prices, and also to what may be termed the *vis inertiae* in the economic mechanism.

Though the determination of money prices often appears to be supported on very airy foundations, it is outside the power of any individual to fix them to suit his own desires. Every individual buyer or seller has to submit to their fluctuations, and any attempt to buy at a lower price or to sell at a higher price must necessarily prove disadvantageous unless his example is immediately followed by the other buyers or sellers of the commodity in question But for the economic system as a whole, there is no tendency for any alteration in a structure of prices which has been once built up. For instance, once a rise in prices has been uniformly dispersed over all groups of commodities, equilibrium in respect to relative prices is once again restored, and relative prices are the only things that really matter so far as production and consumption are concerned.

The recipients of fixed money incomes will, it is true, respond to a rise in prices by diminishing their demand for goods of all kinds, and they will in this way be doing something to restrain the upward movement of prices. But if they are not in a position to hold back their own "wares" from the market, a new position of equilibrium will soon be attained, and they will be receiving a smaller share of the yearly production of commodities while the share of the rest of the community will be correspondingly increased. If, on the other hand, they can hold back their services, as, for instance, with civil servants who can obtain an increase in salaries as a result of a rise in the cost of living, there is then no exception to the general rule And similarly in the case of a general fall of prices

So a fall in the rate of interest, even though it is casual

and temporary, will bring about a perfectly *definite* rise in prices, which, whether it is big or small, will persist as a permanent feature even after the rate of interest has returned to its former value. If the rate of interest remains at a low level for a considerable period of time, its influence on prices must necessarily be *cumulative*, that is to say, it goes on repeating itself over equal intervals of time in precisely the same manner The producer has to pay more for raw materials, wages, rents, etc., but he receives correspondingly better prices for his own products. He finds himself in precisely the same situation as before the rise in prices took place, and he is therefore in a position to pay the same rate of interest as before for the credit which he requires If, however, the credit institutions maintain the lower rates of interest, he will be in a position to offer rather more for raw materials, labour, and land, and competition will to some extent force him to do so. As a consequence, the demands of workers and landlords will be raised, and this will bring about a further rise in the price of consumption goods, and prices will continually rise higher and higher.

An improvement in the terms of credit enabled our business man to pay a higher cash price for the goods which he was going to sell in three months' time, even though he was due to receive no more than the normal sale price At the end of the period he will make the pleasant discovery that he can actually sell his goods at more than the normal price He will now arrange a similar transaction for the next three months and he is likely to base his calculations on the current price. *Even if the terms of credit have by now returned to normal* he will still be able to pay the higher price. And if his bank continues to charge the lower rate of interest he will be in a position to bear still higher costs without involving himself in a loss (and he will in all probability be obliged to do so). In this kind of way an equal rise in prices will take place every three months.

Even more convincing is the case where the money is used for durable investment Let us suppose that there is

a general fall in the rate of interest from 4 to 3 per cent.
We have seen that the value of all permanent capital
goods, for instance of dwelling-houses, will go up by $33\frac{1}{3}$
per cent. It would be possible to raise by anything up to
this extent the prices paid for the materials and services
required for house-building. This is based on the assumption that the net earnings of houses (in particular rents)
remain unaltered in the future. But there will be a rise in
wages, ground rents, etc , and this will bring about a rise
in the money demand[1] for all kinds of goods, including
houses Rents will rise, and while it is true that the owners
of houses will spend proportionately more on such things
as repairs, it is to be presumed that their net return will go
up in proportion This will bring about a further rise in
the price of houses (though not the full equivalent of the
original rise), and so indirectly a further rise in the prices
of everything else. It must be admitted that this line of
reasoning requires some modification  An abnormally
*large* amount of investment will now probably be devoted to durable goods. There may result a relative overproduction of such things as houses and a relative underproduction of other commodities  However, this will
merely mean a more rapid equalisation of relative prices
So long as other things remain equal, it is impossible that
the average level of money prices should fall, or even that
it should cease to rise

We may go further. The upward movement of prices
will in some measure "create its own draught". When
prices have been rising steadily for some time, entrepreneurs will begin to reckon on the basis not merely of
the prices already attained, but of a further rise in prices
The effect on supply and demand is clearly the same as
that of a corresponding easing of credit.

Indeed the effect may be even greater. The effect of
easier credit is confined initially to those who work on
borrowed money. But when prices have already gone up
and are expected to go up further, almost every pur-

[1] ["*Geldnachfrage (moneyed demand)*" in original ]

chaser will be able to offer higher prices and every seller to demand them.

To put an immediate stop to any further rise in prices, it would not be sufficient for the banks to restore the rate of interest to its original level. This would have the same effect on the business world as would a somewhat lower rate of interest at a time when prices are not expected to alter. If, on the other hand, the banks continue to maintain the rate of interest at its lower level, *two forces* will be operating in the direction of higher prices, and the rise will be correspondingly more rapid.

But so long as business continues to be conducted on normal lines, it is not to be supposed that there will be any cumulative movement of prices in the manner of an avalanche [1] Through its influence on supply and demand, an *expectation* of a rise in prices in the future is by its very nature capable in itself of bringing about only a somewhat *smaller* rise than is actually expected For a buyer could not obtain any profit if the whole of the expected rise were included in the actual price, and the seller will almost always prefer a smaller but more secure profit to a profit which is somewhat larger but less certain

After credit ceases to remain easy prices will, for this reason, come sooner or later to a standstill. Let us suppose, for instance, that a further rise in prices of $p$ per cent. over the next three months is generally expected, though without any real foundation Then the rise which actually takes place can only amount to $ap$ per cent , where $a$ is less than unity, or, in other words, a proper fraction Over the subsequent period of three months, it would be possible to reckon on a rise in prices of not more than $ap$ per cent , and this expectation will bring about an actual rise of $a^2p$ per cent And so it will continue If, on the other hand, credit remains easy, prices will indeed rise without limit, but the *rate of annual* increase, so far from being indefinitely high, will at the most arrive at a certain finite limiting value.

The matter takes on an entirely different aspect in the case where the market is under the influence of *speculation* proper. Goods are now bought, not merely to be passed on to other

[1] In an article on "Der Bankzins als Regulator der Warenpreise", *Jahrbucher fur Nationalokonomie und Statistik*, vol 68, 1897, I may have expressed myself rather too hastily. At any rate I had as yet failed to take account of the considerations which follow above.

H

producers and to be distributed to consumers by the normal
methods, but to be hastily disposed of to other speculators.
The time element, which normally plays a decisive part, now
ceases to be of any great significance; and it becomes impossible to make even the roughest kind of estimate of the
probable rise in prices  Insecure sentiment governs the market;
as prices continue to soar and profits are easily earned, the
movement may rapidly reach fever-point. There is almost no
limit to the rise in prices *in spite of the fact* that credit becomes
more and more expensive. But when prices ultimately come
to rest, and the prospect of further profits disappears, the
credit position is so strained and the rate of interest is so high
as immediately to bring about a contrary movement, which
proceeding in analogous fashion may rapidly drag down prices
even below their normal level

For the moment we leave such occurrences on one side. We
are concerned with the organic development of a regular movement of prices.

I can think of but one exception to the rule that easier
credit must lead to a rise in prices  This is the case where
goods are produced *to order*, or the very similar case where
goods are sold for delivery in the future (on a forward
basis). The producer or seller then has to include in his
estimate of costs the interest payments which he incurs
over the intervening interval of time. A fall in the rate of
interest will therefore bring about a *fall* in the selling price.
What would happen if production took place everywhere
on the basis of previously arranged prices may well be
left undecided. In the actual world this factor cannot be
responsible for more than an insignificant counter-current
against the general movement of prices; for the interval
of time over which production takes place to order (or
which elapses before the date arranged for delivery) usually
amounts to only a small portion of the total period of production necessary for providing the goods and for their
subsequent use  Suppose, for example, that a railway company has ordered a consignment of rails from an ironworks.
The ironworks will be able, as a result of cheaper credit,
to charge a somewhat lower price, but the easier credit,
when it has persisted for a sufficiently long time, is likely

itself to cause a far greater *rise* in the costs of manufacture
and in the willingness of the railway company to purchase

This is as much as can be said in favour of a peculiar statement made by Tooke (though it was not, so far as I know,
repeated by his pupils) According to the fourteenth of Tooke's
theses or conclusions, to which we have already made several
references, it is maintained·

"That a reduced rate of interest has no necessary tendency
to raise the prices of commodities. On the contrary, it is a
cause of *diminished cost of production,* and consequently of
cheapness "[1]

This involves a conflict with the well-accredited fact that
a *rise* in the rate of interest has always shown itself to be the
appropriate method of checking an unfavourable balance of
payments and of instigating a flow of bullion from abroad
Tooke tries to meet this difficulty by remarking that such a
rise in the banks' discount rate is not "of such *permanence* as
to affect the cost of production", but, says Tooke, it causes
a·disturbance of credit and "extensive failures", which usually
lead to a slump in prices Tooke would thus appear to maintain that the same procedure has precisely opposite consequences according as it is applied for a long or for a short
period This seems a doubtful possibility.

The opposite case of a *favourable* balance of payments leads
to equally absurd consequences A favourable balance would
cause an inflow of bullion, and this clearly would, or at least
could, bring about a lowering of the rate of interest The result
according to Tooke would be a still further *fall* in domestic
prices (unless some fundamental distinction is admitted here
too between the effects of an easing of credit which is temporary and of one that is permanent), so that the balance of
payments would become more and more favourable and money
would flow in on an ever-increasing scale

In any case, the proposition that prices of commodities depend on their costs of production and rise and fall with them,
has a meaning only in connection with *relative* prices [2] To
apply this proposition to the general level of money prices
involves a generalisation which is not only fallacious but of
which it is in fact impossible to give any clear account It
can be concluded then that, with the one exception referred to

---

[1] *An Inquiry into the Currency Principle,* p 123, *History of Prices,*
vol vi , Appendix xv , p 636 The italics are mine.
[2] See p 27

above, Tooke's proposition must be regarded as *false*, both in theory and in practice.

In other passages of the *History of Prices* Tooke repeats his statement, but in a somewhat modified version in the sense that it is given a particular application to those groups of commodities of which the production involves the use of large amounts of capital So long as it is a question of *relative* prices, this application is perfectly correct, but it has no relation to the question under discussion

We had arrived at the conclusion that, so long as the situation in the market remains unaltered, any permanent fall, no matter how small, in the rate of interest maintained by the credit institutions will cause the general level of prices to rise to an unlimited extent in a continuous and more or less uniform manner. And in the same way, a *rise* in the rate of interest, no matter how small, will, if maintained for sufficiently long, result in a continuous and unlimited *fall* in the prices of all goods and services

These statements sound extremely bold, and indeed paradoxical But it has to be remembered that the rate of interest referred to as the "previous" or the "normal" rate, away from which our deviations are imagined to originate, does not always remain the same and cannot be thought of as so much per cent. It merely means that rate which, having regard to the situation in the market, would be necessary for the maintenance of a constant level of prices. That there must always be such a rate was the implicit assumption underlying our whole argument In the next chapter we shall consider whether it really exists, how it could be attained with the object of fulfilling its purpose, and similar questions about the causes determining the rate of interest.

It should now be clear that, in so far as our hypothetical conclusions are in accordance with reality, the movement and equilibrium of actual money prices represent a fundamentally different phenomenon, above all in a fully developed credit system, from those of *relative* prices The latter might perhaps be compared with a mechanical system which satisfies the conditions of *stable* equilibrium, for instance a pendulum. Every movement away from the position of equilibrium sets forces into operation—on a scale that increases with the extent of the movement—which tend to restore the system to its original position, and actually succeed in doing so, though some oscillations may intervene.

The analogous picture for *money* prices should rather be some easily movable object, such as a cylinder, which rests on a horizontal plane in so-called *neutral* equilibrium. The plane is somewhat rough and a certain force is required to set the price-cylinder in motion and to keep it in motion. But so long as this force—the raising or lowering of the rate of interest—remains in operation, the cylinder continues to move in the same direction. Indeed it will, after a time, start "rolling". the motion is an accelerated one up to a certain point, and it continues for a time even when the force has ceased to operate. Once the cylinder has come to rest, there is no tendency for it to be restored to its original position. It simply remains where it is so long as no opposite forces come into operation to push it back.

It is, of course, clear that such forces can never be entirely absent, no matter how developed the credit system may be, if a precious metal or some other material substance serves as a monetary basis. The simple quantity theory is no longer adequate to deal with the nature of these reactions and with the manner of their operation. It is this question which we shall shortly be considering

# CHAPTER 8

## THE NATURAL RATE OF INTEREST ON CAPITAL AND THE RATE OF INTEREST ON LOANS

THERE IS a certain rate of interest on loans which is neutral in respect to commodity prices, and tends neither to raise nor to lower them. This is necessarily the same as the rate of interest which would be determined by supply and demand if no use were made of money and all lending were effected in the form of real capital goods. It comes to much the same thing to describe it as the current value of the *natural rate of interest on capital.*

It is usually said that in modern communities capital (of the mobile kind) is lent *in the form of money.* But this is a metaphorical and inexact manner of speaking which can easily lead to error. Liquid capital, which is what we are considering, or in other words goods, are never lent—they are never given and taken by way of borrowing—they are simply *bought or sold.*

Even merchandise credit does not involve any lending of commodities, either from the legal or from the economic point of view. It represents a sale where payment is temporarily postponed, or, if you like, a *cash* transaction combined with a *money* loan. Otherwise it would be necessary to pay back the same or an identical parcel of goods, together with accrued interest; or there would have to be a guarantee that in exchange for the stipulated sum of money the same quantity of commodities would be obtainable at the time of payment as at the time of purchase, but this is never the case.

We shall now try, by means of a suitable illustration, to find a more precise basis for our proposition. Let us take an entrepreneur who possesses no capital of his own, or at least no liquid capital. He will require money for the purchase of raw materials and for the payment of wages and rents, and also for his own living expenses during the period of production. (There are other requirements, for

102

instance taxation, but for the sake of simplicity these will be neglected.) All this money may be supposed to be devoted to the purchase of *finished consumption goods*, with which the workers and property owners, and also the entrepreneur, meet their own requirements ; in so far as it is used for the purchase of raw materials, the manufacturers of the raw materials pay it out in their turn on wages and rents (and keep some of it for themselves), and it is all once again exchanged for finished consumption goods. Now liquid capital must originate from somewhere. For the sake of simplicity it will be assumed that the present owners of the available consumption goods are *capitalists*, that is to say, that they have no immediate need either for the goods themselves or for such proceeds as they obtain for them in the form of other goods or of money. They are in a position, if necessary, to postpone payment up to a period of, let us say, one year

It may be supposed in theory that the entrepreneur borrows these consumption goods from the capitalists *in kind*, and then pays them out *in kind* in the shape of wages and rents  At the end of the period of production he repays the loan out of his own product, either directly or after exchanging it for other commodities (relative prices being assumed to remain unaltered)  If this procedure were adopted by all entrepreneurs who work with borrowed capital, competition would bring about a certain *rate of interest* that would have to be paid to the capitalists in the form of some commodity or other. The amount of this rate of interest would be determined by the "supply and demand" for capital. However, this phrase tells us very little  But it is possible to set for the rate of interest an *upper limit* which has a more palpable significance. This limiting value is the amount by which the total product (or its equivalent in other commodities) exceeds the sum of the wages, rents, etc., that have to be paid out. The magnitude of this excess depends on the productivity of the business on the one hand, and on the other hand on the level of wages and rents. This is a matter which will be

discussed more fully in the next chapter. It is clear that the
entrepreneur cannot pay more than this limiting amount.
Moreover, he will be forced as a result of competition with
other entrepreneurs to pay very nearly as much, for unavoidable risks cancel out in the course of a long succession
of economic periods, and the entrepreneur's own profit is
confined to the amount which corresponds to the actual
mental effort of the entrepreneur (and to the rents on such
elements of monopoly as he may possess, like business
secrets, special advantages of situation or of *clientèle*, unless these are regarded as additional sources of income)

But for reasons connected with the conception of subjective
value, the probability that an entrepreneur will make a profit
must always be somewhat greater than the probability that
he will make a loss  For otherwise his "moral expectation"
would be negative. In many cases, however, the entrepreneurs'
gambling spirit will prevent this rule from applying to their
behaviour

Now if money is loaned at this same rate of interest, it
serves as nothing more than a cloak to cover a procedure
which, from the purely formal point of view, could have
been carried on equally well without it  The conditions
of economic equilibrium are fulfilled in precisely the same
manner  In such a case, there is no occasion for any
alteration in the level of prices. In a developed credit
system, the various transactions involve the use of an
indefinitely small amount of money, and if cheques (or
uncovered notes) are in general use, there is no need for
metallic money at all  All that happens is that the banks
extend to the entrepreneurs credits against which they
draw cheques. These cheques (or notes) pass into the hands
of workers and property owners in the form of wages and
rents, and are then passed on in payment for the ordinary
purposes of consumption into the hands of the capitalists,
who for the sake of simplicity will be supposed at the same
time to be traders. Finally, they are presented by the
capitalists to the banks, where they are transformed into
deposits. The difference between the rate of interest ob-

tamable by direct lending to others and the rate paid by
the banks to depositors, is compensated by the greater
security and convenience offered by the banks (Furthermore, creditors and debtors may gradually sever their
temporary relations with their bank and enter into direct
relations with one another[1], but we are abstracting from
this possibility ) At the end of the period of production,
when the finished products become available, the trader-
capitalists renew their stocks. They draw on their credits
with their bank by means of cheques (or in the form of
notes), and so buy the entrepreneurs' produce  The entrepreneurs in their turn present these cheques at the bank
and so liquidate their liability to the bank. If they desire
to continue in production, as would normally be the case,
they will soon draw out once more almost the same sum
by way of a credit  And so the procedure will repeat itself.

There is here nothing calculated either to raise or to lower
prices  It is true that as a result of changes in the conditions
of production, due for instance to technical progress, first
one and then another group of commodities will be obtainable with a smaller expenditure of labour and other factors
of production, and that this must cause continual disturbances in *relative* values  But there is no apparent reason
for any alteration in the general level of *money* prices
An increase in the supply of certain groups of commodities
means an increase in the real demand for all other groups
of commodities. Why then should it bring about a fall in
the average level of prices, it being assumed that money
is obtainable in any desired quantity on terms which correspond to the real advantages entailed in the use of credit[2]

Now let us suppose that the banks and other lenders of
money lend at a different rate of interest, either lower or
higher, from that which corresponds to the current value
of the natural rate of interest on capital. The economic
equilibrium of the system is *ipso facto* disturbed  If prices
remain unchanged, entrepreneurs will in the first instance
obtain a surplus profit (at the cost of the capitalists) over

---

[1] See p. 74 ff

and above their real entrepreneur profit or wage. This will continue to accrue so long as the rate of interest remains in the same relative position. They will inevitably be induced to extend their businesses in order to exploit to the maximum extent the favourable turn of events. And the number of people becoming entrepreneurs will be abnormally increased. As a consequence, the demand for services, raw materials, and goods in general will be increased, and the prices of commodities must rise.

If the rate of interest rises, the opposite situation is created So long as prices remain unaltered, entrepreneurs suffer a deficiency below their normal incomes, and there is a tendency for business to become confined to its more profitable elements. The demand for goods and services falls off, or at any rate lags behind the supply; and prices fall The result in both cases is just those conditions as were depicted above.

But there we were proceeding on the assumption that the condition of the market was stationary Retaining the formal part of our argument, we have now found our way to an important and necessary extension of its material basis. The natural rate[1] is not fixed or unalterable in magnitude. The causes that determine it will be discussed somewhat more fully in the next chapter In general, we may say, it depends on the efficiency of production, on the available amount of fixed and liquid capital, on the supply of labour and land, in short on all the thousand and one things which determine the current economic position of a community, and with them it constantly fluctuates

An *exact* coincidence of the two rates of interest is therefore unlikely. For changes in the (average) natural rate may be presumed (on the basis of the Law of Large Numbers) to be continuous, while the money rate of interest is usually raised or lowered only in discontinuous jumps of one-half or one per cent , at any rate in so far as it is regulated by the large monetary institutions. But

[1] [From now on, "natural rate" will be used to denote "natural rate of interest on capital".]

the money rate of interest can lie sometimes above and sometimes below the natural rate, and there is no reason for not expecting a sufficient degree of coincidence to prevent substantial fluctuations in prices  Our problem is, therefore, to show that in those periods when upward movements of prices have been observed, the contractual rate of interest—the money rate —was *low* relatively to the natural rate, and that at times of falling prices it was relatively *high*. It is only in this relative sense that the money rate of interest is of significance in regard to movements of prices. It can at once be seen that it is quite useless to try to demonstrate the existence of any direct relation between absolute movements of the rate of interest or of the discount rate and movements of prices.

In other words  If it were possible to ascertain and specify the current value of the natural rate, it would be seen that any deviation of the actual money rate from this natural rate is connected with rising or falling prices according as the deviation is downward or upward. But if the middle term of the comparison disappears—if the usual direct comparison is made between the level of prices and the rate of interest —a rise in prices is compatible, not only with a lower rate of interest, but equally with a constant or a higher rate, a fall in prices is as compatible with a constant or a lower money rate of interest as with a higher rate, for the natural rate may move further than the money rate

It is mainly because this obvious possibility has been overlooked that discussions on the subject have been so barren In the place of attempts to discover whether high prices are accompanied by high or by low rates of interest, it would have been well to elucidate the real meaning of a high or of a low rate of interest. It might then have been seen that it is an essentially relative conception, and that a further datum must be supplied, namely, the level of the *natural* rate, before it is possible to determine whether any particular rate of interest is to be regarded as high or as low.

Such investigations will provide the subject-matter of Chapter 11. We must now consider whether it is possible for credit institutions to maintain their rates of interest at any desired level, or whether they are obliged sooner

or later, as a result of the operation on the money market
of the forces of supply and demand, to come into line with
the natural rate. The latter is the view generally held by
economists. *In principle* they are perfectly right; but they
usually omit to provide any clear account of the *manner*
in which the two rates of interest are brought together.
The money rate of interest depends in the first instance
on the excess or scarcity of *money*. How then does it come
about that it is eventually determined by the excess or
scarcity of *real capital*?

"What is interest?" asks F. A Walker,[1] and proceeds to give
the answer. "It is the compensation paid for the use, not of
money, but of capital Money is only one of many forms of
capital, and in loans is usually only the agent of effecting a
transfer of other forms of capital than itself If I borrow money,
the chances are that I at once, or shortly afterwards, purchase
with it articles suitable for my business or my personal necessities. . . These were what I really borrowed. These are what,
in any philosophical view of the subject, I pay interest on,
not upon the money. The money was but the means to this
end ."
This kind of generality is too metaphorical to take us very
far. Walker should have indicated the mechanism by which
the same results are reached in real life as are suggested by
"any philosophical view of the subject". For *in actual fact* it
is money which is lent, not the goods purchased by means of
money. The rate of interest is a matter for negotiation with
the owners of money and not with the owners of goods

The most eminent of writers have contributed very peculiar
views on this subject. W. S. Jevons remarks that under a
system of credit the business man is not the real owner of the
goods which he has bought on credit "Though the merchant
does not own the goods there must be someone *to own them*,
to advance capital, or, as it is said, to discount the bills arising out of the transaction. *Now this capital is limited*, and the
available amount is reduced during the period of permanent
investment, from which a rise of prices proceeds. *It is the exhaustion of this capital which limits credit*, it is the limitation
of credit which must sooner or later bring prices to a stand,
or even cause them to recede to a rate much lower than they

---

[1] *Money in its relations to Trade and Industry*, p 80.

had reached. . . While the elasticity of credit, then, may certainly give prices a more free flight, the inflation of credit must be checked by the well-defined (*sic*) boundary of available capital, which consists in the last resort of the reserve of notes, equivalent to gold, in the . . Bank of England "[1]

It is almost impossible to obtain from these observations any kind of "well-defined" picture. At one moment Jevons seems by "capital" to mean the stock of goods, at another moment the gold or note reserve of the Bank of England. But on neither interpretation do his words carry any intelligible meaning. The stock of goods will certainly fall off when there is any undue conversion of liquid capital into fixed capital. But how can a scarcity of goods be regarded as a cause of a rise in the rate of interest or of a fall in prices? On the contrary, the smaller the available amount of commodities the smaller, other things being equal, is the demand for money. It follows that the rate of interest will fall rather than rise and that prices will go up still further. As for the stock of money, it is clearly impossible for this to alter *at all* as a result of a conversion of liquid capital into fixed capital.

Such mistakes on the part of distinguished writers provide a good indication of the difficulties of the subject. To avoid them, it is, I think, best for the moment to leave on one side variations in real capital, which only complicate the argument, and to concentrate on changes in the money or credit markets, assuming that the situation in the commodity market remains unaltered. It will then be possible later on to combine the two forces, and this in fact is the line of treatment which we shall pursue.

If an attempt had been made to search for the real cause, instead of being satisfied with such catch-phrases as "capital loaned in the form of money", it would have been seen that the connecting link is supplied by the *level of commodity prices*. The only possible explanation lies in the influence which is exerted on *prices* by the difference between the two rates of interest. When the money rate of interest is relatively too low all prices rise. The demand for money loans is consequently increased, and as a result

[1] "A Serious Fall in the Value of Gold", *Investigations in Currency and Finance*, pp 31, 32 [second edition, pp 27, 28]. The italics are mine. A similar treatment is to be found in Nasse, *loc. cit*., p. 149 ff., and also in Scharling, *Preussiche Jahrb.*, 1895 (see p 115, below)

of a greater need for cash holdings, the supply is diminished. The consequence is that the rate of interest is soon restored to its normal level, so that it again coincides with the natural rate.

At the same time it is clear that in an elastic monetary system, where there is only a small reaction against an alteration in prices, a fairly constant difference between the two rates of interest could be maintained for a long time, and the effect on prices might be considerable.

The various practical obstacles which stand in the way of ideally perfect mobility of money are gradually being removed as a result of concentration in the hands of the banks of cash holdings and of the business of lending, and of the use of bills and notes, cheques and clearing methods. Money is continually becoming more fluid, and the supply of money is more and more inclined to accommodate itself to the level of demand We have seen that in our ideal state every payment, and consequently every loan, is accomplished by means of cheques or *giro* facilities It is then no longer possible to refer to the supply of money as an independent magnitude, differing from the demand for money. No matter what amount of money may be demanded from the banks, that is the amount which they are in a position to lend (so long as the security of the borrower is adequate). The banks have merely to enter a figure in the borrower's account to represent a credit granted or a deposit created. When a cheque is then drawn and subsequently presented to the banks, they credit the account of the owner of the cheque with a deposit of the appropriate amount (or reduce his debit by that amount). The "supply of money" is thus furnished by the demand itself.[1]

The banks need not worry whether the dates on which their deposits become due correspond with the periods over which their loans have been granted. From our assumption that every withdrawal of a deposit *must* directly

[1] *Cf* Emil Struck, "Skizze des englischen Geldmarktes", Separatabdruck of the *Jahrbuch fur Gesetzgebung*, Jahrg X , p. 45 ff.

entail the deposit of an equal sum elsewhere or the repayment of an equal loan, it follows that the banks, or rather the aggregate of banks taken as a whole, can within limits to be stipulated in a moment lend any desired amount of money for any desired period of time at any desired rate of interest, no matter how low, without affecting their solvency, even though their deposits may be falling due all the time. It follows that if the rest of our theory is correct the banks can raise the general level of prices to any desired height.

In the next chapter we shall be discussing incidentally some of the ensuing consequences They are the more interesting in that they run completely counter to the ordinary view. For instance, it can be seen that the credit institutions, by supporting long-term enterprises, can to some degree *force* the necessary real capital out of the public

It is also possible for the banks to maintain their rates of interest *above* the normal level for any length of time They are thus able, within certain limits, to exert a continual downward pressure on prices.

We now have to investigate the limits which on one side or the other restrict the power of the banks.

It is, of course, clear that our discussion would have *no* application whatever to the case of an *individual* bank trying to pursue a discount policy different from that of the other banks Such action is impossible If a single bank were to maintain either too low or too high a rate of interest it would rapidly bring about either its own insolvency or the loss of all its borrowers, and the dividends of its shareholders would disappear. An individual bank must in some degree conform to the general movement.

The banks of a single country of which the money is based on a metallic (international) standard are in the same situation *vis-à-vis* foreign banks If rates of interest are maintained at too low a level the precious metal flows away; and if rates are too high the domestic market becomes saturated with foreign metal, which *must* be accepted by the banks in the form of deposits on which interest has to be paid, for otherwise it would cause competition against them in their capacity as lenders.

The classical view is, of course, that these effects are brought about as a result of changes in the domestic price level, and consequently in the balance of trade and in the rate of exchange. According to Tooke, on the other hand, a fall in the domestic rate of interest causes an immediate outflow of the country's money capital, attracted by more profitable opportunities for investment abroad, before it has had time to exert any influence on prices [1]

Which explanation is correct can be regarded as a matter of indifference, for the final result is in both cases the same, nor does the one exclude the other  But the older view seems to have the advantage of greater generality. A country's rate of interest can be low in relation to its natural rate without standing so much below the foreign rate of interest as to compensate for the costs and risks of a movement of capital The effects of easier credit are then confined to its influence on domestic prices This influence is cumulative, and the domestic price level must soon be so much above the foreign price level that exports fall off, imports increase, the balance of trade begins to become unfavourable, and money begins to flow out of the country.

Still more so if the natural rate happens to be *higher* at home than abroad. If the money rate of interest were to remain the same at home as abroad, then, according to those who deny that the banks' discount policy has any influence on prices, no influx of foreign capital could take place, in spite of the difference, possibly considerable, between the two natural rates This seems unplausible Actually domestic prices would constantly rise, and as a result the balance of payments and the rate of exchange would gradually deteriorate until the credit institutions would find it necessary to raise their rates of interest above those of foreign countries An influx of foreign capital would ensue, possibly for a considerable period of time, though as a result of the difference in the two price levels, this influx would take the form, not of money, but of commodities. In other words, a portion of foreigners' claims on goods would be utilised, directly or in-

---

[1] *Cf History of Prices*, vol. iv , pp. 197-202. But here Tooke himself admits that a low rate of interest tends to stimulate enterprise and so indirectly to *raise* prices, in peculiar contradiction to his view, referred to above, that low rates of interest must lead to *lower* prices

directly, for the purchase of domestic securities, debentures, and shares, and for the acquisition of bank deposits  Meanwhile foreign countries would become relatively poor in respect to real capital, and domestic wealth would increase, and the natural rate of interest on capital would rise abroad and fall at home, so that finally economic equilibrium would be restored

Interest and dividends would now have to be paid to foreigners, and consequently, as we shall see later, the equilibrium level of domestic prices would be somewhat *lower* than that abroad.

Recent investigations of international movements of money seem to me on the whole to have confirmed the comparative validity of the older point of view.[1]

If, on the other hand, taking an international point of view, we suppose that the same movement is undertaken, consciously or unconsciously, by every bank in the world, or at any rate in the gold-standard countries, the matter assumes an entirely different appearance

The question with which we are faced is whether the banks could continually maintain a rate of interest *below* the natural rate, and so drive up prices *higher and higher*. If we are looking at the matter purely with regard to the banks' *solvency*, and are assuming that the credit system has been fully developed in every country, there is clearly no other limit than that which arises out of the absorption of the precious metal in *industrial* uses  A fall in the purchasing power of money discourages the production of gold and, other things being equal, it increases the consumption of gold in industry. As soon as consumption began to outstrip production the deficiency would have to be supplied out of the banks' stocks, for no other source is allowed for.

But under actual conditions there is a considerable quantity of coin in circulation—or of notes, which under the banking laws of many countries comes to the same thing. The limit is now, of course, much narrower. A rise

---

[1] *Cf.* Carl Heiligenstadt, "Beiträge zur Lehre von den auswärtigen Wechselkursen", *Jahrbücher für Nationalökonomie*, vols 59-61, 1892-3

in prices exerts its influence, not only on the relation between the production and consumption of gold, but to a much more important extent on the demands of the monetary circulation  The quantity of coins and notes circulating in the hands of the public is usually much larger than the available reserves of the banks  It follows that quite a small rise in prices may bring about a very significant contraction of the banks' reserves

It, is, however, unlikely that, other things being equal, a rise in prices will cause a proportional increase in the quantity of gold and notes in circulation, particularly not of the former. Just as the richest of us does not need to carry with him more than fifty pfennig or one mark in nickel and about ten marks in silver, so there is a certain limit beyond which most payments are made, no longer in gold, but in notes, and a further limit above which they are normally effected by means of cheques. A general rise in prices will bring an increased proportion of the aggregate of payments above one or other of these dividing lines, so that in direct consequence the ratio of notes and cheques to gold coins is increased  (At the same time the constant development of banking technique is responsible for a displacement of coins and notes by cheques.)

But it is very doubtful whether this limit has ever actually been reached, particularly during recent years  For gold has been accumulating in the shape of banking reserves and the uncovered note issue frequently falls short of the legal limit. The operation of this limiting factor can least of all be maintained by those who deny the existence of any connection between the magnitude of available stocks of gold and the level of prices  For if the banks were in practice prevented out of regard for their reserves from lowering their discount rates, what answer would be available in reply to the *bimetallists*, who find in this factor the very cause of falling prices [21]  It is irrelevant to point out that the rate of discount has stood at a lower level in recent times than in the period before 1873. We have already indicated that it is never a question of the absolute level of the rate

[1] *Cf*  O. Arendt, *Die vertragsmassige Doppelwahrung,* vol. i , p. 166 ff.

of interest, but of the level of the lending rate relatively to the uncontrolled rate [1] (the natural capital rate).

Once it is admitted that at the present time the banks' reserves are unnecessarily large and could be diminished without endangering their solvency, it must also be admitted that the banks could lower their rates of interest still further if they desired to do so; at the most it could only be the unnecessary stringency of legal restrictions which prevents them.

It is difficult to understand the view expressed by W Scharling that "gold does not accumulate in the banks because it can find no use as a commodity, but because great stocks of capital which can find no profitable use are represented by the gold lying in the banks, and require this gold to represent them".[2] It must be left undecided whether unused real capital, that is to say, stocks of commodities awaiting sale, are greater to-day in relation to the volume of production and consumption than was formerly the case  Even if it were so and if it were desired to regard the gold lying unused in the banks as "representative" of stocks of commodities, which it could be instrumental in purchasing and disposing of when trade improved—this manner of speaking is purely metaphorical—there would still be no reason why the banks should not at once offer the gold by way of loans  If they are unwilling to do so, that is to say, if they cannot bring themselves to lower their rates of interest, they must have their reasons, some of which we shall set out in a moment  Here lies the direct cause, and in no other "scarcity of gold", for falling prices

As a matter of fact, Scharling himself, at the end of his very noteworthy discussion, admits that at the present time the banks' stocks of gold are from every point of view unnecessarily large.

We turn now to the opposite question. Is there anything to prevent the banks from maintaining the rate of interest *above* the natural rate? It is clearly no longer a question of the banks' solvency—provided that in other respects the banks are solvent in the ordinary sense of the word, their

[1] ["*Verkehrszins*" in original ]

[2] *Preussiche Jahrb* , 1895  See also *Nationalokonomisk Tidskrift* (Copenhagen), 1895

assets exceeding their liabilities. It is now a question purely of the banks' economic interests [1] Our theory tells us that such behaviour will result in a continual *fall* in prices and a continual rise in the purchasing power of gold. The production of gold will become more profitable, and, other things being equal, its output will increase, though possibly not by very much; while the consumption of gold will be curtailed, and, more important, larger and larger quantities of gold and notes will flow out of circulation into the banks as a result of the change in prices It is true that any simultaneous increase in population and in economic welfare and any development of the monetary system (at the expense of the natural system of economy) will exert a somewhat moderating influence. On the other hand, the development of the monetary system carries with it a continual expansion in the use of credit and of banking facilities, and consequently the tendency for money to pass out of circulation is accentuated.

We have already seen that the banks have to accept these sums on deposit and pay *interest* on them even though they do not really want to, and they have to pay a rate which falls only a little short of their own discount rate, for otherwise they would suffer from competition with private lenders (There is an exception in the case of central banks, for reasons which need not here be discussed In any case, most of the gold which accumulates in the central banks does not reach them by way of deposits, but as a result of exchange against notes, part of which then remain in the tills of the other banks.) The banks may dispose of these deposits in interest-earning securities and stocks, but this does not curtail the superfluity of money, for the money which is thereby released has in its turn to find a use Ultimately the banks have no alternative but to lower their discount rates, so as to stimulate the diminishing demand for money This checks or overcomes the upward movement of prices, and a point is soon reached where

---

[1] It will become clear that this factor plays a part also in setting a *lower* limit to the rate of interest

the circulation is once again sufficient to absorb the excess of gold and notes.

It is thus confidently to be expected that the Bank rate, or more generally the money rate of interest, will always coincide *eventually* with the natural capital rate, or rather that it is always *tending* to coincide with an ever-changing natural rate  But whether this result is achieved with sufficient *rapidity* to prevent a continual rise in prices at times when the capital rate is rising (so that the money rate is left *below* the natural rate), or to obviate a gradual fall in prices at times when the capital rate is falling (and consequently the money rate is left *higher* than the natural rate), seems *a priori* very doubtful. This question involves a survey of various complications which unfortunately requires a far more intimate insight into the secrets of banking technique than is at my disposal, particularly as the matter is partly associated with forces tending in *contrary* directions.

For instance, it is in the interests of the banks of issue to have as large a note issue as possible, in so far as they can issue notes against a purely banking [1] cover. They can content themselves for a time with a somewhat low rate of interest inasmuch as the rise in prices, and the consequent increase in the demand for instruments of exchange, will soon enable them to raise their rate. If notes constituted the sole means of exchange, the extent of the note issue would be a matter of indifference; for the value of money would then vary in inverse ratio to the size of the note issue. But this is no longer true if the banks can with their notes displace, in whole or in part, such other instruments as bills, cheques, and cash.

Precisely in the opposite direction lie the interests of those banks which do not issue notes and at the same time possess much capital of their own. A high rate of interest increases their profits, and the consequent fall in prices does them no harm— indeed, the higher the purchasing power of gold the greater is the value of their own property. Finally we have those banks which neither issue notes nor possess much capital. To them the level of prices and the magnitude of the rate of interest are both matters of almost complete indifference (their profits

---

[1] ["*bankmassige*" in original.]

originating principally out of the *difference* between the rates
for borrowing and for lending) Here, however, we have to deal
with a new, and very subtle, consideration If the banks maintain a discount rate, and consequently a deposit rate, which is
too low in relation to the natural rate, many capitalists will
withdraw their deposits in order themselves to become entrepreneurs in such guises as those of shareholders and sleeping
partners. This will not imperil the banks' *solvency*, or at any
rate not nearly so much as would at first sight appear In a
pure cheque economy, the withdrawal of deposits must *always*
(for the banks taken as a whole) bring about either the making
of fresh deposits or the repayment of loans In the case which
we are considering, it is the latter effect which must be realised.
As a result of the assumption by a large number of capitalists
of the rôle of entrepreneur, there is a necessary decline, *ceteris
paribus*, in the activity of those businesses which work on borrowed capital Their owners find no further use for part of the
credit which they have been employing, and repay it to the
banks There is consequently a *contraction* in banking activity,
or at any rate it fails to expand in the same measure as prices
rise, *i.e* as the value of money declines. The opposite would be
the case—banking activity would *expand relatively* to the level
of prices—if the banks maintained too high rates on loans and
deposits. It follows that it is in the interests of the banks to
maintain their rates of interest at a high rather than at a low
level. But there is always the danger of stifling the spirit of
enterprise, a consideration which tells in the opposite direction

I am unable, as I have said, to assess the importance in actual
banking practice of these various factors.

I content myself with a reference to one feature which
is universally admitted to be of predominant importance
in determining banking policy—the influence of habit and
of routine A bank manager occupies a position of high re-
sponsibility, and a great deal depends on his actions If he
is conscientious it will not occur to him to indulge in unnecessarily dangerous ventures and experiments He is a
servant of routine, and it is only when circumstances are
completely altered that he will deviate from the tradition
which, adopted by his bank, has been tested by experience.[1]

---

[1] Gilbart maintains (*Practical Treatise on Banking*, i , section iv ) that
the director of a bank must always follow certain general "principles";

As regards bank-rate policy, there is a far stronger reason
for the maintenance of fixed rules of conduct. For neither
an individual bank nor the banks of an individual country
can on their own initiative embark on any change without keeping in accord with the procedure adopted by
other banks. The open market may perhaps seem to present a somewhat more lively picture, but it is practically
certain that the lending rate of interest never follows
directly on movements of the natural rate, and usually
follows them only very slowly and with considerable hesitation. During the period of transition, the deviation between the two rates has full play, resulting in that phenomenon, often referred to above, which on a superficial
view appears to contradict our theory but in reality is
in complete accordance with it prices rise when the rate
of interest (the capital rate and *consequently* the money
rate) is high and rising, and in the contrary case they fall.

This brings us to a consideration which has for a long time
been emphasised by various writers. When the rate of interest
(both the capital and the money rate) is high, there is an
obvious tendency for money to circulate somewhat more
rapidly, for "hoards" of coin and bullion to be drawn out of
their hiding-places, and for the employment of all credit instruments to become more profitable—in short, there is a tendency
for prices to rise (though only once and for all, not progressively)
A low rate of interest has in all respects the opposite tendency·
certain kinds of credit instrument can no longer be used at all,
because such payments as the stamp duty on bills and the tax
on notes would absorb too substantial a part of the interest.
other things being equal, prices stand at a lower level.

In its essence this is merely a special case of our general
proposition. For it is only so long as these various factors
maintain the money rate of interest either above or below the
appropriate level of the natural rate that prices will continue
moving in the one direction or the other. Eventually the normal
relation between the two rates must be attained, and any
further rise or fall in prices is then impossible.

but he goes much further in emphasising that these principles must
always be *followed* than in defending them against objection In the light
of what is said above, this attitude can easily be understood.

The phenomenon of lending provides our principle with a comprehensive basis; for the only possible limit to the demand for loans, and with their assistance for goods and services, and therefore the only possible limit to a rise in prices, is to be found where the expected gain corresponds to no more than the payment which has to be made for the "use" of the money.

The fundamental ideas of the last two chapters can now be summarised as follows.

At any moment and in every economic situation there is a certain level of the average rate of interest which is such that the general level of prices has no tendency to move either upwards or downwards  This we call the *normal* rate of interest  Its magnitude is determined by the current level of the natural capital rate, and rises and falls with it.

If, for any reason whatever, the average rate of interest is set and maintained *below* this normal level, no matter how small the gap, prices will rise and will go on rising, or if they were already in process of falling, they will fall more slowly and eventually begin to rise.

If, on the other hand, the rate of interest is maintained no matter how little *above* the current level of the natural rate, prices will fall continuously and without limit.

In the interests of accuracy, we have purposely avoided the statement that for the maintenance of stable prices it is necessary that the money and natural rates should be *equal*  In practice they are both rather vague conceptions, if it is a general mean level that is under discussion, and their exact determination, even from the theoretical point of view, involves great difficulties  On the basis of one definition it would be correct to speak of an absolute equality between the two rates, according to another it would be a question of the constancy of the excess of the natural rate over the money rate, corresponding to the unavoidable risks of enterprise and the like. The essential point is that the maintenance of a constant level of prices depends, other things remaining equal, on the maintenance of a certain rate of interest on loans, and that a permanent discrepancy between the actual rate and this rate exerts a *progressive and cumulative* influence on prices.

In two later chapters we shall subject our theory to the test of *experience*, in the shape of actual movements of prices. Some further *theoretical* discussion is, however, desirable We shall begin by examining more closely the causes which determine the natural rate of interest, and we shall deal more systematically with the probable influence on prices of a deviation of the money rate of interest from the natural rate Here we shall base our treatment on certain quantitative relations, and we shall have to resort to highly simplified assumptions which differ widely from the conditions of reality

Many will doubt the usefulness of such an investigation, but it provides, in my opinion, a convenient opportunity for gathering together all the threads of the argument Experience suggests that in any discussion of the complicated conditions of reality there is constant danger of overlooking or losing sight of what may perhaps be the most important elements in the problem

But those of my readers who have no love for the methods of abstraction may omit the following chapter. It does not contain any positive extension of the propositions which have already been set out, and it is not absolutely necessary for an understanding of the argument of the later portions of the book. It is written for those who, like myself, regard as the prime requisite of a scientific theory that it shall be capable of being set out in a form that is self-contained and free of inconsistency, even if at first the assumptions have to be of a purely imaginary character.

# CHAPTER 9

## SYSTEMATIC EXPOSITION OF THE THEORY

### A. *The Causes which Determine the Natural Rate of Interest on Capital*

It is to the brilliant work of Jevons and Böhm-Bawerk that we mainly owe the enormous advance which has recently taken place in our knowledge of the nature of interest and of the part played in production by capital Though they differ somewhat in formal outlook, the substance of these two writers' contributions is very nearly identical.

Jevons opens[1] with the observation that the customary division of productive capital into liquid (circulating) and fixed capital is a scientific conception of little significance, and that its function is better served by the antithesis between *free* and *invested* capital. "The notion of capital", he says, "assumes a new degree of simplicity as soon as we recognise that what has been called a part is really the whole Capital, as I regard it, consists merely in the *aggregate of those commodities which are required for sustaining labourers of any kind or class engaged in work. . . .* The *current means of sustenance constitute capital in its free or uninvested form.* The single and all-important function of capital is to enable the labourer to await the result of any long-lasting work,—to put an interval between the beginning and the end of an enterprise."[2]

Fundamentally this line of approach is certainly correct. But Jevons commits the error of confusing the part with the whole. Even if it is agreed that fixed capital is merely

[1] *Theory of Political Economy,* chap vii.

[2] [*Ibid* , second and later editions, p 223; first edition (worded slightly differently), p. 214 ]

the temporary product of labour and free capital, the costs of production which are advanced out of the latter can never be resolved *entirely* into wages. The rewards of the other factors of production, and particularly of land, must be taken into account.

It might be supposed that even interest itself is partly advanced out of capital This would appear to be the case when interest is paid before the final product is available But from the economic point of view, this is not an *advance* out of capital, but a *retention* of part of the capital, involving an encroachment on its effective amount. While it is usual for the debenture holders of a company, and occasionally even for the shareholders, to receive interest and so-called dividends during the preparations for the work that they are financing, in reality they are merely receiving back a part of their capital which has failed for the moment to fructify, at any rate in this particular enterprise.

Capital in its "free and uninvested form" consists not only of the means of sustenance by which labourers can defray their consumption, but it also provides for the owners of other factors of production, above all for the owners of land. In its essence it is not merely a "wages fund" but also a "wages and rent fund".

This oversight of Jevons' is in keeping with the traditional but fallacious statement of the English economists that the rent of land "does not .. form any part     of the advances of the capitalist" [1] (We shall deal later with the complication which arises when the landlord is himself an entrepreneur )

According to Bohm-Bawerk, [2] the characteristic of capitalist production lies simply in the fact that a portion —in a highly developed capitalist economy usually the main portion—of the available labour and land is employed for the purposes, not of *current* consumption, but of consumption in the more or less distant *future*; and current consumption is mainly made up of the mature

---

[1] J S Mill [*Principles of Political Economy*, book ii , chap xvi , § 6]. *Cf* my *Finanztheoretische Untersuchungen*, p. 44 ff

[2] *Positive Theorie des Kapitales*, first edition, book i., chap. ii.; book ii , chap ii ff [third edition, and Smart's translation, book i., chap. ii., book ii , chap. iii ff.]

product yielded by labour and land employed in the past.
At any moment there are in existence in various stages of
maturity certain preliminary and intermediate products;
these are called capital. But, according to Bohm-Bawerk,
they are to be regarded as *symptoms* of the capitalist process of production rather than as its essence, which simply
consists in the *devotion* to future needs of current productive forces.

This line of approach penetrates more deeply, and for
the case of a monadic economy[1] (or of the economic system
as a whole) it is also the more correct. In a monadic
economy the means of sustenance do not really constitute
capital  it is rarely the case that these are accumulated with
a view to entering on some fresh branch of production, as
is done by the *"Urfischer"* of Roscher (and Ricardo). Consumption goods are usually consumed as soon as they are
ready, provided that the requirements of nature or of
technique do not stand in the way  The thing that is
"saved" is rather a portion of the labour power—available,
though relying on the provision of means of sustenance,—
and of the disposable service of land, which are partly
withheld from meeting current needs and are devoted to
the needs of the future

But the monadic economic system is to-day an exception.
Almost the whole of labour and a large part of land are
employed by their owners in the service of others. The
payment that is received (wages and rents) is devoted by
the workers and landlords purely to the purchase of consumption goods, in so far as they do not themselves accumulate capital. Such a process could theoretically, by
means of payments in kind, be carried on without the use
of money. In this sense consumption goods might be regarded as constituting the original (free) capital by which
labour and land are purchased.

It is not difficult to generalise this proposition. Those
trades in which workers or landlords are themselves
entrepreneurs are always subject in some degree to the

---

[1] [*"isolierte Wirtschaft"* in original ]

general influences of the market. Each such worker or land-lord can be imagined to pay out to himself his wages or rent at the normal rates, as determined in the market, until his product is completed or ready for sale, so that capital is necessary, whether it is owned by the individual himself or borrowed from others, and whether he really spends the money on his own consumption or partly saves it and so converts it into capital.[1]

In this way the whole thing gains enormously in simplicity and clearness, and the lines of approach of Jevons and of Böhm-Bawerk are made to coalesce. With the exception of that part which is consumed by the capitalists them-selves in the form of interest, the total amount of con-sumption goods produced yearly, monthly, or weekly can be regarded, on the assumption of a stationary state, as a *fund* for the payment of wages and rents This fund repre-sents the (real) demand for labour and land An equivalent amount is provided by the combined operation of labour and natural forces and this is added to the country's stock of capital (invested capital), assuming various forms in suc-cession. Beginning with "labour applied to the land", it appears successively as tools, machines, raw material, half-finished goods, and finally in the form of the finished pro-duct (in which, partly or wholly, the capital is once again free). Of this finished product, the capitalist[2] again retains a part for himself as interest or exchanges it against other products for his own consumption The main portion he invests afresh. he employs it, either directly or after ex-changing it for the products of other entrepreneurs, for buying or hiring labour and land for the purpose of further production. Thus at any moment of time a cross section of the actual capital in existence (liquid and fixed) would indicate that nearly all of it (indeed all of it, if we adopt

---

[1] In other words, we separate out the functions of workers, landlords, capitalists (and entrepreneurs) even though they may be actually com-bined in one and the same person.

[2] We assume that normally the entrepreneur receives no profit (*cf* above, p. 104), though we shall see that such a profit may accrue under special conditions.

a more accurate or more ideal point of view) assumes
the form of invested capital. But if a "lengthwise section"
were taken, it would be seen that each individual piece of
capital travels, slowly or rapidly as the case may be,
around a circular path, and that both at the beginning and
at the end it takes the form of free capital, that is to say, of
consumption goods.

For the purposes of a closer treatment of the problem of
capital and particularly of a theoretical determination
of the rate of interest (as well as of wages and of rents),
some further analysis of the meaning of capital is, I think,
indispensable, and it is necessary to turn back to the
classical distinction between fixed and mobile capital.
There are certain products of man's labour which have a
very high and sometimes unlimited *durability* Examples
are provided by houses, streets railways, canals, certain
improvements in land certain kinds of machines While
by *origin*, having regard to the manner by which they are
obtained, they have the attributes of capital and of other
capital goods, they play a part in further production
which comes nearest to that played by *land* I have therefore proposed[1] that they shall be regarded, not as capital
goods, but as a kind of "rent-earning goods", which contribute to output, either with or without the assistance of
further labour and land, and earn for their owners a certain
rent (analogous to the rent of land). Under stationary conditions—which, as the simplest possible assumption, should
serve as a starting-point in all economic discussions—these
goods will not actually be produced at all, they will be
merely maintained; but the labour which is applied to
them can on each occasion be regarded as representing a
new investment of capital Indeed, the gradual replace-
ment of worn-out units (such as houses) by new units can
also be looked at in this way, at any rate from the economic
point of view, if a large body (of houses) is taken as the
unit. On the other hand, it is one of the main character-

---

[1] *Über Wert, Kapital und Rente*, pp 93, 121, 137; *Finanztheoretische
Untersuchungen*, p. 28

istics of a rapidly developing economic system that a considerable part of the available capital is invested for a long term, in other words, it is converted into our rent-earning goods  As soon as the transformation has been accomplished, the new rent-earning good competes only with the other rent-earning goods of the same type. It gives rise to a rent, and unlike real capital goods, it is not offset by the payment of interest.

By capital, in the narrow sense of the word, I mean only tools, machines, improvements in land, etc , of relatively *low* durability (though the dividing line has to be drawn somewhat arbitrarily), furthermore raw materials and semi-manufactured products, and finally stocks of finished consumption goods.

For example, I regard a house, not as a capital good, but as a rent-earning good, which, with or without the co-operation of labour and other factors of production, supplies the consumption good "shelter". Every time that the owner renovates his house (say every ten years) he makes a new short-term investment of capital  The annual rent must in the first place be sufficient, over the period of ten years, to pay for the amortisation and interest on this capital (the cost of repairs), assuming that the house involves no other costs of upkeep  This is equivalent to an annual payment of about one-tenth of the capital sum and, as can easily be seen, to five years' interest on this sum. The surplus is to be regarded as the rent of the house. The fact that at the same time it is equal to the *interest* on the *capital* value of the house is of secondary importance, this capital value depends equally on the amount of the net rent  And it is a matter of complete indifference whether or not this rent corresponds to the interest on the capital originally invested when the house was built, perhaps a hundred years ago  Even the so-called *cost of reproduction* exerts only an indirect influence on the capital value of the site and building. The cost of reproduction may exceed the capital value to an almost unlimited extent (for instance in a regressive community)  The opposite is also often the case, for the new houses which are to compete with the old houses must usually be built in less convenient districts  It is usual to try to draw a distinction between the value of the building itself and the value of the site. But this is a pure matter of book-keeping, because it is in fact impossible to separate the building from the site without heavy cost.

In the above classification, regard is being paid only to the most important economic categories. It is clearly impossible to assign every form of social wealth to one or other of these compartments  For instance, a very significant amount of capital is often invested in the development of human capacities, but these capacities cannot be included under the conception of capital, neither in the narrow nor in the wide sense of the word. They must be regarded rather as the basis for a particular kind of labour (skilled labour), and it must then be remembered that in certain circumstances some of the available capital of a community may be converted into, or invested in, the form of labour (the capacity to do work).

Furthermore, there are sources of income, such as monopolies based on discoveries, patent rights, business secrets, goodwill, which may represent the fruit of capital invested in the past  But they are not imbued with the properties of capital goods in the real sense nor with those of "rent-earning goods"  They are a thing *sui generis*, and follow their own particular laws.

Finally, it must not be forgotten that a very substantial amount of economic production and consumption is connected with the running of the state and of other autonomous bodies, but by its nature this is excluded from the realm of free economic competition and depends on the decisions of the taxing authorities

We are merely concerned with obtaining a sufficiently clear perspective of the general direction in which economic forces operate, and we are not attempting any quantitative estimates. The various circumstances which have just been mentioned can therefore be neglected.

In the same way, we neglect the fact that capital often changes hands before it has completed the full circle. We are supposing, in other words, that once capital has been invested it becomes free only when the finished consumption goods find their way into actual consumption.

Let it be supposed, for example, that in the present year a producer A pays $l_1$ in wages and $r_1$ in rents in order to produce a machine (of low durability). Suppose now that another producer B buys this machine in the subsequent year, and in his turn expends $l_2$ in wages and $r_2$ in rents in producing a certain quantity of raw materials, the machine being worn out in the process. Suppose finally that in the third year C buys these raw materials, and after spending $l_3$ on wages and $r_3$ on rents, produces a stock of finished goods, which he sells at the end of the year. Then, on the basis of the above treatment, the capital that has been devoted to production amounts to

$$(l_1 + l_2 + l_3) + (r_1 + r_2 + r_3) = l + r = k,$$

where $l$ and $r$ represent the total amount of wages and of rent. The average period of investment is

$$\frac{3l_1 + 2l_2 + l_3}{l} = t_l \text{ in the case of wages,}$$

and

$$\frac{3r_1 + 2r_2 + r_3}{r} = t_r \text{ in the case of rent,}$$

and finally

$$\frac{3(l_1 + r_1) + 2(l_2 + r_2) + (l_3 + r_3)}{l + r} = \frac{lt_l + rt_r}{k} = t \text{ years}$$

for the whole of the invested capital. This is all on the assumption that wages and rents are paid out in advance at the beginning of each year. Otherwise the period of investment would clearly be somewhat shorter, but it can always be calculated without difficulty.

If the machine were more durable, and if the final product were disposed of only gradually, the average period of investment could again be worked out without any difficulties that are worth mentioning.[1]

The amount of capital $k$ and its period of investment $t$ can be derived in this manner for each individual industry, or rather for the production of each individual class of consumption good. Then the amount of capital employed in industry as a whole amounts to $K = \Sigma k$, and its average period of investment $T$ is given by the equation

$$T = \frac{\Sigma(k\,t)}{\Sigma k},$$

where $K = \Sigma k$ represents the aggregate value of the con-

[1] Cf. my *Finanztheoretische Untersuchungen*, p. 29.

K

sumption goods invested at any moment in the form of capital, valued either in terms of any one of them or in terms of money.

It is not, of course, easy, and sometimes it is logically impossible, to determine how much labour and land, and consequently how much capital, have been involved in the production of any particular consumption good  The difficulty arises whenever several commodities are produced in the course of one and the same process (the case of by-products--*joint supply* according to Marshall's terminology)  But this does not prevent a theoretical enquiry into the amount of the total "circulating" capital and of its average period of investment.

If $T$ is expressed in years the quotient $K/T$ represents the amount of capital that becomes free in the course of a year—the amount, that is to say, of finished products which are available each year to pay for the services of labour and land (or other rent-earning goods), and it constitutes the *annual* wages-and-rent fund  $K$ itself, the value of the whole of the "circulating" capital, can be regarded as the *aggregate* wages-and-rent fund, although it is not all free and liquid at any one moment, but becomes so only over a period of time, and the conclusions of the prematurely discarded "wages fund theory" can be successfully applied to this quantity, as Bohm-Bawerk has elegantly demonstrated[1] (though it has, of course, to be borne in mind that at any time it lies within the power of the capitalists to increase this fund by new saving or to diminish it by augmenting their own consumption)  It must, however, be remembered that this fund has to last not merely for *one* year, but for a number of years equal to the average period of investment of the capital  This period, like all the other quantities that we are now discussing, is subject to certain variations, of which the nature will shortly be indicated

The matter can be put as follows. If $A$ represents the number of available workers, $B$ the total amount of available land, $l$

---

[1] *Positive Theorie des Kapitales*, first edition, p. 450 [third edition, p  644, Smart's translation, p  419].

and $r$ the average rates of wages and of rent per unit of land, the following relation is approximately true under all conditions:

$$(A \ l + B \ r) \ T = K.$$

This equation simply tells us that all labour and all land, and in its turn all capital, are always seeking employment and are always more or less fully employed.

$B \ r$ really stands for the sum of all "rent-earning goods" (peculiarly durable capital goods), each measured in terms of its own unit (for instance, cubic metres of content in the case of dwelling-houses or factories, kilometres in the case of railways) and multiplied by the corresponding rent.

Everything else now follows from the Economic Principle, viz. that the entrepreneur strives for the greatest possible profit. Furthermore, there is the important fact that we have throughout to deal with fairly plastic, and not with rigidly invariable, magnitudes and relationships.

If it could be assumed that in practice the production of the goods consumed in the course of the year always involves a constant proportion of labour to land (or of other "rent-earning goods"), there would be no principle whatever for the determination of the relative level of the wages of labour and of the rent of land (or of "rents" in general), as they would obtain under free competition. There would necessarily be a permanent excess either in the number of workers or in the amount of available land (assuming that the population was not correspondingly diminished in the one case as a result of emigration, or increased in the other case as a result of immigration or natural growth). Theoretically, such an excess would depress either the level of wages or of rents, as the case might be, to an unlimited extent But this is an assumption which is completely opposed to the facts of reality. In the first place, labour and land can to some extent be substituted for one another (intensive or extensive production) even in the production of one and the same commodity Far more important, there are no two commodities of which the production requires exactly the same proportions of these two factors Suppose now that wages fall as a result, for instance, of an excess in the number of workers. Then the production of those goods which require relatively much labour and relatively little land becomes more profitable than the production of the opposite kind of goods—more profitable, that is to say, to the *entrepreneur as such*, not to the owner of land. The production and consumption of the former kind of goods expands, while there is a relative diminution in that of the latter class of goods  The demand for labour increases, the demand for land (and for other rent-earning goods) diminishes, until finally economic equilibrium is restored, after a certain period of oscillation; and all available factors of production will find employment at prices determined by the market situation—these prices being such that for the individual entrepreneur, or for the aggregate of entrepreneurs, profits are unaffected by a small change in the proportion of labour to land and rent-earning goods.

Actually the complications are greater  We have been making the implicit assumption that the relative values of commodities in exchange remain unaltered  But they are, of course, affected by the change in the conditions of production, and they in their turn exert an influence on the conditions of production. The only scientific method of dealing with the problem consists in paying *simultaneous* regard to all these factors, in the manner first demonstrated very clearly by Léon Walras [1]

The average level of the rate of interest on capital is determined in a completely analogous manner. Let us suppose, for instance, that as a result of increased thriftiness (whether production becomes more efficient or not) there is an increase in the available amount of liquid capital. Then competition between capitalists will raise wages and rents, and there will be a corresponding fall (as compared with the level that it would otherwise have attained) in the earnings of capital, or its rate of interest.[2] But it is to be noticed that it is the rate of interest only on liquid

[1] *Éléments d'économie politique pure*, 1st ed , section IV ; cf also my *Uber Wert, Kapital und Rente*, chap II , section VI

[2] How the process works out in reality, when money serves as a medium of exchange and of payment, will be shown below (p. 151)

capital itself that falls, not the earnings of exceptionally durable capital (rent-earning goods), which, at first at any rate, take part in the rise enjoyed by rents and wages

This effect, which by itself might rapidly depress the rate of interest to a very marked degree, is not decisive. Just as the various branches of production require different proportions of labour and land, so too they require different amounts of (liquid) capital In terms of our definitions, this means nothing more than that the relative lengths of the period of production and the period of investment are different in different cases If there is a fall in the rate of interest, those processes which for technical reasons involve a long period of production will become relatively more profitable, while those processes where the period of production is short will become relatively less profitable There will ensue an expansion in the one and a contraction in the other. The final result of these changes is *that the average period of investment of the aggregate of (circulating) capital is lengthened; and the portion of the wages-and-rent fund which becomes available in any one year is consequently diminished.*[1] As a result, wages and rents are once again lowered, but not of course right down to the level which obtained before the increase in capital took place.

The case of a relative diminution in the amount of circulating capital is exactly the contrary.

The significance of this procedure is enhanced by bearing in mind Bohm-Bawerk's observation, often misunderstood but certainly quite valid, that in almost every enterprise it is possible to increase the efficiency of the factors of production by appropriately lengthening the period of production (by introducing preparatory processes, mechanical methods, etc.). Logically this assumption can now be seen to be by no means indispensable. It is possible to explain the equilibrium, in Bohm-

---

[1] A very clear picture is provided by Bohm-Bawerk's well-known graphical illustration of the varying rapidity with which the product "ripens", *loc cit*, p. 114 ff. [third edition, p 188, Smart's translation, p 107].

Bawerk's sense, of capitalist production without making use of the assumption, a point which raises an objection against opponents of the Bohm-Bawerk theory [1]

It would be necessary for the sake of completeness to consider the influence exerted by all these various changes on capital structure itself. It has further to be remembered that the quantity of *durable* capital goods ("rent-earning goods") is in general capable of expansion; such an expansion will take place when their earnings increase or when the rate of interest falls, so that their capital value now exceeds their cost of reproduction The main characteristic of, and condition for, a stationary state is that this capital value shall be not more than, or a little less than, this cost of reproduction. Such considerations will not be followed up any further in this place They impose no essential restrictions on the above line of reasoning, but they provide a basis for the practical possibility that in a rapidly progressive society the rate of interest may be maintained at a relatively high level over a considerable period of time in spite of continual accumulation of capital

For a further discussion of Bohm-Bawerk's theory of capital, I may perhaps be allowed to refer, not only to Bohm-Bawerk's own fundamental works, but to my *Über Wert, Kapital und Rente* and to the first part of my *Finanztheoretische Untersuchungen*

## B. *The Use of Money*

The nature of the natural rate of interest on capital, and the causes that are responsible for determining its level, should by now have been made sufficiently clear —on the assumption, of course, of universally free competition No distinction has been made between the original [2] (uncontrolled [3]) rate of interest and the contractual [4] (lending) rate of interest.

---

[1] Ricardo was already aware of the possibility referred to in the text, but his treatment, though the same in essence, is rather different in form (*cf Principles*, chap 1, section v).

[2] ["*originaren*" in original ]  [3] ["*Verkehrs*" in original ]

[4] ["*ausbedungenen*" in original.]

In dealing with most economic questions, it is legitimate to make this simplification. For the difference between the two rates, which constitutes the entrepreneurs' profit as such, constantly tends towards zero under the influence of competition among entrepreneurs, or at least it tends towards a certain small amount which is not very different from zero. There is only one case in which the difference cannot be neglected. This arises when it is a question of a change in the average level of commodity prices expressed in *money*. For such a change takes its real origin in the existence of such a difference between the two rates of interest. This has already been explained, and will now be dealt with in a more systematic manner.

It is possible for a considerable difference between the uncontrolled rate and the contractual rate to persist, and consequently for entrepreneur profits to remain positive or negative, as the case may be, for a considerable period of time. It has already been mentioned that this possibility arises out of the fact that the transfer of capital and the remuneration of factors of production do not take place in kind, but are effected in an entirely indirect manner as a result of the intervention of money. It is not, as is so often supposed, merely the *form* of the matter that is thus altered, but its very essence. For real capital goods can no longer be supposed to be actually borrowed and lent, they are now bought and sold. An increase in the demand for real capital goods is no longer a *borrowers'* demand which tends to raise the rate of interest, but a *buyers'* demand which tends to raise the prices of commodities. But money, which is the one thing for which there is really a demand for lending purposes, is elastic in amount.[1] Its quantity can to some extent be accommodated—and in a completely developed credit system the accommodation is complete—to any position that the demand may assume.

The two rates of interest still reach *ultimate* equality, but only after, and as a result of, a previous movement of prices. Prices constitute, so to speak, a spiral spring

[1] *Cf.* above, p. 110

which serves to transmit the power between the natural
and the money rates of interest, but the spring must first
be sufficiently stretched or compressed. In a pure cash
economy, the spring is short and rigid, it becomes longer
and more elastic in accordance with the stage of development of the system of credit and banking.

For the purposes of a complete demonstration of the
influence on prices of a deviation between the two rates of
interest, it is permissible to make a number of simplifying
assumptions These assumptions are made purely for the
sake of simplicity and clarity, not a single one of them is
essential to the validity of the general conclusion. It will
indeed become apparent, as I shall have occasion to point
out, that the transition from our hypothetical assumptions
to the facts of reality will, in more than one respect,
strengthen the plausibility of our conclusions

We imagine a country in which everything is completely
stationary, except for the changes that we are considering
and the effects of such changes We assume, in particular,
that the capital goods which have been invested for a long
time ("rent-earning goods") are subject to no other change
than the repairs which are necessary for their maintenance.
It has also to be supposed that the liquid real capital
which has to be renewed year by year is maintained by the
capitalists at a constant amount. We suppose further that
the length of the period of production is the same in every
business, and amounts to one year, as would be the case if
technical conditions firmly prevented any extension or
contraction Actually the period of production is not only
very different in different branches of production, but in
any given branch it is variable. It is, as we have seen, this
very circumstance, combined with the possibility of transferring capital from one business to another, that is responsible for the determination under conditions of free
competition of the relative levels of real wages, of rents,
and of the rate of interest itself. Now, however, we are not
dealing with changes in these magnitudes. We are trying
to see how their expression in terms of the money unit

would alter if their real value were to remain unchanged
We shall nevertheless take into special account such
factors as actually lead to a change in the average period
of production, and consequently to a change in the level of
real wages, etc.

We may assume further that production begins everywhere at the same moment of time, at the beginning of the
economic year, which need not, of course, coincide with
the calendar year; and we may assume that the final product, the consumption goods, are not completed or available for exchange until the end of the year  This would
correspond in some ways to the situation of former times,
when in many districts the exchange of commodities was
concentrated on one, or a few, great annual markets.

The total quantity of consumption goods is then the
same thing as the quantity of liquid real capital in its free
form, or rather it is the same thing as the quantity of this
capital, inclusive of the amount with which the owners of
capital have the right annually to credit themselves as remuneration for the capital employed in the previous year
and which they consume on their own account during the
current year

In order to make a clear distinction between the rôles of
capitalists and of entrepreneurs, we may imagine that the
latter work entirely on borrowed money and that they derive this money, not directly from the capitalists, but from
a special institution, a bank  At the same time, the capitalists may be supposed to be dealers in commodities. To
make the matter as clear as possible, let us assume that
wages and rents (including rents of houses, etc.) are paid
out in advance at the beginning of the year, and that
the workers, landlords, and also the entrepreneurs themselves, then provide themselves with sufficient stocks
to meet a complete year's consumption  The capitalist
dealers are thus released from the necessity of holding
substantial stocks, and we may imagine that the profit
obtained by actual trade is quite small or we can neglect
it altogether

It goes without saying that this assumption is taking us a long way from reality  Trade must be regarded as an important element in the act of production, and it involves the use of considerable amounts of labour, of advances in respect to capital, etc , for which an appropriate remuneration has to be paid. It might seem better to enrol the traders in the category of entrepreneurs  But we want to be able to assume that the entrepreneurs have to pay off their old debts at the end of the year before they can borrow for the next period of production  This they can do only if they can dispose of their products to somebody who himself possesses money, and, according to our assumptions, this is not yet the case with the majority of actual consumers (workers, landlords, etc.)

Our imaginary procedure is then as follows: At the beginning of the year the entrepreneurs borrow their capital from the banks, in the form of a sum of money $K$  This is equal to the value of the total amount of available real capital, that is to say, of the total amount of consumption goods completed during the previous years *minus* the interest drawn in the previous year by the capitalist  This money capital is now paid to the workers and to the landlords, and at the same time entrepreneurs allocate to themselves an amount (to be considered shortly) as remuneration for their own labour, risk taking, etc , and pay the normal competitive rents for such "rent-earning goods" (sites, buildings, machines) as may be in their own possession. With the aid of this money, the whole of the available commodity capital is now bought up by the consumers, and the money capital $K$ returns once again to the banks in the shape of deposits made by the capitalist dealers.

Strictly speaking, it is a matter of indifference in what form the money is employed  It is true that if use is made solely of metallic money, the banks are unable under normal conditions to provide at any one moment the whole of the necessary amount of money  But we can suppose that they lend as much money as belongs to them—their own capital—to a group of entrepreneurs  This sum is then employed to pay a group of workers, and it next serves to purchase part of the commodity capital. When the money is now returned to the banks by the capitalist dealers, it can be lent out to a new group of entrepreneurs And so on In the end this sum of money will have effected the whole body of transactions, and it will then remain in the banks' tills until the end of the year If the banks have the right to issue notes in excess of the amount of their holding of cash, the quantity of means of exchange which they can issue at any moment is correspondingly greater. It is still greater if all payments are effected by means of cheques, which are normally subject to far more lenient legal restrictions than are notes. In the extreme case, it can be supposed that at one and the same moment the banks open credits to the entrepreneurs to the full amount $K$, that the entrepreneurs pay their workers, etc , by means of drafts on their banking accounts; that these drafts are used to pay for goods, and so reach the hands of the capitalist dealers, and that finally the drafts find their way back to the banks and give rise to corresponding credit balances in the accounts of the capitalists.

The goods are completed only at the end of the economic year, and it is only then that the entrepreneurs can meet their liabilities. It follows that the credit which is granted by the banks to the entrepreneurs partakes of the character of *one-year loans*

In practice, the borrowed money capital is far less in amount than the available (liquid) real capital that is employed in production   The reason is that in many cases the entrepreneur is himself a capitalist (even in the narrow sense in which the term is here being employed). But this concerns us only in so far as it affects the *proportion* between the two quantities We shall return to this question below.

Let the contractual rate of interest be $i$. Then the entrepreneurs have at the end of the year to repay to the banks the sum $K\left(1 + \frac{i}{100}\right)$. The deposits of the capitalists can be regarded as fixed for a term of one year. The rate of interest that is paid on deposits is always somewhat lower than the rate charged by banks on loans.[1] The difference between these two rates remunerates the bank, first of all for the trouble and the risk involved and then for holding in

---

[1] Still more so, of course, for deposits on current account. These do not concern us here.

its till a certain stock of metallic money which earns ı
interest and for holding liquid securities which carry on
a moderate rate of interest. But on our assumptions, t
necessary cash holdings of the banks are reduced to a mıı
mum  (This does not, of course, mean that the bank
its owners need not possess sufficient property of the
own to sustain the confidence of the public ) We are al
neglecting the banks' running costs. We can therefo
assume that the rates of interest on loans and deposı
are equal, or nearly equal—in any case a pretty harmle
assumption.

So the banks have assets on the one side and liabiliti
on the other side, both amounting to $K\left(1 + \dfrac{i}{100}\right)$, and bo
falling due at the end of the year  While the business
lending money and of exchanging commodities remains
a standstill throughout the rest of the year, productiı
sets in at the beginning of the year and continues witho
interruption until the end.

The fruits of production belong in the first place to t
entrepreneurs themselves. Their size, or the price that
obtained for them, determines whether the profits are l
or small or whether a loss has been incurred  In a coı
pletely undisturbed and stationary state, we have seen th
the entrepreneur meets with neither a profit nor a loss;
merely obtains the same return for the trouble of co
ducting his business as he would have obtained for co
ducting a similar business on behalf of others, for ınstan
of a company. (We have referred[1] to the modification
this proposition which is necessitated by the existence
unavoidable risks of enterprise )

Thus at the end of the year the entrepreneurs ha
earned no more on the average than the rate of interest
In other words, the value of the total product at the norm
level of prices is $K\left(1 + \dfrac{i}{100}\right)$. The capitalist dealers nc

[1] P. 104, above

draw on their banking accounts, which amount to precisely this sum. They may, for instance, purchase the finished goods from the manufacturers by means of drafts on the banks The manufacturers then use these drafts to repay their debts to the banks (though they will immediately be desirous of obtaining fresh loans). Their debts amount to exactly $K\left(1 + \dfrac{i}{100}\right)$. It follows that at the end of the year both the banks and the entrepreneurs are cleared of all assets and liabilities. The capitalists, on the other hand, are in possession for the moment of their own capital in its primitive form—in the form of goods.

They first realise the interest that is due to them, which amounts to $\dfrac{i \cdot K}{100}$. We are supposing that they do this by exchanging among themselves a corresponding amount of goods and putting them on one side for the purposes of their consumption during the coming year. The monetary transactions that are involved in this operation may be effected by means of drafts on the banks, but each individual account is finally credited and debited with equal amounts, and consequently each account remains with a zero balance. The rest of the goods, which at the existing price level amount to $K$ in value, are available as real capital for the coming year. This process goes on repeating itself

It has now to be supposed that, for some reason or other, a difference arises between the natural rate of interest and the contractual rate of interest. This may be due, for instance, to a fall in the level of wages (brought about by a relative increase in the number of workers), or to a fall in the rent of land or of other rents, or finally to a rise in the productivity of labour and natural forces as a result of technical progress. Suppose that the natural rate is raised to $i + 1$ per cent, while the banks maintain their customary rate of discount $i$

To whose advantage will this difference accrue? In the first place, of course, it accrues to the entrepreneurs. At the end of the year their product, valued at the normal price level, will amount to $K\left(1 + \dfrac{i+1}{100}\right)$, while the amount that they owe is only $K\left(1 + \dfrac{i}{100}\right)$. They have thus obtained a surplus profit of $\dfrac{K}{100}$, and they can realise this profit by exchanging among themselves the corresponding quantity of goods and laying them on one side for the consumption of the coming year, while they offer the rest of their stocks to the capitalists at the normal prices, that is to say, for a total sum of money $K\left(1 + \dfrac{i}{100}\right)$. In the first place, therefore, the level of prices remains unaltered.

This illustration might be modified in various ways without affecting the nature of the conclusion. Suppose, for instance, that the entrepreneurs offer the whole of their goods to the capitalists, including the one per cent which represents their surplus profit This need not necessarily bring about any fall in prices It is true that the capitalists must apply to the banks for the *excess* of the necessary means of payment over their own capital But the entrepreneurs now realise their surplus profit in the form of money (bank drafts) While they pay in an amount $K\left(1 + \dfrac{i+1}{100}\right)$, they owe only $K\left(1 + \dfrac{i}{100}\right)$, and they are thus able at the beginning of the next year to raise their demand for goods by $\dfrac{K}{100}$ It follows that if wages and rents remain unaltered, supply and demand continue to be equated at the existing level of prices This will still be the case if it is supposed that the entrepreneurs are themselves dealers, or if we allot the function of dealing to yet another group, different both from the entrepreneurs and from the capitalists.

Even if it were desired to associate the increase in the quantity of goods with a tendency for a fall in prices, the fall that could on such grounds be expected would be a very small one More important, it would, so far as I can see, occur only *once and for all*, and it would thus be put completely in the shade by the *cumulative* effect on prices that is to be ascribed to a difference between the two rates of interest.

If entrepreneurs continue, year after year perhaps, to realise some surplus profit of this kind, the result can only be to set up a tendency for an expansion of their activities I emphasise once again that so far it is purely a question of a *tendency*. An *actual* expansion of production is quite impossible, for it would necessitate an increase in the supply of real factors of production, labour and land, or an expansion in the amount of fixed and liquid real capital, so that the available original factors of production could be employed in a longer, and therefore more productive, process. Such changes require time to be effected, and we need not consider them at this point. We suppose that everything remains as before, or that at the most, as a result for instance of longer working hours, there is a certain non-cumulative increase in production, of which the influence on prices is not *progressive* and will therefore be neglected.

It is impossible to endorse the widespread view that under suitable conditions a country's output can be expanded almost indefinitely, by "arousing the spirit of enterprise" and the like This fallacious view is derived by concentrating attention on one single branch of production, provided perhaps with an excess of fixed capital (buildings, machines, etc ). In such a single branch of production it would be possible to increase output immediately, but only at *the expense of the other branches of production* from which labour and liquid capital have to be drawn The impossibility under normal conditions of a *general* expansion of production is, I think, demonstrated by the figures of unemployment at different periods, recently collected in various countries The average number of unoccupied workers is relatively small, about 1 per cent A *general* expansion of production would thus be possible only as a result of longer hours—which are neither desirable nor feasible over any length of time—or as a result of further technical progress

Different in nature is the benefit conferred by a fall in the rate of interest on those enterprises which employ "more capital", *i.e.* in which the period of investment is longer than elsewhere An expansion takes place in their activities, but on the other hand those enterprises which employ less capital are forced to *contract* as a consequence of the resulting rise in wages, in prices of raw materials, etc.

The *tendency* towards an expansion of output is, nevertheless, in operation, and brings about an increase in the demand for labour and other factors of production—and under actual conditions also for raw materials, semi-manufactured goods, and the like. Money wages and money rents are forced up, and although there is no general expansion in production, entrepreneurs are obliged to borrow more capital from the banks for the production of the current year It is impossible to tell directly how much wages will go up, and therefore by how much industrial capital has to be increased But on our assumption it is possible to fix a limit If entrepreneurs are not reckoning for the moment on any rise in future prices, the upper limit to the possible rise in wages is the fall in the rate of interest For the sake of simplicity, it will be supposed thät this upper limit is immediately attained and that the capital demanded from the banks is now $1.01K$.

This increase in the demand for loans can be met by the banks just as easily as the former, or any other, demand. It does not necessitate any rise in the rate of interest, and we shall suppose that this is maintained at $i$ per cent It might, nevertheless, be thought that the rise in wages must deprive the entrepreneurs of the whole of the surplus profit for which they are hoping in respect to the current year. But what actually happens? If the workers and landlords raise their demands for goods for the consumption of the current year to the extent that money wages and money rents have gone up, this increased demand is met by the same amount of commodity capital as before It necessarily results in a *rise in all prices*—a rise which it is simplest to regard as *proportional* to the increase in demand. It follows that the amount paid for the whole of the commodity capital, of which the value was previously $K$, is now $1.01K$. The dealers receive this increased sum in the form of money (bank drafts), but they have to bear in mind that, owing to the rise in prices, this sum represents only the same amount of real capital as before. Let us therefore suppose that they hand over to the banks this money capital, $1 \cdot 01K$. If they do not do so, but in their turn increase their own consumption of commodities, so that their demand more than corresponds to the interest that they are earning, then prices will clearly go up even more, and the workers and landlords, in spite of their increased money incomes, will obtain *less* than the normal amount of consumption goods. This must be the case, because the quantity of real capital will actually decline as a consequence of the increased consumption of the capitalists We neglect such a possibility; we assume that during the process under consideration the quantity of real capital remains constant (either absolutely or relatively to the population).

The position at the beginning of the economic year, after the exchange of goods has taken place, is as follows The banks have obtained claims on the entrepreneurs, falling due at the end of the year, which, inclusive of interest, amount to $1 \cdot 01K\left(1 + \dfrac{i}{100}\right)$, i e approximately $K\left(1 + \dfrac{i+1}{100}\right)$, and they owe to the capitalists the same amount of money, falling due at the end of the year Wages and rents have gone up on the average by 1 per cent , but the same is true of commodity prices, so that real wages and real rents are on the average at the same level as before This does not, of course, mean that a particular group of workers or landlords may not be obtaining rather more than before, and thus attain an actual rise in their real wages and rents at the expense of the real incomes of some other group.

The further developments are a consequence of that law of continuity and inertia to which several references have already been made. According to this law, prices that are once attained persist indefinitely unless some independent cause brings about a fall or a further rise. This persistence is intensified *in practice* by the fact that business is fairly stable and does not proceed in the discontinuous jumps

L

that we are here assuming  This is the reason, unless I am
very much mistaken, why price movements take place
*very much more rapidly* than we have been assuming. For
once a higher level of prices has been established, it may,
after only a few months, weeks, or even days, become the
basis for new contracts, wage agreements, and rent agreements. At the same time there comes into operation that *immediate* rise, to which we referred above, in the demand for,
and the prices of, the raw materials and services employed
in *long-term* enterprises, to the extent that these move in
sympathy with the easing (absolute or relative) in the
terms of credit  It is impossible to make even an approximate estimate of the *extent* of the change in prices which
will be brought about by a given (relative) change in the
terms of credit over a certain period, say a year; but we
need not say more than that in all probability it is sufficiently *great* to provide a perfectly natural explanation of
all such variations in prices as occur in actual practice.
And now it would be as well to return to our hypothetical
conditions

The total amount of consumption goods produced in
the course of the year is no more than it was at the end
of the previous year  Their value was then $K\left(1 + \dfrac{i+1}{100}\right)$,
and since prices have gone up by 1 per cent., it is now
$1\ 01K\left(1 + \dfrac{i+1}{100}\right)$ or approximately $K\left(1 + \dfrac{i+2}{100}\right)$. It follows
that if the entrepreneurs exchange among themselves 1
per cent  of the total amount of goods, just as they did
in the previous year, they can sell the remainder to the
capitalists for a sum of $K\left(1 + \dfrac{i+1}{100}\right)$, and they are then able
to repay their bank loans. Since the capitalists have taken
precisely this sum out of the banks, all the banking accounts once again show zero balances at the end of the
year. It can easily be seen that the entrepreneurs have
earned as a surplus profit over and above their "wage" an
amount equal to 1 per cent. of the capital—precisely that

amount per cent by which the natural rate exceeded the contractual rate.

Let us now suppose that at the beginning of the third year the banks raise their lending rate to the natural rate, $i + 1$. The upward movement of prices now of course ceases, but prices do *not* return to their original level It is true that the entrepreneurs are now deprived of the opportunity of earning surplus profits, and they are under no further inducement to expand their activities or to increase their demand for labour. Equally, they are under no inducement to diminish their demand for labour The workers and landlords will naturally try to maintain wages and rents at the new levels, and these wages can be paid by the entrepreneurs at the new level of prices without incurring "losses", i e without suffering a diminution of their own "wages". It follows that everything is in equilibrium, at a higher level of money prices, wages, and rents [1]

If, on the other hand, the banks maintain the old rate of interest, the whole process described above will be once again repeated Wages and prices rise by another, say, 1 per cent , and when at the end of the year the entrepreneurs have disposed of their stocks at this new level of prices, they once again, in spite of the rise in wages, obtain a surplus profit equal to 1 per cent of the capital

The borrowed capital of the entrepreneurs and the deposits in the banks now both amount to $1 \cdot 02K$, and on both the rate of interest $i$ is paid. But since prices have now gone up by 2 per cent., the annual output is worth $1 \cdot 02K\left(1 + \dfrac{i+1}{100}\right)$, while the entrepreneurs have to pay back only $1 \cdot 02K\left(1 + \dfrac{i}{100}\right)$ There is no need to set out the further stages in this process.

---

[1] The entrepreneurs now borrow $1 \cdot 01K$ of capital from the banks at a rate of interest of $i + 1$ per cent They do this without incurring any loss, inasmuch as their annual output is, at the new level of prices, worth $1 \cdot 01K\left(1 + \dfrac{i+1}{100}\right).$

It is possible in this way to picture a steady, and more or less uniform, rise in all wages, rents, and prices (as expressed in money). But once the entrepreneurs begin to rely upon this process continuing—as soon, that is to say, as they start reckoning on a future rise in prices—the actual rise will become more and more rapid.[1] In the extreme case in which the expected rise in prices is each time *fully* discounted, the annual rise in prices will be indefinitely great.

We have already pointed out that our picture does not correspond to reality It has to be remembered that actual processes of exchange and payment do not take place at these annual intervals but follow on one another in rapid succession, so that one transaction is constantly "infecting" another, to use Marx's phrase. Furthermore, one particular lot of goods is in the normal run of business speculatively bought and sold many times over if the prospect of profits provides a sufficient inducement There is thus no doubt that tremendous fluctuations in prices may be brought about by some cause which is quite trivial in itself although it has real and lasting effects.

We have been assuming that the capitalists deposit an ever-increasing nominal amount of money with the banks, and receive the normal rate of interest. It follows that their demand in terms of money for consumption goods expands *pari passu* with that of the workers and landlords. This is equally true of the entrepreneurs, whose "wages" are, of course, calculated on the basis of the current level of commodity prices The distribution of the product of industry is thus the same as before, except for the surplus profit which accrues to the entrepreneurs at the cost of the capitalists.

It must be conceded that in practice these results require some modification. Thus it is certain that some of the capitalists will prefer to become entrepreneurs themselves, in order to share in the higher entrepreneur profits To the extent that

---

[1] *Cf.* p. 96, above.

this happens, there is a necessary contraction in the amount of business carried on by means of borrowed money. Incidentally, this must exert a certain retarding influence on the further movement of prices. The position of workers and landlords, on the other hand, may be worse than we have supposed. The enterprises which *par excellence* are in a position to draw labour and land to themselves as a result of an actual or virtual easing in the terms of credit are those for which the period of investment of capital is relatively long; for it is here that a rise in wages and rents, with a constant price of the final product, has relatively little significance [1] Production will consequently tend to be diverted in such a way as to increase the average length of the period of investment of capital, and liquid capital will tend to be converted into fixed capital The result must be a diminution in the amount of real capital that is annually available, and a fall in real wages and rents. As for the classes who receive fixed money incomes, it is obvious that they must suffer when prices rise [2]

• Little need now be said about the opposite movement of prices which must be set in operation when the lending rate of interest remains permanently *above* the natural rate Not only will the entrepreneurs now fail to obtain any surplus profit, but they will suffer losses, which they will cover in the first place out of their wages or out of the income derived from their own fortunes To prevent this, they will *desire* to confine their activities to the more profitable channels, and there will be a corresponding contraction in their demand for labour and land. But workers and landlords will respond by scaling down their claims for wages and rents, and on the whole activity will be maintained at its former level (It is not, however, to be denied that there may be a more or less permanent, though not progressive, loss of employment by some of the workers —the industrial reserve )

These diminished wages and rents have to be set against an unaltered amount of consumption goods (real capital) The result is a corresponding fall in the prices of commodities, and entrepreneurs are unable to avoid a loss,

---

[1] *Cf.* p. 133 above.　　　　[2] *Cf.* p. 1, above.

which is expressed by the difference between the two rates
of interest, or at any rate by a part of that difference (if it
is possible for the entrepreneurs to transfer the remainder
on to the shoulders of workers and landlords).[1] There
ensues a further fall in money wages, etc , which results
in its turn in a fresh fall in prices. And so the movement
continues. Prices will cease to fall only when either the
natural rate once again rises or the banks decide to lower
their rates of interest.

It remains only to mention that though the facts are
essentially in complete agreement with theory, they often
present a somewhat different *appearance*. The reason is
that a movement of prices, which is here being treated as
an isolated phenomenon, is in practice *superimposed* on
some other and independent movement of wages, etc.,
dissimilar and possibly opposite in nature. Suppose, for
example, that the rise in the natural rate of interest is
caused by a diminution (absolute or relative) in the amount
of real capital (as at a time of war or of a rapidly expanding
population). Then real wages must fall If the money rate
rises with the natural rate, money wages and real wages
fall together, but if the money rate remains unaltered, or
actually falls (as can easily happen, for instance, through
the issue of paper money by a belligerent power), money
wages may remain unaltered or rise but money prices
will then rise more than money wages Incidentally, this
possibility may perhaps constitute the origin of the widespread view that wages rise more slowly than prices.

If, on the other hand, the natural rate falls as a result of
the accumulation of real capital (which at the same time
involves a rise in real wages), while the money rate is
maintained at its previous level, it is easily possible for the
downward movement of prices to leave money wages, etc.,
apparently unaffected. This is precisely the phenomenon

[1] Thus whether the movement is one of contraction or of expansion,
workers and landlords may suffer This is not really remarkable, for the
fact that any violent change is bound up with what Laplace calls a
certain "loss of *vis viva*" applies equally to economics

which characterises the movements of prices of recent decades. It may, therefore, be legitimate to examine the matter more closely.

We are to suppose that capital is continually accumulating, and that, though possibly with some delay, the efficiency of production is always increasing (that is essential—for otherwise the natural rate would soon sink to zero). The downward movement of prices then proceeds somewhat as follows. The money rate of interest remaining unaltered, entrepreneurs continue at first to borrow from the banks the usual quantity of money, which they employ for the payment of wages and rents at the full rates But against this "money capital" now has to be set, not a constant, but a somewhat *increased* amount of real capital. For the capitalists do not themselves consume the whole of the product that was due to them in respect to interest at the end of the previous year, part of it they save It follows that their demand for commodities is diminished a little, let us say by 1 per cent. of the capital. Prices must therefore fall, and wages and rents, which remain unaltered in terms of money, really go up somewhat. Now it is always simplest to assume that a price level which is once attained will persist until there arises some adequate reason for an alteration Thus prices may remain at the lower level at the end of the year, and the entrepreneurs, who were previously making neither profit nor loss, must now suffer a loss, which will amount to 1 per cent. of the capital.

The result, other things being equal, would be a diminution in the demand for labour, etc , and a fall in (money) wages and rents. But, as a result of industrial progress, average productivity will have increased, and the output of the current year might be expected to increase by 1 per cent.[1] It would thus appear as though entrepreneurs could carry on in the usual way and pay the usual wages

[1] If production had increased already in the first year, there would be no divergence whatever between the two rates of interest. Prices would continue at their previous level, and everything else—wages, capital, and interest—would merely have risen uniformly.

and rents; for the expected increase in output compensates for the fall in prices that has already occurred.

At the same time, however, the amount of real capital must be supposed to have increased yet further as a result of new saving  (It is to be noted that it has already increased by the one per cent  which the entrepreneurs had to reckon as a loss and which they will now make good by diminishing their consumption in the current year, without the intervention of the capitalists, it would thus be maintained at the same amount as at the beginning of the previous year.) A further fall in prices is the inevitable consequence  Real wages and rents rise still further, while remaining unaltered in terms of money, and in spite of the increase in productivity, the entrepreneurs are again unable to avoid a loss

The process might continue in this way, the fall in prices becoming ever greater while money wages and rents remain unaltered  The total quantity of money lent by the banks and the total quantity of their deposits would remain constant[1] while the amount of real capital and annual output continually increases. It might thus appear as though the downward movement of prices took its origin "on the side of goods", to use the usual manner of speaking, rather than "on the side of money". The immediate cause, however, of the fall in prices is in this case just the same as in the case where the quantity of capital and of output *remain unaltered·* the immediate cause is the excess of the money rate of interest over the natural rate of interest  If *no* such divergence had existed—if, for example, at the very beginning of the period under consideration, the banks had lowered their lending (and deposit) rate of interest so as to bring it into line with the natural rate (lowered by the increase in the amount of real capital)—the quantity of "money" would have kept step with the quantity of goods, and there would have been no fall whatever in prices  This can easily be shown as follows·

---

[1] But the capitalists enjoy the fruit of their savings, for the constant amount of money capital is ever growing in value

Let us assume that the banks had already lowered their rate of interest to $i - 1$ per cent. at the beginning of the first economic year To the entrepreneurs is again offered a surplus profit of one per cent of their capital—at any rate, so it appears to them, and that is all that matters The entrepreneurs' demand for factors of production is therefore increased, and there is a rise of, say, one per cent.[1] on the average in all wages and rents. The process has already been discussed,[2] but in the case that was described above, the surplus profit was retained by the entrepreneurs because the rise in wages brought about an immediate rise in prices This will not happen in the present case, for we are assuming that the amount of real capital has simultaneously increased by some one per cent. as a result of the savings of the capitalists It follows that prices remain unaltered The entrepreneurs have to pay out one per cent. more in wages and rents, so that it is clear that at the end of the year there is no surplus profit available for them. They have borrowed "money capital" amounting to $1 \cdot 01K$, and, including interest at the rate of $i - 1$ per cent., at the end of the year they owe $1 \, 01K\left(1 + \dfrac{i-1}{100}\right)$, or approximately $K\left(1 + \dfrac{i}{100}\right)$ The year's output is as yet unaltered, and at the current level of prices amounts in value to $K\left(1 + \dfrac{i}{100}\right)$ The entrepreneurs thus make neither a profit nor a loss, just as under normal conditions.

If everything else remained the same, they would be able (as a result of the maintenance of easier credit conditions) to continue to pay the higher level of wages and rents; but they would now be under no incentive to raise their demand for labour, etc. Now, however, there are introduced those improvements in technique which, without any increase in costs, would lead to an increase in out-

---

[1] In fact the rise would be somewhat smaller, but that is of no consequence.

[2] P 144 ff , above

put. The hope of surplus profits is once again aroused, the demand for factors of production is once again stimulated, but the result is the same as before—the level of wages and rents (of real wages as well as of money wages) is raised. Entrepreneurs are once again disappointed in their expectations, for the rise in prices which would have secured them surplus profits again fails to take place— because of the simultaneous increase in the amount of real capital.

At the beginning of the previous year, the real capital amounted in value to $1.01K$, and an equal sum was deposited by the capitalists in the banks. At the end of the year, the capitalists are thus credited with $1.01K\left(1 + \frac{i-1}{100}\right)$, and with this they purchase the goods produced during the year. But their share in respect to interest now amounts only to $\frac{(i-1)K}{100}$, and but for the new savings, the amount of capital would remain the same as it was at the beginning of the year, viz. $1.01K$ We are, however, assuming that there are new savings amounting to $0.01K$, or in other words, that the capitalists devote only $\frac{(i-2)K}{100}$ to the consumption of the following year. It follows that the amount of real capital at the beginning of this year amounts to $1.02K$

Whether the capitalists, whose incomes have diminished as a result of the fall in the deposit rate of interest, will be able or willing to save the same amount as before is a separate question which need not concern us here.

---

Many of the above statements must, in their relation to the traditional treatment, appear almost paradoxical. It would appear, for instance, that the distribution of the product of industry between capitalists and entrepreneurs depends on nothing more than their subjective dispositions or caprices. It has, however, to be remembered that we are here dealing with moods and influences which, arising out of a single motive, are common to all individuals and call for uniform treatment. The effect is, therefore, the same as though there were *conscious* co-operation for a common end. At the same time, it is scarcely open to doubt that by means of economic

co-operation the capitalists and entrepreneurs, who control
the subsistence-fund of society, could diminish the share of
labour and other factors of production to an almost unlimited
extent, and bring about a corresponding increase in their own
share in the product. On the other hand, the individual capitalist or entrepreneur is in this respect practically powerless. He
has to follow the stream—and while it is true that he himself
forms a part of this stream, its force is irresistible

It might further be asked whether we are right in suggesting
that it lies in the power of the credit institutions, acting in co-
operation only with the entrepreneurs, to determine the direction of production and consequently the period of investment
of capital, without paying any heed to the actual capitalists, the owners of goods  Here too there can be no doubt that
this really is the case (though in practice this power cannot be
so absolute as we are supposing)  We have been assuming
throughout that the period of investment of (liquid) capital is
*one year*  Suppose now that the banks lend a portion of the
"money" at their disposal (*i e* of the credit that is extended)
for *two* years, while the whole of their deposits remain fixed
for only one year  Will not this lead to the insolvency of the
banks, or at least to great commercial difficulties? Nothing of
the sort  The actual consequence will merely be that at the
end of the first year a somewhat smaller amount of consumption goods will be completed, for those entrepreneurs who
borrowed money for a term of *two* years have probably devoted it (and the productive services which they have purchased with it) to a process of production that lasts two years
and is consequently not yet complete  When the capitalist
dealers come to purchase the available quantity of finished
products at the normal prices (as is likely to be the case), they
do not require to use the whole of their capital and leave a
portion of it deposited at the banks (corresponding to those
bank loans which are not yet due). If, however, the capitalist
dealers do devote the whole of their capital to the purchase
of goods, this can only lead to a rise in prices, and the excess
now accrues to the producers of the available consumption
goods, and can be employed as capital by them. No matter
what view is taken of the matter, it will be found that the money
immediately flows back to the banks, or that the sum withdrawn by means of cheques returns in the form of deposits.
The *real saving* which is necessary for the period of investment
to be increased is in fact *enforced*—at exactly the right moment
—on consumers as a whole, for a smaller quantity than usual

of consumption goods is available for the consumption of the second year  At the end of the year (the beginning of the next year), when the two years' period of production comes to an end and the available quantity of consumption goods has increased correspondingly, the consumers will receive some reward for their abstinence

These considerations are of extreme importance in relation to actual economic events, but they are usually overlooked in the customary treatment of the theory of money, being regarded as relevant only to a natural economy.

# CHAPTER 10

## INTERNATIONAL PRICE RELATIONSHIPS

IN order to subject our theory to the test of experience, it would be necessary to observe the simultaneous movements of rates of interest and prices in some *closed* economic system. But the only closed system to-day is the world as a whole, and for the world as a whole we have no reliable figures of commodity prices The statistics that are so far available refer purely to single countries, or rather to single markets. We have then to ask whether such data are of any use whatever for our purpose We have to ask, in other words, whether and how far a movement of prices in one country is an indication of a similar movement in other countries, and whether and how far the fluctuations of prices at the ports are related to the prices that rule in the interior.

It has long been recognised that the general level of prices in a single country cannot be altogether independent of the prices that rule in the countries with which it trades The manner in which equilibrium between the various price levels is restored after it has been upset by some disturbance is explained by the familiar classical theory. If domestic prices rise, other things remaining equal, the import of foreign goods is encouraged, and the export of domestic goods is made more difficult. There consequently results a balance of payments in favour of foreign countries, and this has to be met in money Money flows abroad and causes some rise in foreign prices, while at home the relative scarcity of precious metals brings prices down to their former level.

Fundamentally, this explanation must be correct. It is, however, clear that international equilibrium of prices is usually restored far more rapidly and far more directly.

157

The increase in the supply of foreign goods and the diminution in the demand for exports must themselves exert, directly and indirectly, a pressure on domestic prices which is quite independent of any simultaneous movement of precious metals—and will be felt equally where the one country employs gold and the other silver as the standard of value, or where one or both of them have a paper standard In these latter cases, however, there can be no question of a complete and definitive mutual regulation of prices. It is true that as a result of the unhindered rise in the rate of exchange (of the country in which there has been a relative rise in prices), the excess of imports will sooner or later disappear, and equilibrium will be restored. At the same time, the movement in the rate of exchange merely acknowledges the deviation between the two price levels, and supplies a measure of the alteration in the value in exchange of the one standard in terms of the other (for instance, gold in terms of silver), and this alteration must be regarded essentially as a *consequence* and not as a *cause* of the movement in relative prices,[1] though this does not mean that the relationship between the two price levels, and so indirectly the relative values of the two precious metals, cannot be influenced by a change in the conditions of production of these precious metals.

Even if two countries employ the same metal as a standard of value, the general level of prices need by no means be the same. Considerable, and fairly permanent, deviations have to be reckoned with Such deviations were more marked in former times—for example, in the first third of the nineteenth century, as Nassau Senior demonstrated by his well-known and thorough comparison of the costs of living of a worker in America, England, and India [2] The explanation given by Senior himself depends on the varying distances of these countries from the sources

[1] *Cf* Professor Marshall's Evidence before the Gold and Silver Commission, and especially his Memorandum (*Appendix to Final Report*, p 47) [*Official Papers*, p 170 ff ]
[2] *Three Lectures on the Cost of obtaining Money*, p. 1.

of the precious metal, and above all on the greater *efficiency of labour* in the more civilised countries This explanation cannot be regarded as correct The latter factor, as Mill points out,[1] accounts for differences in real wages (which, as a matter of fact, were at that time abnormally low in England) but not differences in prices. If prices moved with money wages, real wages would be no higher in civilised countries than in uncivilised countries· what then would be the advantage to the worker of his greater efficiency?

Mill himself suggests as the most important cause of the differences in prices—the magnitude of which he considers in any case to be exaggerated[2]—the higher cost of transport of goods imported into England as compared with exported goods But in any case, according to Mill, prices will tend to stand highest "in the countries for whose exports there is the greatest foreign demand, and which have themselves the least demand for foreign commodities".

This view may be correct when it is a question purely of the *direction* of the deviation of prices and not of its *magnitude* For no matter how eagerly the products of one country may be demanded by another country—the two countries may be separated by a political frontier or they may consist of two neighbouring ports—*no* appreciable difference of prices can persist when there is a free interchange of goods In finding an answer to the above question, it is important to differentiate between these two factors (the direction of the deviation on the one hand and its magnitude on the other), for they take their origin in different, though partly interconnected, causes.

Let us suppose that there are two countries, A and B, which are absolutely identical so far as the conditions of production are concerned, or, what comes to the same thing, that in every branch of production A possesses a

---

[1] *Principles*, book iii , chap. xix , § 2

[2] In Mill's time (about the middle of the nineteenth century), English prices had, in the course of the previous twenty years, sunk considerably—probably more than in most other countries

*uniform* advantage over B  Then, in accordance with Ricardo's well-known law, no trade whatever can take place between these two countries, neither directly nor indirectly  If they are isolated from the rest of the world, the level of prices in *either of them* may exceed the level of prices in the other up to the point where the difference in prices amounts to the lowest possible cost of transport (including tariffs) of any one commodity. The costs of transport (and tariffs) constitute a double-sided threshold up to which (but no higher) the difference in prices can rise on either side

But now let it be supposed that the conditions of production are the same except that in country A a certain commodity can be produced which it is impossible to produce in country B, or which can only be produced in country B at great cost  This commodity will, of course, be partly exported to B  If the price level in B were the same as in A, there would be no commodity which it would be profitable to export to A, and the imports into B would at first have to be paid for by means of *money* (precious metal). The result would be that the general level of prices would rise in A and fall in B until eventually it became profitable to export some commodity from B to A. When this point is reached, the general level of prices in A *permanently* exceeds that in B to the whole extent of the particular transport costs that are involved—except for that commodity in the production of which A has *special* advantages· this commodity is, of course, dearer in B than in A, but it is likely to play an insignificant part in the determination of the general level of prices.

We can now see what it is that determines the *direction* of the deviation of general price levels  It does not depend on the fact that one country is superior to other countries in *all* branches of production, but rather on the fact that its superiority is confined to a *small number* of branches of production, while the other countries either possess no advantages whatever or possess advantages only in respect of commodities of which the value is small compared with the necessary costs of transport On the other hand, the *magnitude* of the deviation is determined by the general level of costs of transport It therefore depends in particular on the distance between the two countries, on the height of the tariff walls, etc.

It can easily happen that the general level of prices is higher in a country which imports the standard of value, for instance gold, than in a country where it is produced; provided that gold does not constitute the sole or the main export of the latter country.

It can already be seen that the relative price levels of different countries cannot be related to their relative distances from the sources of the precious metal This would only be the case if the conditions of production in all the countries were identical (or uniformly different), so that they all had to compete for the precious metal by means of the same products

It is, however, broadly true that if two countries exhibit no particular distinguishing features and if their distances from the sources of the precious metal are fairly equal, then prices in these two countries will be at the same general level· they have to deliver up the same amount of goods in order to obtain a given quantity of gold

On this point W Lexis is responsible for a curious confusion [1] He tries to deprive Ricardo's law of "comparative costs" of practical significance by maintaining that if a country is superior to another country in all branches of production, the *immediate* effect of removing tariff barriers would be devastating competition in the production of every kind of commodity The reason why Lexis arrives at this conclusion is that he assumes that so long as the original tariffs are maintained "the general level of money prices would very probably be about the same" in both countries, and *consequently* also "the money price of the unit of labour" But this would be an impossible situation. If the general (average) level of prices is the same in the two countries, the price of the unit of labour *must* (other things being equal) be correspondingly *higher* in the better situated country than in the less productive country. If Lexis means that the one country is inferior to the other only in his two branches of production (cloth and iron), then it has

[1] *Schönberg's Handbuch*, 3rd ed , vol. ii., art xxiv (Handel), § 65, p 903

M

to be realised that, according to Ricardo's theory, *both* these types of production would be completely abandoned after the introduction of Free Trade. On this count Lexis' proof falls completely to the ground.

It can easily be seen that international or inter-local debt payments operate in the same way. Here doubtless is to be found the simplest explanation of the fact that prices and the cost of living are usually much lower in the more remote parts of the country than in the big towns and their environments. (This deviation was formerly even more significant than it is to-day.) The open country is always having to render payments to the towns for rents, legacies, taxes, etc. It follows that even if there were no *exchange* of commodities between the towns and the country, there would have to be a flow of goods from the country to the towns, and the level of prices in the country is depressed below the level in the towns by an amount equivalent to the costs of transport. Specifically urban products, which are of course somewhat cheaper in the towns than in the country, are not of great significance.

It is now clear—and it has frequently been pointed out —that the continual improvement in transport that has taken place throughout the greater part of the nineteenth century, and the disappearance of many tariff barriers, must have brought about a gradual *equalisation* of price levels in different countries and districts This effect would have been more widespread and more deep-seated but for the revival of protectionist ideas at the present time.

This has to be borne in mind if correct conclusions are to be drawn from the price movements indicated by index numbers.[1] These are almost exclusively concerned with wholesale prices in certain ports such as Hamburg and London. It is probable, and indeed certain, that at times when these index numbers are falling, the fall is partly due to this process of equalisation between prices in the

---

[1] But the influence of tariffs can only be an *indirect* one, for foreign goods are, of course, valued in "bond" and their prices are reckoned duty-free.

interior and prices at the port; and it follows that the average level of European prices must have fallen much more slowly. On the other hand, in the fifties and sixties, when index numbers were on the whole rising, the rise in the interior, and therefore also the average rise, was probably more rapid. No material is available for a more precise investigation of this question

In the next chapter we shall pay particular attention to prices in England. There are here two points that have to be specially borne in mind, in respect of the first half of the nineteenth century there are the changes in the conditions of transport during and after the war, and in respect of more recent times there is the great alteration in the constitution of England's exports. At one time England's exports consisted almost entirely of highly compact textiles and other manufactures, but ever since the removal of the export tax on coal at the beginning of the forties, England has been exporting an enormous quantity of precisely that commodity of which the weight and volume are greatest in relation to its value England's imports, on the other hand, now involve relatively low freights—in some cases the cost of transport is purely nominal—whereas formerly the situation was probably the opposite There can be no other country which has experienced anything like the continuous and vigorous fall of prices that has taken place in England, except for the period 1850–1873.

It remains true that if a country is in trading relations with the rest of the world, the movements of its price level must theoretically accord with the laws that have been developed above. The increase in imports, which is the concomitant of a rise in domestic prices and prevents any further rise, can be regarded as an increase in the country's liquid capital. The result is a fall in the natural rate of interest, which, other things remaining equal, prevents any further rise or causes an actual fall in the domestic price level. This explanation was suggested above[1] and could be

[1] P. 112 ff.

illustrated in terms of the example employed towards the end of the last chapter.

Thus the main principle always remains the same, but it has to be admitted that its verification becomes considerably more difficult as soon as the relatively simple conditions of an isolated community are complicated by the intricate relationships involved in international trade. The difficulties are accentuated further when it is necessary to discuss the movements of prices in individual towns.

It is just on account of these very difficulties that it has seemed to me necessary to present a detailed statement of the *essentials* of our theory, and to try to make it convincing I will now attempt to test the theory somewhat more closely by the facts of reality.

# CHAPTER 11

ATTEMPTS have often been made to demonstrate a parallelism between changes in prices and changes in the rate of interest. It has already been mentioned that these attempts have never yet been successful Some of them have been directed to ascribing both changes to a common cause It has, for instance, been suggested that a "surplus of gold" leads both to a rise in prices and to a more or less permanent fall in the rate of interest ("cheap money", in *both* senses of the term), and, on the other hand, that a scarcity of gold results in falling prices and a high discount rate Others have regarded a low rate of interest as a stimulus to production and speculation, and have in this way tried to ascribe rising prices to a low rate of interest. But the facts have never conformed to the theories. It has always been observed that, broadly speaking, a low discount rate accompanies *low* and not high prices, while an abnormally high discount rate is scarcely ever found to prevail except when commodity prices are *high*. R. Giffen [1] has recently tried to rescue the theory by relating the rate of interest to the movement in prices of a *somewhat later period of time* The results obtained by Giffen are somewhat better, but they cannot on the whole be regarded as convincing.

It was soon noticed that it would be more satisfactory to regard the movement of prices itself as the cause and the rate of interest as the effect. This point of view has its theoretical justification, for if other things remain equal,

---

[1] *Essays in Finance, Second Series*, 1886, p. 70 *Cf* the criticism of his views by Irving •Fisher, *Appreciation and Interest*, 1896, p 57, note.

a continual, and therefore expected, rise of prices is calculated to raise the rate of interest on loans.

This, in fact, is the point of view that has recently been adopted by Irving Fisher He points out [1] that when prices are rising, entrepreneurs are in a position to pay a higher rate of interest on their loans (and that as a result of a rise in the demand for loans, they will gradually be compelled to pay a higher rate). For "business profits . . . are the difference between gross income and expense, and if both these rise, their difference will also rise" This passage is based on a misconception If this were the cause of the rise in business profits, profits could rise *only in proportion to prices*, i e. at an annual rate not exceeding *a small percentage of the net profit itself*; and entrepreneurs could not possibly be in a position to meet on the *whole of their borrowed capital* a rise in the rate of interest that corresponded to the rise in prices (On Fisher's assumption, they have really obtained no surplus profit at all, for their own costs of living have gone up in the same proportion.) The assumption which forms the logical basis for Fisher's argument is that entrepreneurs incur their "expense" (wages, rents, etc ) when things are cheap, and dispose of their product after prices have gone up. But it is then necessary to suppose that the rise in prices originates from some quite *independent* cause, which has nothing to do with the behaviour of the entrepreneurs According to my view, a rise in prices, at any rate an international rise in prices, is usually due to a rise in the entrepreneurs' demand for labour and other productive services. Such a rise in prices is thus the consequence of a previous, no matter how far from uniform, rise in money wages and rents, and it merely serves to compensate the entrepreneurs for the rise in costs of production It does not provide them with the means of paying a higher rate of interest—except in the case where the prevailing rate of interest is lower than the *natural rate*, i e. than the profit which the entrepreneurs would obtain if prices did not alter.

The actual cause, however, of the change in prices remains in obscurity, and contradictions arise as soon as an attempt is made to elucidate it. It is impossible to conceive that a change in prices has no connection whatever with the situation in the money market (such a view,

---

[1] *Appreciation and Interest*, p. 75

as we have several times had to point out, has no basis
either in fact or in logic). But the explanation suggested
by the Quantity Theory—that rising prices are due to an
excess of money, falling prices to a scarcity—does not accord
with actually observed movements of the rate of interest.
If it were correct, we should expect that at a time of rising
prices there would be a temporary reduction in the rate of
interest, at a time of falling prices a temporary increase; and
that when prices had become accommodated to the change
in the stocks of precious metal, the rate of interest would
once again return to its normal position. Observation
teaches us, however, that when prices are rising there is a
continual *rise* in rates of interest, and that when prices are
falling there is a continual *fall* in rates of interest

All these difficulties and complications at once disappear
when it is changes, brought about by independent factors,
in the *natural rate of interest on capital* that are regarded as
the essential cause of such movements. These changes can
be regarded as the cause, not only of the movement of prices,
but indirectly of the analogous but somewhat later alteration in the money rate of interest  Abundance or scarcity of
money, and in particular the quantity of cash held by the
banks, is now imbued with a merely secondary importance. Such factors are to be regarded as consequences of
changes in the demand for instruments of exchange brought
about by changes in the level of prices. It still remains true,
however, that they *may* take their origin in independent
causes (the production of precious metals, issue of paper
money, development of the credit system, etc.), and that
they then have an independent significance in regard to
movements of prices, in so far as they accelerate or retard
the movement of the money rate of interest to the new
position of the natural rate (they may even cause the
money rate to move in the opposite direction to the
natural rate).

No matter how plausible all this may appear, it is only the
facts themselves that can provide final confirmation. Now,
how is such confirmation possible if one of the significant

factors is practically an unknown? No statistics of the natural rate of interest are available. A precise investigation would necessitate an *ad hoc* enquiry, and for the past this is as good as impossible While the *general trend* of the natural rate over decades can be observed in the movement of the money rate itself, of the banks' discount rates and the so-called open-market rate, and of the prices of debentures and Government securities, this can be done only by assuming that on the average the two rates of interest are *equal* to one another. What we are looking for is the extent of the *divergence* between them, and for this there are practically no data available.

It might be possible to obtain some information from the accounts of individual enterprises and from the annual reports and dividends of companies. But it has to be remembered that the thing that is commonly regarded as interest does not correspond to the use to which we are applying the term, for it usually covers not only interest on *liquid* capital, but consists far more largely of rents of every kind rents of land, monopoly rents, the return on buildings and durable machinery These rents are not affected by movements in the rate of interest in the narrow sense of the word, or if they are affected it is only very slowly as a result of the competition from additional capital goods of the same type. An excess of liquid real capital will have a tendency, as was shown above, to raise not only real wages, but also the real rewards of all factors of production It raises *for a time* the rents obtained by fixed capital, and it *permanently* raises the rent of land, while the actual rate of interest will fall by a corresponding amount
In recent times agricultural rents have remained unaltered, or have actually fallen This is sometimes regarded as a consequence of the general tendency of rents on capital to fall. This explanation is fallacious. The phenomenon is in fact peculiar to western Europe, and can be explained as the result of increased agricultural competition from countries overseas and from Russia.

To deal with each of these difficulties individually would at present be impossible. We shall now try, nevertheless, to give in the light of our theory a short review of the history of prices of the nineteenth century, and particularly of its second half, so far as material is available.

In his article on "The Variation of Prices and the Value of the Currency since 1782",[1] Stanley Jevons worked out index numbers, based on Tooke's tables,[2] for forty groups of commodities. These index numbers are calculated both for various individual groups and for the aggregate of the forty groups. The results show that at the beginning of the seventeen-nineties there set in an enormous *rise* of prices, which culminated in 1809–1810, when prices had gone up since 1790 by 80 per cent. in terms of gold and by 90 per cent. in terms of the somewhat depreciated paper. There then ensued a *downward* movement of prices, beginning in 1809 in terms of gold prices, and in 1814 in terms of paper prices This downward movement persisted with few interruptions until the middle of the century, by which time prices had fallen in the ratio of 5.2, *i e* by *considerably more than half*, as compared with the gold prices of 1810. The further movements of prices will be referred to below

In order to discover the causes of these enormous variations in prices, it is essential to ascertain how far the phenomenon was matched in other countries and how far it was peculiar to England. Although no figures are available for a precise comparison, there can be no doubt that *to some extent* the position of England was peculiar Ever since the development of her manufactures, and as a consequence of this development, the general level of prices has presumably stood higher in England than in other European countries, and *a fortiori* than in India But this presumption can only refer to the *direction* of the deviation--to its algebraical sign, which was constantly positive for England The *magnitude* of the difference depends, as was explained in the last chapter, on the general level of costs of transport. For several reasons, these were artificially raised during the war Later on they were considerably diminished

---

[1] *Journal of the Royal Statistical Society*, 1865, also *Investigations in Currency and Finance,* p. 119 ff. [second edition, p 112].

[2] *History of Prices*

as a result both of the renewal of friendly relations and of the gradual development of sea and land transport. This would explain why the rise in prices before 1815 and the fall in prices after 1815 were more considerable in England than in most other countries.

But in the case both of the rise and of the fall there remains a residue, which must be ascribed to other causes. Jevons himself maintained that Tooke was too one-sided in explaining the causes of the rise in prices during the war (as being due to bad harvests, etc.), and that a principal cause was the effect on the money market of the suspension of cash payments by the Bank of England. Large issues of irredeemable paper money were made at that time also in other countries—in France, Austria, Russia, Sweden, and Denmark. But in these countries the paper money was usually issued either by the Government itself or through the banks in the form of advances to the Government. In England it was different: bank-notes were issued in excess of the sum corresponding to the Bank's capital (advanced long before to the Government) purely by way of commercial credits covered by normal banking security. At the same time, the Bank pursued a very liberal discount policy. While bank rate continued, during the whole period of restriction, to be maintained in the normal way at the legal maximum of 5 per cent., it gradually became the case that loans were granted at this rate of interest without any restriction, so long as adequate security was forthcoming (whereas formerly, when the notes were redeemable, there were frequent occasions when the willingness of the Bank to lend became drastically curtailed). That this procedure was wrong in principle is conceded even by the followers of Tooke, though they maintain[1] that an "over-issue of notes" would have been possible only if bank rate had accidentally stood lower than the rate in the open market, the "market rate"[2] I am unable to accept this

[1] Wagner, *Geld-und Kredittheorie der Peelschen Bankakte*, p 57
[2] Not to be confused with what we called above the "bond rate" (the rate of interest on long-term investment)

argument. The so-called open-market rate (which usually refers to bills and securities of the very first quality, so that in respect of liquidity they can be regarded almost like actual cash) always stands under normal conditions below bank rate, whether this is high or low. The real question is whether bank rate (and consequently rates of interest in general) stood high or low in relation to the current level of the *natural rate*. It now appears extremely probable that bank rate was low in relation to the natural rate. In no sense was the war a period of depression for English industry. Quite the reverse· as Jevons emphasises, it was just in the period from 1782 to 1815 that "the very foundations of our home industries were being energetically laid".[1]

This fact makes it all the more difficult to explain the rise in prices on the basis of Jevons' treatment, which clings closely to the Quantity Theory With our theory, on the other hand, it fits in extremely well. A rise in industrial productivity raises in the first instance the natural rate of interest, so that prices rise if the money rate is for the moment kept unaltered. It is only later, when the banks are driven by the contraction in their reserves to push up the money rate, that prices recede. This factor was completely absent during the period of restriction of payments.

There now ensued the inevitable consequence of a war— a relative depletion of liquid capital. It is thus extremely probable that the natural rate remained very high during the whole period, presumably far higher than the rate asked for by banks or bill-brokers; and prices rose in consequence The one peculiarity lies in the fact that so great a rise in prices failed to bring about a more rapid and considerable fall (to use English terminology) in the rates of exchange and an efflux of gold. The explanation must be that there was, for the reasons already given, a simultaneous rise in prices in other countries; furthermore, we have seen that a rise in the costs of transport would *in itself* be

---

[1] [*Journal of the Royal Statistical Society*, 1865, p. 303], *Investigations in Currency and Finance*, p. 132 [second edition, p. 124].

responsible, other things remaining equal, for a relative rise of the English price level.

It is my opinion that essentially the same explanation holds good for the contrary movement of prices which characterised the long period of peace after 1815. While the development of industry continued unceasingly, it gave rise at the same time to a tremendous accumulation of capital, of which the influence on England would have been still more marked had it not been for the constant lending to other countries and subsequently for the inauguration of domestic railway building. There must have been a rapid fall in the natural rate of interest The money rate followed only slowly and with hesitation. Bank rate remained at 5 per cent. until 1824, and then at 4 per cent. until 1836 (though the open-market rate was lower). According to our theory, a rapid fall in prices must have been the result. (In actual fact the collapse of prices was practically at an end by 1832 Prices then rose and fell in turn, after the crisis of 1847 there was another fall in prices, but it was of short duration )

Jevons regards the fall in prices since 1815 as "less difficult to understand"[1] than the previous rise Among other factors, he ascribes it to the fact that the "production of almost all articles has been improved, extended, and cheapened during this period". But he admits that this argument "tells two ways", for there had been no check to the development of industry during the previous period.

According to my treatment, increased productivity cannot by itself be responsible for any general fall in prices. If entrepreneurs and capitalists appropriate the increase in output for the purposes of their own *consumption*, the money demand for consumption goods expands uniformly with their supply. If, on the other hand, entrepreneurs and capitalists diminish (or fail to increase) their own consumption, in order to accumulate capital, then it is true that with money wages and rents for the moment unaltered, an increased quantity of consumption goods is offered to workers and landlords, and prices have to fall. But *ipso facto* the natural rate of interest has fallen too, and when it comes to rest below the money rate, a further

[1] *Loc. cit.*, pp. [303], 131 [123] respectively.

(progressive) fall of prices must be the usual consequence of the resulting pressure on money wages and rents.

It is a matter for wonder that so rapid a fall in English prices was not more effective in causing an influx of precious metal. The explanation may well be analogous to the one that we have suggested for the contrary phenomenon which was exhibited in the previous period. In the first place, there was a simultaneous, though less considerable, downward movement of prices in other countries, and secondly, the constant difference, positive in sign, between the English price level and that of other countries must necessarily have been diminished through improvements in transport. The cheapening of foreign produce at English ports exceeded the cheapening at foreign ports of the less bulky English produce. Finally, England's foreign loans during this period exceeded the interest due to her on her old loans, and must, therefore, have contributed to the same result, by hindering or postponing the influx of sums that would otherwise have fallen due. It follows from the above that continual willingness to lend exerts a negative influence on a country's price level, while the drawing of interest from abroad acts in a positive direction.

For the second half of the century, we have Sauerbeck's tables for England and those of Soetbeer, continued by Heinz, and later those of Conrad, for Germany (Hamburg).[1] They agree among themselves to a remarkable extent, though the downward movement of English prices in recent times is somewhat more pronounced, perhaps in accordance with the explanation that I have put forward above. The general effect is to reproduce, though on a somewhat smaller scale, the picture of England's price movements in the two earlier periods.

An upward movement of prices started in the fifties, which, interrupted by the world crisis of 1857 and then by

---

[1] A valuable compilation of these and other tables of prices, some of them previously unpublished, is to be found in the Appendix to Irving Fisher's *Appreciation and Interest*.

the crises of 1864–66, did not really culminate until 1873. Then began the gradual fall in prices, so often discussed, which has continued up to the present time, so that the general price level of to-day[1] is lower than it was in the middle of the century.

The explanation seems to me completely analogous to that of the movement of prices in the years 1790–1815 and 1815–50. Though the period 1851–73 was not, as was the Napoleonic era, a time of uninterrupted warfare, it comprised, among other wars, the Crimean War, the extremely exhausting and expensive American Civil War, and the wars between Germany and Denmark, Germany and Austria, and finally Germany and France. On the other hand, this period was distinguished, not only by a general progressive movement in industry, but in particular by the freezing of enormous quantities of liquid capital as a result of the completion of the west European railway system. For both of these reasons, the natural rate of interest is generally admitted to have stood abnormally high. While the widely oscillating money rate of interest was on the average definitely higher during this period than either in the preceding or in the succeeding period, it seems very doubtful whether it rose as much as the natural rate, partly because the large increase in the production of gold and the issue of paper money in America, in Austria, and finally in France, were working in the opposite direction It is remarkable and significant that in England, for instance, bank rate was on several occasions lower, or no higher, than the market rate, and was presumably exerting an overwhelming downward pressure on the market rate. The upward movement of prices is in no way inexplicable. On the contrary, it is to be expected that for Europe as a whole, and particularly for the more remote portions of our continent, the rise in prices was relatively even greater.

Since 1871 western Europe and the United States have enjoyed uninterrupted peace It must be admitted that in

[1] [1898 ]

Europe *intentions* have not always been so peaceful as actual *relations*—witness the frightful growth of armies and armaments. But no matter how many milliards have in this way been swallowed up, there can, of course, be no comparison in point of capital wastage with an actual war [1] Railway building, though it was continued on an enormous scale, took place mainly in countries outside Europe, or in its more remote regions. In short, there was a considerable lack of really profitable openings for the additions to liquid capital which arose out of the savings of almost all classes of the community. The increase in real capital served rather to raise real wages and the rewards of other factors of production. The natural rate of interest consequently fell everywhere, and this would, in my opinion, be even more noticeable if it were possible to distinguish the return to actual (liquid) capital from the rents of land and monopolies.

The money rate of interest also fell, but whether it fell to *a corresponding degree* must be regarded as doubtful. For effect cannot precede cause, and furthermore there were monetary influences operating in the opposite direction. The production of gold was slackening (it has caught up again only in the last few years), cash payments were resumed in several countries (France, the United States), and finally silver was extensively demonetised. But the extent of the banks' reserves, particularly in recent years, warns us against following the bimetallists in attaching undue importance to these influences It has rather to be supposed that the banks, as a result either of discretion or of routine, have often been reluctant to allow their rates of interest to accommodate themselves immediately to the situation in the market, and have preferred to allow an ever increasing amount of their cash resources to lie idle, earning no interest.[2]

The fall in prices of recent decades is thus provided with

---

[1] See for instance Giffen's well-known calculations (*Essays in Finance, First Series*, p 1 ff.) on the cost of the Franco-Prussian War The American War was even more costly

[2] *Cf* W Schailing. *Preussiche Jahrb*, 1895, conclusion

an adequate explanation, which is free of the contradictory and arbitrary elements which run through most of the explanations hitherto put forward. It has furthermore to be noticed that the extent of this movement is perhaps somewhat exaggerated by the index numbers. In the first place, the *equalisation* of prices, to which we referred above, was presumably still in operation between various countries and districts. (We have, in fact, noticed that Sauerbeck's index numbers for England, when brought to the same scale as Soetbeer's for Germany, indicate a somewhat greater fall in prices ) Secondly, and most important, the constituents of the cost of living which take the form of personal services, house rents, etc., have fallen far less in price than actual commodities In this connection it is to be observed that expenditure on travel and on urban fares, which to-day is indispensable to so many, was formerly far less important

It is, of course, to be understood that these considerations can claim to indicate only very broad agreement between our theory and the facts. A detailed demonstration would be as interesting as it would be difficult. I do not yet feel myself to be in a position to undertake it. The theory must, therefore, be regarded for the moment as a mere *hypothesis*, the complete validity of which can be established only by further resort to the facts of experience.

If it turns out eventually to be correct the practical consequences are of enormous importance. Banks and credit institutions have hitherto exerted only an *involuntary* influence on prices, and consequently it has sometimes been in a favourable direction and sometimes in an unfavourable direction. Now, however, they will be able in full consciousness to pursue their objective, to the indisputable benefit of the world economy. It lies outside the terms of reference of a purely theoretical treatment to show how this might be brought about My purpose is to lay down the theoretical principles which underlie these phenomena, and once they are correctly understood their application can be confidently left to the experience and insight of practical men. But the matter is one of great importance, and practical applications should be the goal of every theory. A few final remarks on this theme may not, therefore, be out of place.

# CHAPTER 12

## PRACTICAL PROPOSALS FOR THE STABILISATION OF THE VALUE OF MONEY

IF there is any truth whatever in the above considerations, they must enormously influence our opinion of the practical proposals that have hitherto been put forward for stabilising the value of money. Let us begin with the best known of these proposals, that of so-called *bimetallism*, by which is to be understood the system under which both gold and silver are legally recognised as means of payment and are freely accepted for coinage at a certain fixed ratio in terms of value.

The discussion of bimetallism has proceeded for many years, but from a practical point of view it has up to the present been rather unfruitful. The upshot, in my opinion —and this is becoming more and more generally admitted —is that the bimetallists have succeeded in providing a theoretical proof of *one* of their main assertions. They have succeeded in demonstrating the possibility of maintaining a constant ratio between the two metals by means of international co-operation, which need not necessarily comprise every country (leaving out of account the casual and inconsiderable *agio* which may appear in favour of the less bulky metal on account of the greater ease with which it can be transported—an *agio* which in any case may sometimes appear between gold and notes redeemable in gold, in favour of the notes).

Extreme monometallists would deny this possibility. A fixed ratio between gold and silver is to them "as unnatural and unthinkable" as, for instance, a fixed ratio between copper and iron or between beef and corn. These extreme opponents of bimetallism have two alternatives. They can resort to the conception of an intrinsic value

178

inherent in gold or in silver. This view must to-day be regarded as out of date. Or they have to ascribe to the proposed measures an enormously strong influence on the conditions of production and consumption of the precious metals. They have to imagine that the production of the under-valued metal (gold for the moment) ceases almost completely while its consumption enormously increases; so that it must soon disappear from circulation, while the over-valued metal is thrust into circulation by the opposite tendencies In other words, the bimetallic system would, according to this view, pass over sooner or later to a monometallic silver system.

It cannot be denied that bimetallism would be associated with some such *tendency*. It is impossible to say how this tendency would work out if the legal ratio deviated *too much* from the actual ratio in exchange of the two metals. The whole thing depends enormously on factors about which we know nothing, the future conditions of production of the precious metals, the attitude of Asiatic races in regard to hoarding gold instead of silver or in regard to keeping up their present habits of hoarding in general, and finally the general causes which determine the relative amount of so-called industrial consumption. In so far as its use in industry can be regarded, not simply as consumption of the precious metal, but at the same time as a kind of hoarding, it may perhaps be supposed that under a bimetallic system it would be largely diverted to silver (the value of which would now be guaranteed)

The closer the approximation between the ratio that is introduced and the present ratio of the values of uncoined gold and silver, the smaller, of course, is the fear of a diminution, not to mention a complete disappearance within a measurable space of time, of the world's stock of monetary gold.

All such anxiety is dispelled by the stability which past experience shows this ratio to have maintained, particularly in the present century until the demonetisation of silver of 1873 and the following years. This stability was

maintained in spite of several important changes in the
conditions of production of the precious metals.

A substantial advantage of bimetallism, and of any
fixed ratio established by law, lies in the fact that considerable portions of the world still base their currency on
silver. A fixed ratio between gold and silver is thus calculated to make a significant contribution towards the
introduction of order and security into the ever growing
trade relations with the more remote portions of the world.
But this argument would be deprived of much of its
strength if other silver countries were to follow the example
of India and decide to give up the free coinage of silver.

That, it seems to me, is about all that can be said
in favour of the bimetallists' proposals. As regards the
practical difficulties of the transition, these have been discussed so fully by the monometallists that they need not
occupy much of our attention.

It is only reasonable to rule out a restoration, or at any
rate a sudden restoration, of the old ratio of $15\frac{1}{2}$ . 1, in
other words, a *doubling* of the present exchange value of
uncoined silver in terms of gold. Such a restoration would
inevitably involve a real price revolution, not only in silver
countries but in gold countries too. For it has to be realised
that a rehabilitation of silver would to-day have an entirely different significance from its former demonetisation. Its demonetisation may be illustrated by the *closing*
of a sluice at a moment when the water level is the same on
both sides, while its rehabilitation would be like *opening*
(or rather demolishing) the sluice when the levels are unequal.

It is remarkable that so distinguished a monetary expert as
W. Lexis does not appear to have realised the consequences
correctly. He maintains[1]—curiously enough, he is arguing
*against* the bimetallists—that it is "very likely that an increase
in the quantity of silver money" (brought about by the intro-

[1] "Die Währungsfrage in der neuesten Zeit", *Schönberg's Handbuch*,
4th ed , p  407.

duction of bimetallism) "would, in the course of years, have as little influence on prices as the increase in gold production of recent years". The new silver could simply be stored up in the vaults of the banks, just as the gold has been hitherto.

This could occur only if there were no silver countries at all in the narrow sense of the term. The effect of suddenly doubling the value of a kilogram of silver in European markets would clearly be to cause an enormous rise in the demand for European products on the part of the silver countries. The flow of silver to the East would cease altogether or be reversed. Equilibrium would not be restored until prices had risen in Europe, or had fallen in the silver countries, or, more probably, both— to such a degree that gold prices in Europe had *doubled in terms of* silver prices in the silver countries [1]

It is possible that, owing to the undeveloped state of the monetary and credit systems, prices in the silver countries are more stable. If that is the case, the greater part of the relative change in prices would have to be borne in Europe, and the rise in European prices would be very great To Europe as a whole this would be of no advantage, on the contrary, we should be obtaining for our valuable products merely a mass of useless silver Certain classes of producers would obtain considerable profits during the period of transition (but not beyond), and the real burden of all debts expressed in terms of money would be permanently diminished In particular, the change would be enormously beneficial to "the agricultural debtors" (Lexis seems to me to be wrong in questioning this), while their creditors, great and small, would suffer a corresponding loss.

Thus it appears likely that a return to the so-called bi-metallic parity would bring about a rise of prices in the gold countries. It must not be concluded that the suspension of free coinage of silver has been the *cause* of the fall in prices of recent years A rather different point of view must be adopted If the link between the two metals were replaced, the level of gold prices in gold countries *relatively* to that of silver prices in silver countries would return to about the position that existed at the beginning of the seventies. As gold prices have fallen, since that time and silver prices have risen, the two

---

[1] Let us begin with both prices denoted by 100, in terms of gold in the one case and of silver in the other case  Then they would subsequently have to stand as 150 : 75, or 133⅓ : 66⅔, etc —at any rate in the ratio of 2   1.

price levels might also be restored to somewhere near their former *absolute* levels  But the movements in prices that have actually taken place since the link between the two metals was severed depend essentially on independent influences that have applied alike to both sets of prices. Their nature was indicated above with reference to the gold countries. The change in the ratio between gold and silver must, as has been emphasised above, be regarded, at any rate in part, as an effect rather than a cause of these changes in prices.

The introduction of a ratio which was much closer to the one which prevails in practice need not, of course, give rise to any considerable qualms. But it would almost certainly involve melting down and increasing the size of the silver coins that circulate to-day. The cost would be enormous, and the advantages, apart from those which we have referred to, would not be very great.

And when the change had been accomplished, what then? Would we now have attained the ideal monetary system, and would the stability promised by supporters of bimetallism really be provided? Such a point of view, derived from the assumption of free coinage of silver, is quite untenable— though free coinage of silver would now be necessary in order to maintain good relations with the silver countries. We are told that if two commodities are employed as a measure of prices, their value in conjunction must be more stable than of either taken separately. That may be true, but it is improper to proceed by way of the "Law of Large Numbers" when it is a question purely of the transition from the number one to the number two. Circumstances can easily arise under which the bimetallic standard of prices would be less stable than gold  Let us imagine— what is, after all, not unthinkable—that we have now reached the lowest point of the downward movement of prices, and that the continual production of gold and the excess of bank reserves must necessarily tend to depress the money rate of interest and force up prices  In the immediate future, however, fairly stable prices might be attained, inasmuch as new countries, such as Austria,

Russia,[1] and perhaps finally India, may turn over to gold coinage. But the introduction of bimetallism, even at a moderate ratio, would under such conditions bring about a continual, and perhaps very considerable, rise in prices, with all the associated disadvantages

The same essential considerations apply to the "composite standard" or "symmetalism" proposed by Marshall, Edgeworth, and others Under this system, a country's, or the world's, coinage would consist of a mixture in certain proportions of gold and silver The system would not even have the merit of avoiding fluctuations in the rate of foreign exchange with silver countries.

L. Walras has proposed a method,[2] not really bimetallism at all, which theoretically is less objectionable. He would maintain the use of gold as a standard, and he would not permit the free coinage of silver, but silver is to be used as a *billon régulateur*, the size of the stock of monetary silver being managed according to circumstances, with the object of achieving the highest possible degree of constancy of the value of money in terms of commodities. Unfortunately, Walras has not, so far as I know, ever entered into the details of his proposal, but, unless I am mistaken, it does not in its essence come to more than that when prices are falling the banks should *buy* silver (at the market price) in exchange for bank notes, and *sell* silver when prices are rising. It does not appear to matter very much whether this silver is used for the purpose of coinage or not. The important point lies in the variation of the total quantity of means of exchange as a result of notes being issued or withdrawn against silver

It seems to me very probable that such a plan would be successful if it were set in operation on a sufficiently energetic scale by a fairly large number of gold countries, though it is necessary to assume that analogous measures in regard to *gold* would not be adopted by the silver

---

[1] Russia's transition to a gold standard is, of course, now [1898] complete

[2] *Théorie de la monnaie*, p 75 ff

countries. But individual attempts in this direction cannot achieve very much  The history of the Bland and Sherman Bills indicates that even a country as large as the United States cannot accomplish much if it is acting alone.

Lexis goes too far, I think, when he maintains that "the regulation of prices by Walras' plan . . . is impracticable" [1] Lexis' objection is derived from his view that "the effect on prices of an increase or diminution in the quantity of money cannot be determined *a priori*, and may vary greatly both in magnitude and in direction"  It is hard to see how the *direction* of this effect can be open to doubt, though opinions may vary as to its *magnitude*  Lexis does not succeed in proving his assertion[2] that the accumulation of gold in the vaults of the banks during recent years has had no influence on prices  It is impossible to say how high the market rate of interest would have been, and how far it would have depressed prices, if this accumulation had not forced the banks to lower their rates of discount.

Silver purchases by banks or governments in accordance with Walras' plan would have two effects  It would increase the quantity of monetary instruments available for lending, and so bring about a *fall in the rate of interest*; and it would raise the price of silver, and so increase the silver countries' demand for commodities. Both effects would tell in the direction of raising European prices  The sale of silver would, of course, lead to the opposite result  It has, however, to be supposed that the silver countries maintain throughout a completely passive attitude. It is, in particular, assumed that a cheapening of gold in Europe will not cause an efflux to the East. These assumptions are bold ones, and they constitute a weak point, not only in Walras' plan, but in bimetallism itself.

A plan proposed before the English Gold and Silver Commission[3] by J. Barr Robertson goes deeper than Walras' project, with which it has considerable affinity, though it too is somewhat confused  Robertson was of the

---

[1] *Jahrbucher fur Nationalökonomie und Statistik*, vol 51, 1888, p. 74.
[2] *Schönberg's Handbuch, loc cit*
[3] *Second Report*, p. 24 ff., Q 6287-6304

opinion that the total amount of gold and silver in the world was *insufficient* for the price level of the future to be maintained either under the present monetary system or after the introduction of simple bimetallism  This view was possibly more justifiable in 1887 than appears to be the case to-day.

Robertson estimated, from sources which are unknown to me, that the total quantity of circulating medium (gold, silver, and paper) was about £900 million in the gold countries and about £450 million in the silver countries (the silver being valued at its old ratio to gold of $15\frac{1}{2}$ . 1). The *Economist's* index numbers of that time (1887) indicate that English prices had fallen since 1875 in the ratio of 100 : 69, and in India in the ratio of 100 . 91. (This corresponds fairly exactly to the ratio that then existed between gold and silver ) According to Robertson, the introduction of bimetallism at a ratio of $15\frac{1}{2}$ . 1 would lead to a rise in the monetary stock [1] of the gold countries to £987$\frac{1}{4}$ million, and to a fall in that of the silver countries to £362$\frac{3}{4}$ million  The general index number for both countries would now stand at 75$\frac{3}{3}$. Robertson then worked out the consequences of introducing bimetallism on the basis of the ratio of about 21 · 1, which at that time prevailed  Silver coins would now have to be increased in size, and as a result there would be a considerable fall in the nominal value of the total stock of money. The aggregate of circulating medium in gold countries would contract to £856 million and in silver countries to £428 million. The index numbers would stand at 65$\frac{1}{2}$ and 86$\frac{1}{2}$ respectively, so that *both* price levels would have fallen

These calculations can, of course, be accepted only in a very broad sense. To-day, when prices in India have *risen* very definitely, they do not apply at all.

Robertson proposed that in addition to the adoption of a fixed ratio between gold and silver, the total quantity of circulating medium in all countries should be expanded by the addition of a certain amount of irredeemable notes  The extent of this addition would be a matter for constant international arrangement, and the object would be to stabilise the general level of prices. These notes were not to serve as international means of payment, the provision

---

[1] [*Goldvorrat* of original is presumably a misprint for *Geldvorrat*.]

of which would continue to be reserved for the precious metals, gold and silver.

I do not entirely comprehend the plan. If the notes are not to be redeemable, how can it be certain that gold or silver will always be available at par for the purpose of international payments? According to Robertson's own view, unduly pessimistic though it is, the output of gold was insufficient even to meet industrial consumption. The result would be that if the price level was kept constant (and still more if it was raised), an *agio* would finally emerge on gold or metal as against the irredeemable notes.

But Robertson's fears were, of course, exaggerated. Soetbeer's estimate indicates that even at that time the consumption of gold did not exceed two-thirds of the annual production. Even this figure may be too high. Lexis maintains[1] that at the present time industrial consumption amounts to scarcely more than *a quarter* of the production, which has meanwhile, it is true, greatly increased.

It is, however, necessary to recognise the possibility of the industrial demand for precious metals permanently exceeding production. If this were to happen, it would certainly call for the introduction of irredeemable paper money, unless the whole monetary and economic situation of the world were to be left to the caprices of the production and consumption of gold. Measures would then have to be devised to enable notes to serve as an international means of payment; and *paper*, rather than *metal*, would become the standard of value.

A proposal put forward by Hertzkas[2] takes us one step further According to this suggestion, gold coinage would be retained, but the transport of gold would be avoided by means of the introduction in all countries of "gold certificates" as legal tender, the gold itself being kept in some central depository. The practicability of this, proposal essentially depends, it seems to me, on the willingness of each central bank to pledge itself to redeem these

---

[1] *Jahrbucher fur Nationalökonomie und Statistik*, vol 66, 1896.
[2] *Ibid.*, vol 65, 1895.

certificates, when it is asked to do so, at their par value in the country's currency, gold or notes. But if such willingness could be relied on, then the same end could, I think, be attained in a far simpler and at the same time very much more effective manner. It would only be necessary for the central banks to accept, without charging any *agio*, the notes *of one another* for redemption or in payment, as is already the case among the Scandinavian banks (of Denmark, Norway, and Sweden). From time to time foreign notes could be exchanged between the banks by means of an international clearing, and any outstanding differences could be paid in gold or met by arrangement through the accepting of deposits, the exchange of securities, etc.

An arrangement has existed since 1885 (in one case since 1888) between the Scandinavian Central Banks by means of which sums of more than 10,000 kronen (£550) can always be transferred *without* any charge for interest or costs But each Bank is under an obligation to remit any balance in gold on demand, and it has no right to exercise this power *on its own account* The Banks can utilise the claims that arise in this way, and indeed the whole of their net claims on foreign countries, as a basis for their note issue. Their stocks of gold [1] thus constitute to some extent a single reserve, and gold is actually transported between them only on a very limited scale.

Such an arrangement would be the logical sequel to the constantly growing importance of the part played by the banks in equalising the balance of international payments. Even to-day there are certain countries which very rarely send gold abroad, though their coinage is of gold and they rigorously maintain the redeemability of their notes. Their banks prefer to deliver bills on account of their foreign commercial activities, and if necessary to pay interest on them. We have already noticed the example of Sweden, though here gold is never employed even in domestic business, notes being issued in small denominations (down to 5 kronen), and the stocks of gold in the

---

[1] [*Geldvorrate* of original is presumably a misprint for *Goldvorrate*.]

private banks of issue remain untouched for years on end, though like the Reichsbank they are under an obligation to redeem their notes on demand in gold.

— — — — — — — — — —

One general observation is applicable to all the above proposals for stabilising the value of money, or for raising prices or preventing their further fall  According to our line of approach, they can attain their objective only in so far as they exert an indirect influence on the *money rate of interest*, and bring it into line with the natural rate, or below it, more rapidly than would otherwise be the case.

The possibility of equalising prices between gold and silver countries provides in its essence nothing more than an illustration of this general principle. A rise in the demand of the silver countries for European products resulting from a rise in the price of silver would mean surplus profits to European entrepreneurs. The diminution in importers' profits, which would result from the decrease in the supply of the products of the silver countries and from the rise in their costs of production, is of no great consequence, for importers play a relatively small part in the provision of such commodities (production, transport, etc ).

(It is by now superfluous to remark that profit to the entrepreneur is in no way identical with profit to the economic system. In this particular case it would be bound up with a net loss to society.[1])

Suppose for example, though it seems scarcely possible, that under Walras' scheme the issue of notes in exchange for silver (or the expansion in the issue of silver coin) merely resulted in a corresponding amount of gold or of notes being deposited at the banks, without providing any stimulus to the banks to reduce their rates of interest. Clearly then the policy would be perfectly useless (apart from its effect on the price of silver and the consequent reactions)

The question thus arises whether the object in view

[1] *Cf* p. 181, above.

could not be obtained far more simply, far more cheaply, and far more securely through the monetary institutions of the various countries agreeing among themselves to undertake *directly* that alteration in their rates of interest which is necessary and which alone is effective—the whole purpose, according to our theory, being to bring the average money rate into coincidence with the natural rate.

Under Walras' system silver would not serve as a standard nor as an international means of payment; even if prices were to rise, very little more *silver* would be required for the purpose of transactions. Why then burden the banks with useless stocks of silver? Why not let them issue notes (or credits) against government bonds, debentures, or—bills? In other words, why not take *direct* measures to lower the banks' rate of interest?

This does not mean that the banks ought actually to *ascertain* the natural rate before fixing their own rates of interest That would, of course, be impracticable, and would also be quite unnecessary. For the current level of commodity prices provides a reliable test of the agreement or diversion of the two rates. The procedure should rather be simply as follows: *So long as prices remain unaltered the banks' rate of interest is to remain unaltered. If prices rise, the rate of interest is to be raised, and if prices fall, the rate of interest is to be lowered, and the rate of interest is henceforth to be maintained at its new level until a further movement of prices calls for a further change in one direction or the other*

The more promptly these changes are undertaken the smaller is the possibility of considerable fluctuations of the general level of prices, and the smaller and less frequent will have to be the changes in the rates of interest. If prices are kept fairly stable the rate of interest will merely have to keep step with such rise or fall in the natural rate as is inevitable.

In my opinion, the main cause of the instability of prices resides in the inability or failure of the banks to follow this rule.

A different jargon has become common in recent times,
and it is sad to find a man like Lexis, in his recent discussion in *Schonberg's Handbuch*, maintaining that "the
money (in the banks) lies there at the disposal of everybody on the most favourable conditions obtainable". As
a proof of this, we are told that, for example, "the Bank
of France has at last given up the principle" (it should
rather be called the routine) "of not lowering its official
rate below 2½ per cent., and has accommodated itself to a
rate of 2 per cent."[1]

But a rate of 2 per cent. does not imply "the most
favourable conditions obtainable". It is favourable only
if the borrower can earn *more* than 2 per cent per annum
on the capital that he borrows; it is very unfavourable,
indeed ruinous, if after deductions for costs and risk there
remains a profit of only 1⅞, 1¾, or 1½ per cent. on the capital.

The objection that a further reduction in rates of
interest cannot be to the advantage of the banks may
possibly in itself be perfectly correct. A fall in rates of
interest may diminish the banks' margin of profit more
than it is likely to increase the extent of their business. I
should like then in all humility to call attention to the
fact that the banks' prime duty is not to earn a great deal
of money but to provide the public with a medium of exchange—and to provide this medium in *adequate measure*,
to aim at stability of prices. In any case, their obligations to society are enormously more important than their
private obligations, and if they are ultimately unable to
fulfil their obligations to society along the lines of private
enterprise—which I very much doubt—then they would
provide a worthy activity for the State.

It has now to be asked whether a policy of co-operation
between the banks of the whole world (or of the gold-
standard countries) lies within the realm of possibility.
The banks of any single individual country, and above all
its central bank, must in fixing their rates of discount
allow themselves to be directed by the state of foreign

[1] *Schönberg's Handbuch*, 4th ed., p. 406

trade, of the balance of payments, and of the rates of exchange. How then could they allow their rates of interest to be prescribed by others? This difficulty would still remain even though the central banks of the various countries accepted one another's notes at par. An unfavourable balance of payments would then make itself felt, not primarily by an efflux of precious metal, but by the balance of the domestic banks at the international clearing becoming more and more passive This balance would eventually have to be liquidated by a transfer of gold or would have to be converted into some form of interest-bearing debt The bank or banks of the country concerned would thus be subject to a direct pressure to raise their rates of discount. They must then in all circumstances retain a free hand to be used *in the last resort,* if not earlier, over bank-rate policy.

This is a serious difficulty, which has to be met in deciding the *manner* in which our policy should be put through, without constituting any logical objection to its practicability

It is frequently observed that the difficulties which arise through a highly one-sided balance of payments or through a large difference in the price levels of two or more countries can be overcome by measures undertaken, not only by the "unfavourably" situated country, but also by the "favourably" situated country or countries Suppose that money is flowing from country A to country B. This flow can be stemmed and reversed not only by a *rise* in the rate of interest in country A, but also by a *fall* in the rate of interest in country B, and also, of course, by a simultaneous movement in both countries It is only the *difference* between the two rates of interest which is of consequence. And a change in the rate of interest which was undertaken by both countries *in the same direction,* and to about the same extent, would have *no* influence on their mutual trade relations. In other words, to adopt once again a mechanical metaphor, international prices, like prices in general, can be compared to a system which possesses not one but "two degrees of freedom": they can be moved in opposition to one another, but they can also be moved in *conjunction*. There is first of all the individual regulation of *relative* rates of interest, which aims at maintaining the rates of exchange, the balance of payments, and the *relative* level of prices, and which, by the nature of the case, must proceed in *opposite* directions in different countries or groups of countries. At the same time, and more important, there can, and should, on occasion come into being a co-operative regulation of the rate of interest, proceeding everywhere *in the same direction* with the object of maintaining the *average* level of prices at a constant height

Co-operation between the banks of a single country for the regulation of rates of interest is already, of course, a matter of everyday procedure. Co-operation between the banks of different countries could easily take place, at any rate in times of peace, as soon as it was clear what objective was being aimed at. It would be sufficient if a scheme of co-operation were accepted, and fairly loyally adhered to, by a majority of countries; any individual country would deviate from the ruling rate of interest, unless for some pressing cause, only to its own disadvantage.

It would still remain to provide a satisfactory measure of the average level of prices and its fluctuations. The problem is a difficult one but cannot to-day be regarded as insoluble. Its nature is such that it would be clearly best to hand it over to an international commission on the lines of the Metric Commission. As soon as this body had discovered a divergence of the world price level from its normal level (which would, of course, be fixed quite arbitrarily), it would be the duty of the banks to pool their efforts and restore equilibrium This suggestion may sound strange, and perhaps comic (reminiscent of the Astronomical Society of Laputa), but it represents the logical development of the idea underlying the deliberations, until to-day at any rate quite ineffective, of all monetary commissions.

With their present stocks of gold, which could be

enormously reinforced by the issue of notes in small (though not too small) denominations, the banks would be able fully to maintain the present level of prices for a reasonable space of time. That is not a matter for doubt. It is rather to be feared that if gold continues to be produced on the present or on a higher scale, the monetary institutions will be finally compelled to lower their rates of interest to such an extent that a rise in prices will be unavoidable. For my part (for reasons which I have already given), I regard such an eventuality as no less undesirable than a further fall in prices. If the banks are not to suffer too obvious losses (through failing to make use of interest-bearing deposits), it would be possible to avoid such a rise of prices only by the *suspension of the free coinage of gold* This would mark the first step towards the introduction of an ideal standard of value. Monetary discussions of recent years have made us more and more familiar with such an international paper standard. While it is usually regarded as a means of meeting a growing scarcity of gold, it might just as well, I think, and must, come into being as a consequence of an over-abundance of gold.

In any case, such a prospect need not, on closer investigation, provide cause for consternation On the contrary, once it had come into being it would perhaps be the present system which would sound like a fairy tale, with its rather senseless and purposeless sending hither and thither of crates of gold, with its digging up of stores of treasure and burying them again in the recesses of the earth. The introduction of such a scheme offers no difficulty, at any rate on the theoretical side. Neither a central bureau nor international notes would be necessary.[1] Each country would have its own system of notes (and small change) These would have to be redeemable at par by every central bank, but would be allowed to circulate

[1] On the grounds of convenience, it would be very desirable to adopt a uniform unit of value or at any rate to modify the existing units (in the manner of Laveley's proposal) so as to simplify their arithmetical relationships.

only inside the one country. It would then be the simple duty of each credit institution to regulate its rate of interest, both relatively to, and in unison with, other countries, so as both to maintain in equilibrium the international balance of payments and to stabilise the general level of world prices. In short, the regulation of prices would constitute the prime purpose of bank rate, which would no longer be subject to the caprices of the production and consumption of gold or of the demand for the circulation of coins  It would be perfectly free to move, governed only by the deliberate aims of the banks.

----  --- ------ --- ---

The possibility of establishing a stable measure of value and of maintaining prices at a constant average level was questioned by Ricardo but is to-day affirmed by many outstanding economists. The upshot of our own investigations is that such an aim is attainable, not only in theory but in practice  Its fulfilment calls for every effort on the part of statesmen and thinkers  It is a thing unworthy of our generation that without pressing cause the most important economic factors are left to pure chance.

But it must not be supposed that stabilisation of prices would overcome the economic depression which for more than twenty years has provided a constant source of complaint on the part of certain classes of the community; nor would economic progress again resume that very rapid pace to which we have become accustomed since the middle of the century. This depression must be regarded as the cause rather than the effect of the fall in prices  It has its own peculiar relations to the popular catch-phrase "economic depression". The productivity of labour and land has, in our portion of the globe, quite definitely not fallen off. Wages have not fallen, in fact they have on the average, taken in relation to the prices of the most important articles of consumption, undoubtedly risen. Even rents have definitely risen, while agricultural rents have had to give way (in western Europe) to the competition in the production of corn exercised by various parts of the world, the rise and expansion in other kinds of rents, including urban ground-rents, have been all the more tremendous  The enormous growth in national and communal budgets provides an unmistakable sign of increasing welfare. What has fallen is the rate of interest on liquid capital and the thing that is usually termed entrepreneur profit, *i.e* the *surplus* profit, over and above the remuneration for services rendered, which accrues to the entrepreneurs at times of prosperity.

We have already recognised the main cause for this phenomenon  The transformation into fixed capital of the new liquid capital which comes into being has now to follow a far less profitable course, and the increase in the amount of capital has in part to serve to raise wages and rents.

It is true that, on a purely quantitative view of the expansion of population and of output as a whole, progress has been somewhat less rapid in recent decades than earlier in the century  It is, however, premature, and indeed ridiculous, to indulge in the hope that the conditions of earlier times will again return. Such a hope is derived from nothing but the short-sighted desires of mankind.

The economic development which has characterised the present century, particularly in the older European countries, is in this respect to be regarded as anything but a regular phenomenon. It is a peculiar and rare *exception* to a general rule  The unlearned multitude may fail to comprehend, and many educated people may be *unwilling* to comprehend  But the economist should shun the popular prejudice, and should attempt to fight it with all the power at his command. For by the nature of his studies he can view these matters in a better light, and he, more than anybody else, is under an obligation to proclaim the truth concerning them.

Progress in the *qualitative* sense, increase in economic

welfare, is possible, or at least conceivable, to an almost unlimited extent, but only on the assumption that progress in the *quantitative* sense, expansion of population, is very severely restricted. The assumption of even a slow growth of population and output leads in the last analysis to a *reductio ad absurdum*. It is clear that a constant rate of growth, in accordance with the familiar geometrical progression, is in many degrees *absurdius*; while the idea of endless, and above all accelerating, progress, both quantitative and qualitative, can only be described as *absurdissimum*. Those who expect *monetary measures* to perform miracles might well remind themselves of the well-known fact that coins do not give birth to offspring, and that even if they did, precious metal and bank notes would constitute neither sustenance nor clothing

But liberated from all unhealthy fantasies, the question of monetary reform on rational lines definitely remains among the most important of economic problems. That its realisation depends on international co-operation, which would have to be both permanent and somewhat thorough in nature, is to my mind a positive recommendation I joyfully welcome every fresh step towards the uniting of nations for economic or scientific ends, for it adds one more safeguard for the preservation and strengthening of that good on which the successful attainment of all other goods, both material and immaterial, ultimately depends —international peace.

# APPENDIX

## THE MONETARY PROBLEM OF THE
## SCANDINAVIAN COUNTRIES

# THE MONETARY PROBLEM OF THE SCANDINAVIAN COUNTRIES [1]

## I

NOT long ago I was asked by Professor Davidson to write something about the recent rise in the Danish and Norwegian exchange rates I am afraid that I consented rather too hastily, for starting off with the whole question of the rise and fall of prices during and after the War, I soon became assailed by very strong misgivings as to the completeness, if not the validity, of the explanations usually provided with such unanimous conviction by economists, especially here in Sweden. I began further to wonder whether practical men of affairs, in spite of some obviously wrong and illogical conclusions, have not in some directions advanced further than we have towards an understanding of these phenomena The consequence is that my treatment of this side of the question has become disproportionately extensive For this I have to apologise

The main question at issue has referred on the one hand to the relation between a *scarcity of commodities* and the rise of prices and on the other hand to the relation between the cessation of such a scarcity and the subsequent fall in prices That commodities were scarce during the War cannot be denied In the belligerent countries this was due to the fact that a large percentage of productive workers were called to arms or to the production of munitions At the beginning of the War the deficiency of ordinary commodities could in part be made good by drawing on stocks, of which Germany in particular had large quantities, or they could be replaced, as in the case of the Entente countries, by imports But as the War went on and covered a wider field these sources were of course no longer adequate In the neutral countries the scarcity of commodities was more indirect in origin, taking the form partly of obstacles to import, partly of an unduly large export of goods to belligerent countries. Nevertheless, it is a well-known fact that a very marked scarcity made itself felt even in neutral countries By what means, and in what order, this scarcity was first alleviated on the conclusion of the War, and

[1] *Ekonomisk Tidskrift*, 1925.

was finally eliminated, is a matter far more difficult to ascertain (and one to which I shall return). There is, however, no doubt that in most countries the degree of scarcity which existed during the War has been alleviated, or even more than alleviated.

It is the scarcity of commodities that business men have regarded as the chief if not the sole cause of the rise in prices, at any rate in those countries whose exchanges did not entirely collapse during the War, and similarly it is increased supplies which provide their explanation of the marked post-War fall in prices. The expansion and subsequent contraction in the medium of exchange would according to them be merely the consequence, indeed the almost inevitable consequence, of the rise and fall in prices which had already taken place. The theorists, on the other hand, have tried to prove that a scarcity of commodities in itself can cause at the most a proportionate rise in prices, whereas in most cases the rise was very much greater. The theorists would argue that if the total quantity of money in circulation had decreased *pari passu* with the decline in supplies of commodities, no rise in prices would have taken place, if the quantity had remained stationary, there would have been no more than a proportionate rise in prices, which in the countries least affected would amount to 10 or 20 per cent But the actual rise in prices amounted to several hundred per cent The main cause is, therefore, to be sought in the monetary sphere, in an over-liberal credit policy on the part of the note-issuing banks, and above all in a too great benevolence toward the demands of governments. Even in the country where such a measure was least to be expected, namely, England, the government took it upon itself to issue notes.

The most pregnant formulation of the arguments on the two sides is perhaps to be found in Professor Cassel's well-known *Money and Foreign Exchange after 1914* (March 1922). I take the liberty of quoting the following passage· [1]

Whenever this suggestion has been made [that the driving force in the rise in prices has been what is termed inflation], the usual answer from the central banks has been that they could not suppress the demand. When the scarcity of commodities became aggravated, the public clung as long as possible to their claims upon life, and bought, in spite of the fact that prices rose. It was commonly imagined that the public were·by no means limited in this buying up of goods by the amount of their current incomes, but that they could draw on their balances at the banks for as much as they wanted, and could thus procure

---

[1] English edition, p 55.

the purchasing power they needed in order to supply themselves with goods at however high a price. This reasoning is rather alluring,[1] and it may not be out of place to say a few words in explanation of where the error really lies. The public's deposits at the banks are, as a rule, loaned out to industry and trade. If the public withdraws any part of its deposited funds in order to gain extra purchasing power, then a corresponding amount of funds must be withheld from industry and trade. In consequence of this the purchasing power of enterprises, and ultimately also that of the workers, is diminished, and therefore no increase takes place in the total purchasing power which the community has at its disposal This is only the case if the banks create fresh bank currency in order to be able to pay back the deposited funds which the public demands to withdraw, and therefore do not make the reduction in their granting of credit to industry which this consumption of the savings should rightly have required But thereby we find ourselves involved in a regular process of inflation, with a rise in prices as the inevitable consequence

The weakness in Professor Cassel's argument, as well as in the argument of those whose opinions he opposes, seems to me to lie in the lack of a clear conception of the term *purchasing power* It is only *money* purchasing power which here comes into question. It therefore stands to reason that a general rise in the market prices of both goods and services *itself* creates the purchasing power required for meeting the higher prices If the rise in prices were absolutely uniform, then each individual, whether it was goods or services that he had for sale, would obtain exactly the amount of purchasing power which he needed in his capacity of buyer. Should the rise in prices be less uniform (in the War it was far from uniform), then some naturally get more and others less for their goods and services, but the sum total of purchasing power is still sufficient for the purpose and does not need to be supplemented by the banks. This monetary purchasing power will *not*, of course, no matter how great it becomes, be sufficient to procure the quantity of goods which each individual would like to consume, for if it were, everybody, taken together, would obtain more goods than the amount actually on the market, and that is an absurdity But it is this very scarcity which causes the rise in prices, and the monetary purchasing power so created is adequate to pay the sum actually demanded for the available goods and services

---

[1] [These two words are translated from the Swedish edition The English edition reads "quite false" ]

What *is* needed is *an increase in volume of the medium of exchange*. If all payments were made on a cheque basis this increase would, of course, take place quite automatically. All drafts on banking accounts, with the resultant transfers from one account to another, would constantly increase in amount as prices rose  At first, however, there would be no increase either in the average amount or in the aggregate of these accounts. In the course of time they would become inconveniently small in proportion to the increased volume of monetary payments. They would consequently need to be adjusted upwards  In the final analysis this presupposes an increase in bank credit. But as prices rose, bank deposits and bank loans would swell more or less automatically

Again, if other instruments of exchange, such as bank notes (and coin) are employed, then a general rise in prices will cause the banks of issue to increase their issue of notes (and coin)  Should these banks flatly refuse to expand their circulation, they would doubtless cause an embarrassing shortage of the medium of exchange, and as a result the rise in prices would meet with difficulties and might perhaps be hindered  But it does not seem likely that these banks could actually prevent the rise or force prices down to their original level  For in the first place, resort could be had to payment by cheque to almost any desired extent—as happened in the United States during the crisis of 1907, secondly, if an extension of credit were refused by the private banks as well, an increase in the velocity of circulation of notes and cheques might roughly compensate for the insufficiency in quantity. According to a statement by Bortkiewitch in the *Schriften des Vereins fur Sozialpolitik*, 1924  170, the rise of prices in Germany eventually amounted, if I remember rightly, to 37 times the increase in the circulation of bank notes  The conditions, it is true, were extraordinarily abnormal, but a doubling or trebling of the normal velocity of circulation of money ought not, even during fairly stable conditions, to meet with *insurmountable* difficulties.

The quantity theory is, of course, entirely based on the thesis that the velocity of circulation of money at any given time is approximately constant, a thesis based in its turn on the supposed conservatism of our habits of payment. Such conservatism cannot be denied, but our deeply ingrained habits of consumption are far more conservative, and if the two come into conflict, it should be fairly obvious which will get the upper hand, in spite of the fact, or rather for the very reason, that our habitual requirements can no longer be satisfied.

It should *a fortiori* prove futile to prevent a rise in prices merely by raising interest rates so as to make it more difficult to obtain credit A rise in the rate of interest is certainly an almost infallible means of restricting the demand for credit on the part of all *producers*, but it can hardly have a similar effect on those who merely desire to strengthen their cash position in view of the increase in the volume of exchange

It is clear that this premise, namely, the shortage of goods, regarded as the primary cause of the rise in prices, leads us to an entirely different presentation of the problem from the one on which monetary theory has hitherto been based [1] Under normal conditions, when production and consumption proceed in almost unchanged proportions, a rise in prices (apart from a rise due to an abnormal increase in the production of gold) can actually be caused only by too liberal a credit policy on the part of the banks, making it possible for speculators to obtain an increase in money purchasing power which no longer corresponds to such increase as may be simultaneously brought about by voluntary saving. In this case the remedy is obviously to be found in a tightening of credit, brought about for instance by raising the rates of interest on advances and deposits This would lessen the demand for credit and possibly encourage saving In the present case, however, it is not a question of additional purchasing power (for this, as we have seen, is provided automatically by the rise in prices). Here too a relative shortage in the means of payment can at a time of high prices make payments more or less difficult, but it cannot entirely prevent them so long as purchasing power exists.

Suppose that there were a real market in the physical sense, for instance, a yearly fair at which the population of the neighbouring communities exchanged their produce A rumour that there would be a shortage of goods in the future would unquestionably cause an increased demand for goods, and a general rise in prices. For this to happen it would not, of course, be necessary to suppose that the amount of legal tender on the market increases, but only that on the last day of the market, when all business transactions are finally settled, claims and

---

[1] It is the more remarkable that this fact has been overlooked—if indeed it has—inasmuch as all economists are familiar with the phenomenon that scarcity of any given commodity, say grain, may lead to a much more than proportionate rise in its price In such a case it is generally supposed that the money prices of other commodities *fall* to a corresponding degree, but I know of no instance where this has actually happened

debts are cleared on a larger scale than usual, and at the same time that the available money circulates somewhat more rapidly, which does not alter the fact that the money brought to market is generally in proportion to the expected amount of business.

It is indeed true (and this would to a certain extent seem to strengthen Professor Cassel's argument) that the intimate relationship between the money market and the capital market means that every measure on the part of the banks which tends to restrict the quantity of means of payment has a very restraining influence on producers' demand for credit (and encourages saving), with the obvious result that prices tend to fall *pro tanto*. The strength of such influences as may be brought about in this way should not, however, be exaggerated It is certain that if such measures for checking the demand for credit are to have any effect whatever, they must be taken in hand *at the very commencement of the rise in prices.* Once prices have started to rise, it is too late for these factors to play any rôle What is the significance of a rise in the rate of interest of a few per cent per annum in checking the demand for credit when producers may already reckon with a progressive rise in prices of perhaps as many per cent a *month?*

On the other hand, the bankers were definitely illogical when they gave as their reasons for not raising rates of interest during the War, firstly, that such a rise would not have been able to check the rise in prices, and secondly, that higher rates of interest would be harmful to "legitimate business enterprise" It is obvious that the two sections of this argument are mutually contradictory Just to the extent that a rise in rates of interest would have failed entirely to check the rise in prices it would not have been harmful either to legitimate or to illegitimate business enterprise—at the most it would have served as a slight check on the enormous profits which were being made.

But it might be asked, granting the above-mentioned premise (I should like to emphasise that I do not personally guarantee its validity but have accepted it as a hypothesis on the strength of the opinion of practical men of business), how, apart from a return to normal conditions in regard to production and consumption, could stabilisation of prices be at all possible? This question is not easily answered If new credit is entirely withheld, then prices will naturally become stable when the tension between the price level and the amount of available medium of exchange has become so great that it entirely counteracts the tendency towards a rise in prices. If on the other hand the banks offer capital, though at higher rates of interest, then theoretically at least the rise in prices might be expected to continue, for it cannot cease until a balance has been attained between the supply and the demand of goods, and this *never* takes place so long as there is a general endeavour to maintain a degree of consumption which it is physically impossible to meet But such an attempt must eventually cease When scarcity is permanent, people will at last resign themselves to the inevitable and give up the attempt to maintain the normal standard of living to which they had been accustomed. Thus demand and supply will again correspond to each other on a lower plane, and there will be no cause for a further rise in prices If, however, the scarcity of goods extended to the necessities of life, this transition could not, under conditions of free competition, take place without entailing great suffering for the poorer classes, as the better situated classes would, despite the scarcity, be able naturally to satisfy their needs for these goods It follows, in my opinion, that rationing was a blessing, and that it should have been applied on an even larger scale, so as to have included such things as fuel (which would indirectly have had the effect of rationing housing, so that the laws regulating the letting of houses and flats—which did not entail rationing—would perhaps have been superfluous). However, anybody who tried during the War to procure—sometimes perhaps illegally—an extra pound of butter or coffee or a sack of potatoes, will be able to testify to the difficulty of resigning to the inevitable. And, in fact, prices did not cease to rise until the armistice, and not definitely even then

## II

Through force of habit I have been writing as though I were treating mainly of Swedish conditions. But the above description, in so far as it is correct, applies pre-eminently to the belligerent countries, where the rise in prices must in any case be presumed to originate. It was, as I have pointed out, their governments' heavy demands for goods and services for the purposes of war which directly brought about the scarcity of raw materials and labour necessary to the production of goods for civilian purposes, and this, on our hypothesis, should of itself have caused a general rise in prices [1] There is no doubt that

---

[1] The matter can be simplified by assuming that *every single* member in turn of the population who can serve at the front or work at home has

this rise in prices was very much strengthened because the various governments (who had no goods for sale and consequently were in constant need of new purchasing power) did not from the beginning procure such purchasing power from the public, either by way of taxes or through loans at suitable rates of interest—say twelve to fifteen per cent—but instead procured it partly (as in England) directly by issuing bank notes, partly by loans from the note-issuing banks at nominal rates (as in France, Germany, etc ), and only in the second instance tried to procure it from the public, first of all from the War profiteers, and even this at rates that had been artificially lowered by previous manipulations

In neutral countries, especially in the Scandinavian countries, prices did indeed rise as much as, or more than, in belligerent countries (such as England and America), but this rise was a secondary and derivative phenomenon  This is easily demonstrated  it was in all probability only by prohibiting the import of gold (February 1926) and by forcing the rate of foreign exchange below par that we were able to prevent our price level from rising yet further  If the Scandinavian countries had simply maintained the gold standard during the War—a thing which they unquestionably would have been capable of doing and which in fact Norway is said to have proposed at the beginning of the War—then it would have been impossible to prevent a further rise in prices,[1] and by sending us gold foreign countries would then have been able at their pleasure to draw notes from the Bank of Sweden, thereby assuring themselves of our goods (unless there had been a complete embargo on all exports)  In this way we should have obtained a great deal of gold, but the maintenance of the gold standard *after* the War would have been made harder rather than easier, for the deflation necessary to bring this about would have been still more comprehensive  To avoid it we might have been forced in the end to cancel payments in gold, precisely on account of the superfluity of gold, and at the present moment all three Scandinavian countries might have had a depreciated paper currency,

for some weeks every year to go soldiering *on his own provisions* and work at the munitions factories *without pay*; in this way a proportionately lessened supply of labour power (and to some extent of capital) would remain over for the production of ordinary goods.

[1] In the Netherlands, where the Central Bank at least claimed to be prepared to accept at par all gold offered—although certain restrictions no doubt were in force—the wholesale price index during the last years of the War rose *above* our own, notwithstanding the fact that their import difficulties were hardly greater than ours

as is the case in Spain in spite of the enormous amount of gold which she acquired during the War Our financial and political leaders are therefore at the most to be blamed for having refrained from preventing the rise in prices, not for having actually brought it about, and if our theory is correct, prevention might have proved impossible, although our leaders should have been able to manage considerably better than they did.

We know that in regard to all these questions Professor Cassel is of the opposite opinion. But his views, especially in his *Money and Foreign Exchange after 1914*, are so vaguely expressed that I am unable to grasp their real meaning Professor Cassel was one of those who recommended the exclusion of gold in 1916, and he is even said to have been the author of the very sensible plea for this measure which was originally intended to be placed before the Diet. Professor Cassel regrets—as I do, and, I believe, the majority of Swedish economists with me—that the exclusion of gold was not carried out more radically, and with a clearer conception of its aim. This failure was partly due to the fact that the agreement of Denmark and Norway to the measure was only half-hearted, and that they subsequently thwarted the intentions of the Bank of Sweden by sending their gold into this country Nevertheless, Professor Cassel subsequently claims in his book that it would have been better if we had not declared the exclusion of gold,[1] and he claims further (p. 271)[2] that the economists who during the summer of 1918 continued to urge a more energetic enforcement of the exclusion of gold were "badly informed", because at this time, according to Professor Cassel, the value of our currency was "considerably below its gold value" He praises the "clearer insight" of the practical bankers "who on the same occasion pointed out that it would be desirable if the Bank of Sweden were less averse than heretofore to the influx of gold, and expressed the opinion that the status of our country might be such (after the War) as to necessitate the export of gold on a large scale"

---

[1] He says (English edition, p 94) "After the end of the War Sweden would have had an effective gold currency, and the former parity between the Swedish krona and the dollar might at any rate approximately have been maintained." Can anyone believe such a statement? Why, then, did Holland (not to mention Spain) let her currency drop far below the dollar and, from 1921 onwards, below the Swedish currency as well?

[2] [Henceforth references are to the Swedish edition, unless otherwise stated.]

Up to the present date the Bank of Sweden has scarcely been *obliged* to export gold. What it actually has exported it has no doubt been only too pleased to get rid of. I therefore find it hard to see where the "clearer insight" of these bankers comes in  On the other hand, it would have been very advantageous from a purely business point of view to increase the supply of gold at the expense of the supply of foreign exchange if it had been possible to foresee that certain currencies would subsequently depreciate, but as a matter of fact there was nothing to prevent the private banks from importing gold for their own needs instead of buying foreign currencies, a procedure that, as far as I know, was never adopted. For that matter, if Professor Cassel's theory were valid, the advice of the private bankers to the Bank of Sweden would have been as vain as the contrary advice of the economists  If the value of Swedish currency was below its gold value, the Bank of Sweden could in any case only import gold at an excessive price  But how does this tally with Professor Cassel's statement? The fact is, as Davidson points out, that the dollar rate at that time was 91 ore, *i e* more than 20 per cent. *below* parity  It follows that, according to Professor Cassel, dollar notes would have been still lower, say 30 per cent. below their gold parity, a thing very difficult to imagine, for shortly afterwards, without any deflation either previously or subsequently, they could be redeemed in gold.

What Professor Cassel probably means to say is that Swedish prices during the War were forced to such a high level by *internal* inflation (principally as a result of "official" waste) that *if the trade balance had been level*, our currency would have proved to be considerably below the dollar, and therefore also below gold parity  But it was difficult for us to import, and as a result our balance of trade and of payments was "favourable" —Professor Cassel has not gone into this matter in detail. Consequently our currency (and also to a lesser extent that of our neighbours) was valued *abroad* above its *real domestic worth* and even above its parity with the dollar  This is not impossible, but if it had really been so, it would, in the case of Sweden, prove difficult to explain why the inferiority of our notes was not disclosed as soon as a free gold market was established in America through the resumption of the redeemability of the dollar and the free export of gold, and why furthermore the Swedish crown, after a temporary depreciation, resumed its parity in relation to the dollar as early as December 1922 without our taking any drastic measure to raise its value. This contingency Professor

Cassel obviously did not foresee (see p. 276), in spite of his oft-vaunted prophetic powers.

I see the matter in a different way The abnormally high level of prices in Sweden during the War is to be ascribed to three factors, which would have made themselves felt to an equal, if not to a greater, degree even if we had remained entirely passive and had accepted all the gold that was offered us The first factor was the general inflation, to the extent to which it extended over a gold-standard country such as the U.S A The second factor would have led to European prices rising higher than American prices even if currencies had been kept at their parities. This factor took the form of the very *excessive exports* of American goods (during and after the War), which caused the already enormously high freight rates to rise considerably more for eastward than for westward trade [1] The result was indirectly to raise the prices of our imports, in spite of the fact that our direct imports from America during the last years of the War were insignificant (they grew in volume later on) Finally, we have the well-known restrictions on imports, which for certain reasons made themselves more felt in Sweden than in the other Scandinavian or neutral countries, and which obviously had the same effect that high or prohibitive import tariffs would have had, viz of raising the general price level Even this rise in prices would have taken place on a full gold standard, indeed, the rise would have become even sharper, until perhaps it would eventually have prevented any excess of exports Instead, we refused to accept gold and the rates of exchange perforce fell below parity. This no doubt inclined exporters and their financial backers, the banks, to extend credit at cheap rates abroad, or, if it was stipulated that payment must be in Swedish currency, it induced the foreign buyer to seek credit, even on onerous terms, in the hope of a future profit on the exchange. This inducement would have been lacking if we had received our payments in gold. It is quite possible—and this is not denied by Professor Davidson—that the *tension* between the exchange rate and the price level would not then have become *quite* as great as it actually did become—for instance, during the autumn of 1917 I naturally do not venture to claim that every detail of this explanation would tally with the truth, but it seems to dispense with the necessity of presupposing an "internal inflation"—it depends only on the

[1] This phenomenon probably became more noticeable when the United States shipped her armies and war materials to Europe, and less so when the return movement set in

P

absence of any internal deflation, which if it had come to pass
would have caused the dollar exchange to sink yet further
Wherein then lies "the fatal miscalculation" which Professor
Cassel ascribes to the above-mentioned economists?

## III

As to the period *after* the War, with its irrational and often
puzzling price fluctuations, I am loth to confess that I would
far sooner listen to somebody who could express an authoritative opinion on these matters than essay an explanation myself. I feel that some very general remarks are all I have to offer

We (and the other neutral countries) were now able to import freely, and the trade balance, instead of showing an excess
of exports, showed a very decided excess of imports (principally from America)  It is clear that the discrepancy between
a dollar rate which was far below parity and a price level, or
rather price index, which was more than 50 per cent. higher
than in America, had soon to disappear, [1] whether this would
come about by a sudden fall in our commodity prices or by a
rise in the dollar exchange rate to far above parity, would of
course depend on circumstances  If Professor Cassel had had
his way in the spring of 1919, when the dollar first rose above
parity, and had induced us to re-establish a full gold standard
with free export of gold, then we should obviously have chosen
the former alternative  Whether this would have been to the
benefit of our country is a question into which I shall not enter.

Even at as late a date as March 1922, Professor Cassel regards his advice in this matter as having been sound, and
claims that if it had been followed "no violent fluctuations
need have taken place." [2] The result, so far as I can see, would
have been that our price level would have behaved in the same
way in terms of crowns as it actually behaved *in terms of gold*,
i.e divided by the dollar exchange rate's ratio to parity. In
other words, from an index number of 369 in January 1919 we
should have fallen to 246 in January of the following year,
after which our index would have risen again to about 296 in
July 1920 and then have fallen to 150 in October 1921. The
absence of fluctuations would have been, to say the least,
relative  Towards the end of his book (p 351) Professor Cassel

---

[1] Our price level, as expressed in *gold*, remained higher than the
American level until the end of December 1922

[2] *Op cit.*, p. 280

warns us in the strongest terms against any attempt to make our notes redeemable in gold until the price level has been "brought into conformity with the gold standard one intends to introduce", and in this connection hints that it would be advisable to "procure more sensible managers for the central banks" As far as I know, however, nobody has ever proposed anything so risky as he did in 1919, when he was opposed by the Governors of the Bank of Sweden How is it possible that such contradictions can emanate from the same brain?

Professor Cassel had for that matter come to the conclusion that (p. 352) "it was hardly possible for a small European country independently to resume the redemption of notes with gold". The lack of relation to the facts may be left on one side; but how does this statement tally with Professor Cassel's adherence to the point of view which he first put forward in 1919?

The fall in our prices was at first gradual, and was actually interrupted in 1920 by a fresh rise, mainly confined, however, to wholesale prices.[1] On the other hand, the dollar rate rose almost continuously, until in December 1920 it reached its maximum (37 per cent. above parity)—though only after *deflation* in America had been going on for several months

This severe deflation, in which many countries—though not all—were gradually involved, is undoubtedly a unique phenomenon in monetary history It seems futile to try to find a purely monetary explanation of the whole, or of the major part, of this deflation, as being due to "deflationist policy" of the Federal Reserve Board and other Central Banks It must, indeed, be admitted that a high rate of interest, *ceteris paribus*, renders all sellers anxious to sell for cash, and all buyers *less* anxious to buy for cash, and that it therefore has a certain tendency to force down cash prices, i.e the actual price level And I think that I may also safely maintain that a rate of interest which permanently either exceeds or falls below the actual earnings on capital invested in productive enterprise would have a

---

[1] It would be hard to deny that this rise was caused—as pointed out by Davidson in part at least by the premature lowering of the discount rate by the Riksbank. Judging merely by Cassel's comments (p 275 ff), the uninitiated reader would hardly be able to draw any conclusion other than that Cassel himself had opposed this step. As it happened, however, barely a week had elapsed since he recommended a still more thoroughgoing lowering of the discount rate, for the strange reason that the dollar had already risen above its parity. This, to say the least, was an original way of introducing his simultaneous recommendation that the export of gold be resumed

*cumulative* influence on prices.[1] But that an increase of a few per cent. *per annum* (it has never been a question of more) would be able in itself to lower prices as much as 5 per cent *a month*, as happened during the memorable year 1921, seems *a priori* unplausible, and I cannot see how such a causation can be theoretically maintained. If, on the other hand, such a catastrophic fall in prices should be due to *other* causes, it seems equally futile to attempt to check it by a more liberal credit policy, unless the banks are simply to lend money without demanding interest or repayment—a thing which doubtless did actually occur on a considerable scale (*vis-à-vis* the State) in those countries, such as Austria, Russia, Germany, and to some extent also Italy and France, which did not participate in the general deflation

Here too it is tempting to adopt the view of those who lay most stress on the "side of goods", and on the closely related "psychological factor". The deflation in the United States was, as we know, preceded by a severe rise in prices (far more severe than that in Sweden) during the latter part of 1919 and the beginning of 1920 The cause is doubtless to be sought in the relative shortage of goods brought about by the enormous excess of exports (amounting to over four billion dollars) from America during the year 1919 The fall in prices which followed was at first, as is often observed, in the nature of a recovery, of a

---

[1] This point of view is, strangely enough, opposed by Professor Cassel, although it would seem in itself considerably to strengthen his own argument On this point Schumpeter ("Kreditkontrolle", *Archiv für Sozialwissenschaft*, 1925, no 1, p 295) goes even further than Cassel, he holds that a permanently high bank rate, though at first it brings about a lowering of prices, must finally *lose all effect*, as it tends to decrease production and thereby to increase the scarcity of goods For my own part, I have assumed that the volume of production—leaving out those phenomena which are caused by a crisis—will, on the whole, remain *constant* as long as the real factors of production, land, labour, and real capital, remain unaltered Bank rate affects only the competition between producers for the possession of these factors, causing their prices, and other prices, steadily to sink, or to rise, as long as an abnormally high or low bank rate is in force If Cassel's view, and still more that of Schumpeter, were correct, it would be possible for the banks to raise or lower their rates *ad libitum* without risking anything more than a *once-and-for-all* rise or fall in prices This seems absurd The extreme complication of the whole question becomes apparent when it is remembered that high bank rate, especially if it also depresses prices, should stimulate *voluntary* saving and should thereby increase the amount of real capital, whereas *low* bank rate, with a resultant rise in prices, will *force* people with fixed incomes to save, and this should *also* tend to increase the amount of capital. It is for future investigations to unravel this tangle.

reaction against the preceding sharp rise in prices But such an explanation does not carry much weight. If a rise in prices, caused by a scarcity of goods, had already been checked by the reluctance of the banks to provide the means for their payment, then even if the scarcity of goods were to cease, the downward tendency would obviously get the upper hand, and prices would fall But if, as has generally been the case, the means of payment keep fairly well in step with the rise in prices, one could hardly expect more than that the rise in prices would cease—and not that it would be followed by a decline—when the supply of goods had risen to normal.

There may, however, in this connection be another factor to consider. When there is a persistent shortage of goods, the tendency for prices to rise must eventually cease, even without any restriction of credit on the part of the banks. This will occur when people in general have become *accustomed* to, and *resigned* to, the restriction in consumption to which they have year after year been forced to adapt themselves When this has become the case, then a more normal supply of goods will have the effect of abundance, of a surplus supply, for which no corresponding demand has as yet made itself felt We should then witness the same phenomenon that I described in my introduction, only reversed However vague this explanation of the phenomenon of deflation may seem, it is probably nearer to reality than the usual explanation of the process of deflation "that there was an abundance of goods but that people were too poor to buy them". For, broadly speaking, that is impossible. It is impossible, at one and the same time, to be both rich and poor, to have goods to sell and yet lack the means wherewith to buy other goods. One *nation* can, of course, have an abundance of goods while another lacks the barest necessities, whether, however, this would lead to a rise or fall in the international price level is not clear. Goods always set up a demand for other goods, as J. B. Say long ago demonstrated.

Finally, it is fairly obvious that the severe deflation which set in a year and a half to two years after the end of the War had all the characteristics of a phenomenon caused by a crisis The cessation of the War did not immediately bring an abundance of goods in its wake. While it greatly facilitated the exchange of goods between most countries, production did not rise to anywhere near its pre-War volume Furthermore, the importers, aided by credits, held their expensive imports in stock, in order to prevent the market from becoming glutted and to assure for themselves a profit Professor Cassel points to the alleged abundance of goods during the years 1919–20: it must, he says, "cause some embarrassment to a theory which wanted to make the scarcity of commodities the true ground of explanation for the rise in prices".[1] This argument, however, hardly carries as much weight as might at first be supposed Gradually the further holding of goods in stock became too inconvenient and risky, partly, no doubt, on account of the high rate of interest, but mainly as a result, in all probability, of the increased production and supply of goods, particularly (as Professor Cassel himself points out) after the belligerent countries had begun to sell off their enormous supplies of war materials In particular, England's military stocks exceeded anything one had been able to foresee, among other things, England had during the War bought the whole Australian wool clip for several years in advance. Another important factor that had a bearing on this matter was the much discussed purchasers' strike.[2] When prices began to fall, everyone postponed his purchases as long as possible in the hope that prices would fall still further, at the same time, merchants tried to force their sales, fearing too that prices might fall still more This kind of purchasers' strike is quite a usual phenomenon, if I am not mistaken, during every crisis, and to some extent it strengthens my argument as to the reason for a fall in prices. A person who postpones an otherwise desirable purchase makes a sacrifice which is less onerous to the extent that he has been forced, by the previous shortage of goods, to lower his standard of living. (In some cases, and in respect to some commodities, the tendency may be in the opposite direction )

Suppose then (although it must be granted that this is not very plausible) that the effect on prices of a shortage of goods is, so to speak, compensated by the subsequent restoration of normal output. There would still remain a very considerable residual rise in prices,[3] and this would have to be looked upon as the cumulative result of *that* inflation which in the meanwhile would be caused on the "side of money" through too liberal a granting of credit. It can scarcely be questioned that bank rates, both during the War and during the first years after the armistice (even in those countries which, relatively speaking, were foremost in protecting their cur-

[1] *Op. cit.*, English edition, p 54

[2] An analogous War-time phenomenon was the underhand withholding of goods

[3] This can probably be best measured by the *cost of living* index, which includes both retail prices and *rents*.

rencies), were too low in relation to the real rate of interest, which must have been forced up by the lack of liquid capital caused by the War. It is unfortunately true that these last-mentioned conceptions are extremely difficult to define and outline, but this does not alter the fact that they constitute the bedrock foundation of economic phenomena, to which a thorough study will amply testify.

Looking upon the matter in this way, it seems to me that the lack of understanding between practical men of business and economists might dissolve into a higher unity, and since there is hardly any reason, short of another world war, to fear that a sudden shortage of goods will occur, a wise and fore-seeing bank policy should, under normal conditions, be all that is needed to give all possible desirable stability to the level of prices and to the purchasing power of money.

## IV

In turning to the Scandinavian countries, we find that whereas Sweden, like two other neutral countries, Holland and Switzerland, and even at an earlier date than these countries, without taking any special measures and without any other difficulties than those involved in lowering the price level, was able to bring her currency to parity with the dollar and with gold, Denmark and Norway, in spite of diverse measures, have not yet been able to attain this end. It is obvious that the cause of this disparity is to be found in the less favourable external circumstances of these countries—the U-boat warfare with ensuing losses for Norway, and miscalculated *transito* transactions and the financing of Sonderjylland, etc , in the case of Denmark—and not in any superhumanly clever measures on the part of our bankers and financiers. Nevertheless, it is legitimate to say that ever since the exclusion of gold in 1916 the Swedish currency has been more rationally managed than those of our neighbouring countries. If the prevailing wholesale price level of the three countries is divided by the dollar rate of exchange, it will be found, as a Norwegian writer has pointed out,[1] that the purchasing power of the dollar was lower in Sweden than in Norway, and highest in Denmark. This would

[1] Emil Diesen, "Price Level, Currency, Exchange Rates, etc.", *Statsök. Tidskr* , 1922  As far as I can see, his figures for Sweden do not quite tally with those given by Davidson in *Ekonomisk Tidskrift*, 1925, no. 1.

seem to prove that the rise of prices in Sweden was principally due to external circumstances, and when these circumstances were removed the currency regained its parity value as against the dollar, on the other hand, the rise of prices in Norway and Denmark, at least after the War, was partly due to *internal* inflation, which became continuous and even accentuated, and made it impossible to bring the values of these currencies up to that of the dollar and of the Swedish crown. During recent years the values of these currencies have fallen as low as 60 ore for the Danish crown and 50 for the Norwegian, reckoned in Swedish currency.

Since then, however, as we know, there has been a change for the better, both currencies having risen by over 50 per cent. According to the latest quotations the Danish crown is so near parity that one may assume that in all probability it will regain parity, especially as the Danish price level (if the figures given by *Finanstidende* are otherwise reliable) was already by October of this year very close to the Swedish one (It is to be noted, however, that it is not a question of the actual price level but rather of the index numbers obtained by using the price level as it was twelve years ago as a basis) Conditions in Norway are unfortunately not nearly so favourable, the exchange rate with Sweden at present being 76 öre, whereas Norway's price level (index number) compared with ours would barely correspond to an exchange rate of 72 öre. In this respect, however, a considerable improvement has set in since 1924.

As this development has taken place principally during the year 1925 I have not any detailed commentaries available It is, however, generally attributed, at least in part, to a factor that we have hitherto only lightly touched on, but which has no doubt during the whole period in question played a considerable part, namely, *foreign bull speculation* in the currencies of the two countries This type of speculation has come into dis-repute since the War. It has been practised on an enormous scale but has led to enormous losses for the speculators, simply because the country in question did not, as it proved, at all wish to improve its currency but on the contrary lived—as long as it could—on its successive depreciations.[1] But even under

---

[1] During the War and the first years of the ensuing peace, speculation in low-value currencies was probably on the whole bullish, as it was believed and hoped that they would improve in the future. As, however, this hope was in regard to certain countries frustrated, it was only natural that bull speculation should eventually be replaced by bear speculation —a continued *deterioration* of the currency was taken for granted, and

normal conditions bull speculation, whether in commodities or in securities, has the disadvantage, where *the bull movement is supported only by the speculation itself*, that when profits are realised and the object of speculation is sold, the price falls again on account of the increase in supply. In a case, however, like the one we are speaking of, the speculators have been supported by the obvious wish, and officially expressed intention, of both countries to regain the parity value of the crown. They have been able to count upon the fact that if the exchange rose and *remained for any length of time* at a higher level as a result of their manipulations, the government of the country would not wish it to fall again and would exert themselves to maintain it at this level. If speculators, for instance, have bought bills or other securities from Denmark, this implies that Danish imports have partly been obtained on credit (or that its exports have been paid for in advance), in which case one may foresee that a foreign loan will be issued to consolidate the floating debt instead of letting this debt again bring the exchange rate down. Unfortunately, speculators do not find it to their advantage to let the exchange remain at a constant level, and if they try to harvest their gains at too early a date, the exchange may be lowered again. This form of speculation, which after all is nothing else but a temporary foreign loan, unquestionably produces a good lever for facilitating attempts at deflation, imports are stimulated, import goods become more abundant and cheaper, the whole procedure runs more smoothly and pleasantly than if it is to be entirely based on measures taken within the country itself, tightening of credit and domestic borrowing

In his above-mentioned article, Schumpeter remarks in regard to *England*, probably rightly, that when England announced her intention of returning to gold parity, and the whole world knew the weighty reasons for this step, speculators generally became bullish of sterling and in this way supplied England with capital, which in a marked degree facilitated her endeavour. Schum-

as the measures adopted by the governments to counteract this new trend of speculation either were inadequate or failed altogether to materialise, the bear speculation, as has been the case in France during recent years, led to a sharp decline in the currency and thereby indirectly in commodity prices, without any corresponding internal inflation taking place (*cf* articles by A Aftalion in the *Revue d'économie politique*, 1924). In Germany it went finally so far that the domestic currency ceased to function as a measure of value— apart from immediate exchange transactions—and was instead transformed, so to speak, into an independent object of wealth, which under the constant pressure of bear speculation was forced down until its value was nil.

peter seems to fear that this would give rise to a troublesome discrepancy between exchange rate and price level in England, but this fear seems to have been unfounded. On the whole the fluctuations of the exchange rate and of the price level seem to influence one another in the same and not in the opposite direction, which would indicate that both have a common source—as Schumpeter himself points out

But everything costs something; an increased consumption of import goods is obtained at the price of a foreign debt, and added to this the country has, on account of the rise in its exchange, to pay a sort of secret rebate on capital corresponding to the speculators' gain on the exchange

The most advisable thing, therefore, especially in regard to Norway, seems to me immediately to resume payments in gold at approximately the present rate of exchange This would not hinder, but would rather facilitate, the Government's consideration of the advisability of granting the compensation that might justifiably be claimed both from the State and from the individual on account of the fall in the value of the currency. This matter, as I have pointed out in an address given before the Society for Political Economy, cannot be regarded as settled even in the countries that have been able to redeem their notes at gold parity, because the value of gold is still far below what it was before the War.

However, as far as I can see, there is no immediate necessity for adopting *a new monetary unit* The notes at present in use can simply be exchanged for new notes of a somewhat lower value, which could be directly redeemable in gold at the former parity. In this way the re-establishment of the monetary union between the three Scandinavian countries would, *inter alia*, be very much facilitated. I, for my part, firmly believe in such a union This monetary union—with such further regulations as were added to it either by express agreement or by the force of established practice, and which led to the three countries having essentially the same monetary system—may be said to have constituted a small-scale pattern for that future regulation of the world's monetary system on a uniform basis which so long has been a favourite idea of economists Now that the realisation of these plans seems to be within reach, it would indeed be a great pity if the failure of the pattern should be used as an argument by those who, as a result of prejudice and mental sloth, are driven to oppose all new departures.

Let me end with these simple remarks.

I understand very well that on this occasion I have called for the indulgence of my readers more than I usually do. What I have written has principally been an attempt to clarify my own thoughts on a difficult and involved question. It would be a great satisfaction to me if I could dare to think that I have induced the reader to attempt a similar process, even if he should in this way reach conclusions very different from my own

THE END

*Printed in Great Britain by R. & R. Clark, Limited, Edinburgh*

Lightning Source UK Ltd.
Milton Keynes UK
UKOW05f0356050915

258084UK00015B/1201/P